STANDING BY THE REPUBLIC

STANDING BY THE REPUBLIC

50 Dáil Debates that Shaped the Nation

JOHN DRENNAN ∿

Gill & Macmillan

Gill & Macmillan
Hume Avenue, Park West, Dublin 12
with associated companies throughout the world
www.gillmacmillanbooks.ie

978 07171 5291 9

Index compiled by Eileen O'Neill
Typography design by Make Communication
Print origination by O'K Graphic Design, Dublin
Printed and bound in the UK by MPG Books Ltd,
Cornwall

This book is typeset in 11/13 pt Minion.

The paper used in this book comes from the wood pulp
of managed forests. For every tree felled, at least one
tree is planted, thereby renewing natural resources.

A CIP catalogue record for this book is available from the
British Library.

5 4 3 2 1

CONTENTS

ACKNOWLEDGEMENTS   IX

INTRODUCTION   1

HOPEFUL FORTIES, HUNGRY FIFTIES   5

1. 'Doomed be damned': Dev loses power and the sky
    doesn't fall in, *18 February 1948*   7
2. Keeping the past for pride as Mr Costello declares
    the Republic, *24 November 1948*   14
3. Protecting mothers and children? Not in our
    Republic, thank you, *12 April 1951*   20
4. The Duke of Plaza Toro returns, leading from behind,
    13 June 1951   28
5. Suffer the little children ... in blind indifference,
    23 April 1954   33
6. Dev steps out, Costello steps in again, *2 June 1954*   37
7. 'National progress has halted': Lemass addresses
    the state of the nation, *13 December 1956*   42
8. Hoping for an 'upsurge of patriotism': Mr Lemass
    is chosen, *23 June 1959*   48

AFTER THE LOST DECADE NEW HOPE BLOSSOMS . . .
BUT OLD PROBLEMS SCOWL   53

9. A turn to the left: Lemass leads on, *23 April 1963*   55
10. In the 'affluent society' even the undeserving poor
    deserve justice, *12 October 1966*   61
11. The reluctant Taoiseach takes to the pitch,
    10 November 1966   65
12. 'So charming as to be dangerous',
    30 November 1966   71
13. The Revenue are not the enemy: Mr Haughey's
    first budget, *11 April 1967*   76

14.   *Hot Dames on Cold Slabs*: The beginning of the end
      of the age of censorship, *10 May 1967*   81
15.   Oliver J. Flanagan's fishy tale, *8 November 1967*   86

      ENTER HAUGHEY AFTER JACK SECURES TOO MUCH
      OF THE LOVE OF THE PEOPLE   91

16.   The Arms Crisis: A state and a party confront
      the enemy within, *6–8 May 1970*   93
17.   Jack's 'exercise in persuasion', *21 March 1972*   100
18.   The original Quiet Man comes to power,
      14 March 1973   105
19.   Honest Jack gobbles the lot as John Kelly plays
      Nostradamus, *5 July 1977*   110
20.   'Tis an 'Irish solution to an Irish problem',
      28 February 1979   114
21.   Mr Haughey 'comes with a flawed pedigree',
      11 December 1979   119

      THE HORRID EIGHTIES AND THE GREAT AGE OF GUBU   125

22.   'I found my foot in some strange doors last week',
      30 June 1981   127
23.   Ephemeral creations bring down the best
      Government we never had, *27 January 1982*   131
24.   A duo of despair, *9 March 1982* and *14 December 1982* 136
25.   Dessie O'Malley stands by the Republic,
      14 February 1985   141
26.   Frankenstein's monster and Pee Flynn stalk the land,
      14 May 1986   146
27.   Mac the Knife confronts Ireland's economic crisis,
      31 March 1987   152
28.   'A further significant development in the political
      degeneration of Fianna Fáil', *12 July 1989*   157

AN EVIL SPIRIT LEAVES AND A WARD BOSS COMES   163

29.   An evil spirit governs the Republic, *31 October 1990*   165

30.   'I have done the state some service', *11 February 1992*   171

31.   Hollow, nervous laughter as they pass the graveyard, *11 February 1992*   175

32.   A bit of a shock as Bruton 'rises as a phoenix', *15 December 1994*   179

33.   We are in surplus: Labour's last budget, *22 January 1997*   185

34.   A rat in an anorak or a humble nort'side Dub? *26 June 1997*   189

35.   Ray Burke draws a line in the sand, *10 September 1997*   193

36.   Bertie sees the Ghost of Tribunals Future, *7 October 1997*   198

37.   Drinking champagne as Charlie McCreevy becomes midwife to the Celtic Tiger, *3 December 1997*   203

38.   Hope and history walk hand in hand, *21 April 1998*   208

39.   The apotheosis of the dragon's teeth of terrorism, *2 September 1998*   213

DEATH OF THE REPUBLIC   217

40.   A man in full: Bertie leaps the second hurdle, *6 June 2002*   219

41.   McCreevy's last hurrah turns into a handful of dust, *3 December 2003*   224

42.   Appeasement challenged: Enda comes of age, *8 February 2005*   229

43.   Three-in-a-row secured as death by tribunal waits, *14 June 2007*   234

44.   'This is a wonderful country, and we are a fortunate people': Seeing through a glass darkly as Brian Cowen becomes Taoiseach, *7 May 2008*   239

45. Handing over the deeds of the country to bail out
the banks, *30 September 2008*   244
46. Ireland has 'turned the corner', *9 December 2009*   252
47. Darkness falls, *23 November 2010*   257
48. 'Where do we leave our cvs for all these jobs?'
19 January 2011   264
49. Mr Cowen sips from the bitter cup for a final time,
1 February 2011   269

EPILOGUE   273

50. Hanging out our brightest colours for Enda,
9 March 2011   275

BIBLIOGRAPHY   280
INDEX   283

ACKNOWLEDGEMENTS

To those who are close to me, in particular Alice, Ciara, Timothy and Michael.

Thanks are also owed to the dedicated, if wildly optimistic, Gill & Macmillan team, including Fergal Tobin, Deirdre Rennison Kunz, Ciara O'Connor, Teresa Daly and the hard-working editor, Ruairí Ó Brógáin, who dealt with a difficult text with such dedication, and to the ever-helpful John McNamee of Eason's, Portlaoise.

Finally I would like to commend the Oireachtas Education Unit, whose own list of historical debates provided me with the idea for this book.

INTRODUCTION

In 1986 John Kelly TD claimed that the Irish politician is

> a hissing and a byword to many people. Wrongly so, no doubt. Perhaps the public do not understand the motives which drive people into it, the bug which gets into them or the psychological deficiencies which force them to try and make up in this arena what they lack in others. They may not have enough sympathy. All they see are a lot of fat cats or people who ride along enjoying a high profile and getting a lot of coverage and publicity on what they think is a lot of unearned money.

Almost thirty years later little has changed, but is such an analysis too reductive? For politics is also an art that, to some degree at least, shapes the destiny of the nation.

Despite—or perhaps because of—our national capacity for talk, one of the unchanging features of Irish politics is the public's distrust of the art of political rhetoric. This opinion is epitomised by the outwardly wise old saw that a new TD, having talked themselves into the Dáil, should keep quiet lest they talk themselves out of it.

However, as John Bruton once noted in an eloquent critique of Sinn Féin, words are the only weapons politicians possess: they are for them the tools that shape the future of the society they represent. And the Dáil is still the great arena in which the battle to reinvent, protect and sometimes even define the nature of the republic we inhabit takes place.

Though eloquence in politics is associated with sophistry, voters still retain a core belief in the status of the Dáil as the national theatre of the people. It may be a dusty old palladium now, but in the public imagination it is still where the future of the state is settled. This status means that the present lacuna, in which there is no collection of the most dramatic debates that have occurred within the Dáil, is all the more curious.

My objective in this book has been to write the story of the evolution of a state as seen through the great clashes that occurred in the political theatre of the people.

In looking at the great cast of kings, pretenders, princes, regicides, turbulent priests and some clowns, we begin, just to vary the atmosphere, in 1948, with the transfer of power from Éamon de Valera to J. A. Costello and the birth of the Republic. This date is chosen because in many respects it marks the natural end of the old Civil War era and the beginning of the process that would shape the development of the modern Republic. It is also relevant for darker reasons, as the final debates in this book tragically chronicle what is essentially the death of that first Republic.

The subsequent debates reveal that for much of the 1950s the new Republic's legs were, in a hostile world, at best unsteady. There were great characters and dramatic moments, but the dominant mood of the age was one of public stagnation, as, aided by the strength of some ghouls from the past, the old dispensation clung on grimly to power. Several of the debates from what should seem to us an entirely different time in fact resemble a prologue to our present fire-song.

The mood picks up dramatically in the 1960s through seminal events such as the arrival of Seán Lemass, the introduction of free education by Donogh O'Malley and the reform of the censorship laws. The wars in the 70s and 80s about divorce, abortion and the Arms Trial, in contrast, are indicative of the arrival of a darker era of uncertainty, one accentuated by the sulphurous elevation of Charles Haughey to office and by the subsequent great corruption wars.

This book will focus on the more dramatic and colourful figures of our parliamentary history—our various Taoisigh, John Kelly, Ray Burke, Dessie O'Malley, the two Brian Lenihans (father and son), Michael Noonan—as well as on some semi-forgotten blossoms such as Oliver J. Flanagan.

I have tried to avoid the temptation to editorialise, and to let, within their context, the politicians of the various ages speak in their own voices.

In selecting the debates I was mostly guided by the historical importance of the events—for instance the election of a Taoiseach or the state of knowledge in the 1950s of the abuse of children—rather than by soaring flights of rhetoric. This means that in some debates, such as that regarding our accession to the European Union, there is little hand-to-hand political combat. In that instance, for example, it was the significance of the occasion—together with its eerily prescient critique by Justin Keating (one of the lost public intellectuals of the era) of the dangers of EU membership—that merited its inclusion.

As well as focusing on how incoming Governments saw the country—on their plans and hopes and how accurate those were—this book also covers a number of critical budgets from the Haughey era to the present.

Mention of Haughey brings us to one of the text's central themes. Over four decades, no politician, outside perhaps of de Valera, possessed such sway over the imagination, and the nightmares, of the country.

Another feature I have noted is that drama and conflict in Irish politics often appear in clusters. The strongest evidence for this is the stark contrast between the Augustan age of Bertie, in which nothing occurred (on the surface, at least) for a decade, and the cataclysmic Cowen era, in which one could be dealing with five national crises a week.

In this regard, readers will also have to excuse me for the high concentration of debates from the last four years; but we must realise that this has been the most traumatic era for politics and the state since the Civil War.

Study of these debates may even become all the more necessary, for when it comes to our recent series of political catastrophes, the flux of events means that we quickly lose touch with the public record of who said what during the banking guarantee or the debates on the EU-IMF bail-out.

Though this book deals with debates that often range over days and weeks, a single speech is sometimes so compelling that it dominates the entire affair. Examples of this are Garret FitzGerald's 'flawed pedigree' oration about the accession of Haughey to the Taoiseach's office, and Dick Spring's coruscating 'evil spirit' critique of the same politician more than a decade later.

I hope to show that, in spite of itself and the voters, the Dáil, often driven by outside events, has provided us with no shortage of dramatic moments, and sometimes of merely farcical rows.

Happily, not all the events described herein are dark and bitter. There are also those days of joy, generally during the accession of Taoisigh or in the wake of the Belfast Agreement, on which Leinster House, all too briefly, hangs out its brightest colours. Some may even recall that the mood was more than jovial during a couple of Charlie McCreevy's budgets. But, like many other things, all that has gone quite out of fashion now.

HOPEFUL FORTIES, HUNGRY FIFTIES

Chapter 1 ～

'DOOMED BE DAMNED':
DEV LOSES POWER AND
THE SKY DOESN'T FALL IN

18 February 1948

The late 1940s were a time of conflicting national impulses. In public life—understandably so, given our economic performance—the language of pastoral decline was endemic. But radical strands of thought, which would fully blossom only in the sixties, were also emerging. In looking at the 'desolate' forties and fifties, the modern eye also sometimes fails to see that the new Free State had come through significant traumas and secured major achievements.

The bloodied entrails of the War of Independence and the Civil War meant that even securing a relatively apolitical police force and a democratic transition of power from the victorious to the defeated side of the Civil War was, in the context of the time, a worthy success. Under Éamon de Valera, Ireland had also gone through a radical era in which the final apron strings of empire were severed just in time to avoid embroilment in the Second World War.

Thanks to the senseless economic war with Britain a new economic regime based on tariffs and self-sufficiency had been developed, and the primacy of the state had been established over the nascent but pleasantly incompetent— well, by fascist standards—Blueshirts as well as over the somewhat less pleasant remnants of the IRA, which had been proscribed in 1936.

Throughout all these changes a Taoiseach formed by the age of political giants such as Charles Stewart Parnell and W. E. Gladstone retained an aristocratic hold on the loyalties of his people. There was, however, an Achilles heel in the political make-up of the man known as 'the Chief', for the closest de Valera had come to an economic policy was his belief that sovereignty on its own could play a key role in socio-economic development. Amidst the bloodshed and terror of the 1940s a policy of elegant pessimism, in which Ireland aspired to be little more than a quaint backwater, had its attractions. And few in Fine Gael would have disagreed fundamentally with de Valera's Arcadian dreams of a land of 'frugal comfort'.

But the mood of the citizens began to shift when the ending of the war appeared to signal an actual deterioration in economic conditions. That old fox de Valera had sensed trouble in 1947 when Clann na Poblachta had won two by-elections. The farcical Locke's Distillery furore saw the ascetic de Valera shrouded with accusations about the sale of the rights to mature whiskey in return for a gold watch. In fact Dev was up to different types of mischief with the *Irish Press,* and his political health had been far more damaged by a teachers' strike and an emergency budget in 1947, which had imposed new taxes on beer, cigarettes and even cinema tickets.

In spite of all these factors, after the results of the snap election came in it looked for a time that de Valera would return to office. Fine Gael, with 19 per cent, won its lowest share of the vote in the history of the state. The eternally unhealthy Labour Party was split into two parties, while the nascent radicalism among the electorate was epitomised by the election of two former chiefs of staff of the IRA—one of those of very recent vintage. Clann na Poblachta was described by one observer as consisting of 'incorrigible Celts, disgruntled IRA and political adventurers', and Clann na Talmhan, which was led by the barely literate Joe Blowick, with 7 seats, was, as Breandán Ó hEithir noted, unique among Irish political parties in having 'no policies apart from the remedying of farmers' grievances—a task beyond human or divine competence.'

The political mathematics were finely balanced. Fine Gael, the Labour Party, the National Labour Party, Clann na Poblachta and Clann na Talmhan had 67 seats, and Fianna Fáil had 68, so the balance of power was held by a curious collection of independents such as James Dillon, whose political style was characterised by colourful pledges to smother Britain in eggs and throw all the rocks in Connemara into the sea.

It had been widely predicted that de Valera would return to power, but the yearning for change meant that suddenly, much to his own horror, J. A. Costello was asked to lead an alternative Government. There can be no doubt that Costello was a reluctant Taoiseach, but, as he prevaricated, one friend tartly noted that 'you have been in politics for thirty years and you cannot refuse the top job. If you play with fire you must expect to get burnt some time.' While he was reluctant, Costello could be fiery. Speaking on de Valera's famous bill to ban the wearing of political uniforms in public, he told Fianna Fáil that 'the Blackshirts were victorious in Italy . . . the Hitler shirts were victorious in Germany, as, assuredly in spite of this bill . . . the Blueshirts will be victorious in the Irish Free State.'

Ultimately, on the day de Valera finally lost power, it would be the ebullient independent Dillon who summed up the mood of the new Government when he roared 'Doomed be damned' in the direction of those nervous TDs who thought Ireland would never see prosperity again.

The different nature of the politics of the era was epitomised by the speech of the leader of Fine Gael, General Richard Mulcahy. He had proposed Costello for the Taoiseach's post after it became clear that the antipathy that existed between Mulcahy and Seán MacBride (of Clann na Poblachta), who had fought on opposite sides in the Civil War, meant that no Government could be formed under his own leadership. Significantly, Mulcahy began by referring to the death of the agricultural reformer James Hughes and to the

> message he had preached so often here—the harmony that lay between the animal and the plant and the soil and the climate; the harmony that made it possible for the farmer to take from the soil of this country what gives us our sustenance and the things that go to build up our cities and our towns.

Mulcahy admitted that this was

> a house that has from time to time gone through very difficult days . . . [But] just as there is a harmony between the animal, the plant, the soil and the climate . . . there is a harmony between men's minds that has to be studied reverently and worked for as assiduously as any harmony that God established in the soil of the country we live in.

It was this motive force that had driven the decision for the eclectic coalition to be formed

> in harmony and in reverent thought for their responsibilities and their duties to their country, as against the ideas that have been preached contrary to that harmony during this recent election campaign.

Mulcahy's speech, with its references to unhealed wounds from the Civil War, its quasi-mystical Catholicism and its emphasis on agriculture, shows how deeply Ireland's elite had been infused with the romantic nationalism of the late nineteenth century. More significantly still, it was indicative of how little their world view had changed.

Mulcahy somewhat ornately noted of Costello that 'his selection has not been a question of bargaining but a manifestation of that [Christian] spirit that is deep in our tradition and deep in our faith.' Looking at a deeply uncertain world that was spinning towards the Cold War, Mulcahy felt that there was 'a move in this country to realise what it is the Irishman and the Irishwoman hold as a faith and that a sincere and successful effort is going to be made to see that that faith is translated into good works for the glory of God and for the benefit of our country.' In Mulcahy's view Costello was 'the man to hold together and to bind that spirit and to lead it to achievement,' if only because of 'the sacrifice he is making in turning his back on his professional life and professional work—a sacrifice of mind in addition to many other sacrifices—in order to preside over that great experiment.' The image of Costello the reluctant Taoiseach would become one of the defining themes of the politics of the 1950s.

William Norton, leader of the Labour Party, wasn't impressed by Fianna Fáil's continuing attempts to raise hares over the new coalition Caliban. It was true that

> this country has not so far had inter-party government. We have had for the past twenty-six years one-party government, but considering the nation's economic position, and reflecting on the economic, social and agricultural maladies which afflict it, one can see no special virtue in one-party government.

Seán MacBride meanwhile defended what was a startling new development, observing that 'the people, by 750,000 votes to 500,000 votes, clearly indicated that they wished to terminate the virtual political monopoly which has existed for some sixteen years.' Though MacBride, like so many of his generation, appeared often to be more interested in events in the one section of the country he didn't govern, he acknowledged that there were real domestic problems too, such as emigration, rural depopulation, tuberculosis and the fall in agriculture. Most importantly of all, there was a sense that the nation was on the ebb.

After the vote that elected Costello as Taoiseach the colourful independent Oliver J. Flanagan was first out of the traps, with a pious ejaculation of 'Thanks be to God that I have lived to see this day.'

After a nervous Ceann Comhairle snapped, 'Order—Deputy Flanagan should not start off on the wrong foot so early in this Dáil,' Costello expressed his appreciation for his nomination in language you wouldn't hear from any latter-day politician, as he claimed: 'The position was not sought by me nor wished for by me in any way.' Instead he had bowed to the perceived need for a leader who was 'detached from the controversial bitterness of the past.' It had only been in response 'to the urgent desires of all those parties that I laid aside my own personal interests in order that this should come about.' He warned of feeling that 'there are very onerous tasks in front of the new Government which must now be formed' and that he would 'have to shoulder serious responsibilities for which I am in no way fitted', and others were equally lacking in confidence.

Three TDs appealed for a 'national government' (one of all parties), with one deputy noting of de Valera that 'it is a pity he cannot see his way, after all these years, to sacrifice his will by having his party included in any Government that may be today born.'

James Dillon, as noted earlier, was rather more sanguine, observing that, while others might be in despair,

> Fianna Fáil is going out, and thanks be to God. I welcome that development, because by the action which Dáil Éireann will take today, in the name of the Irish people, it will reassert before the world that this country depends on no individual for its existence as a sovereign and independent nation.

Dillon, an unashamed apologist for parliamentary democracy, in a country that was still lukewarm about the concept, celebrated the decision to reject

> the facile freedom dependent upon the rule of one man for the complex and difficult liberty of a parliamentary democracy operated by those who love this country more than they love their party.

The love of party above country would be a continuing theme in Irish politics, but Dillon, who had a somewhat broader world view than most of his contemporaries, was equally concerned about the gathering shadows of communism and fascism. He defiantly observed that

> what we do here today will demonstrate not only to our own people but to all who hate this country that, at a time when one small nation after another in the Europe in which we live has lost its freedom and surrendered its destiny into the hands of one man, this small nation confidently and courageously takes its liberties out of the hands of one man and places them in the safe keeping of a group of democrats who believe that parliament under a democratic government is capable of carrying this country through any perils that may confront it in the future.

Seán Lemass was most assuredly not in the mood for good wishes. In an angry speech he dismissed the pious claims about no bargains and said, 'It is, I think, not a secret that many discussions have taken place'. In his view anxiety about the new Government's intentions could be relieved only by a 'clear statement'. The future Fianna Fáil leader issued a sharp offer of help to 'the Taoiseach, or Deputy Mulcahy, whoever is the most authoritative spokesman of the proposed new Government,' and expressed the hope that we would not see a reprise of 'the Fine Gael industrial policy in the past' that left the country 'with a legacy of ruined mills and derelict factories.'

Hearing this, some of the new Government became a tad restive, but they were swiftly silenced by Lemass's observation that 'the deputies opposite are perhaps forgetful of the fact that they have now acquired the dignity of membership of a government. They are still inclined to behave like a lot of paid hecklers at a public meeting.' In a sign of the times, Lemass proudly claimed of Fianna Fáil's legacy that the six-ounce butter ration was 'the largest in Europe', and that, 'so far as tea is concerned, there is at the present time enough tea in the country to abolish rationing.' This was followed by the promise, often made but rarely lived up to, that Fianna Fáil, as an opposition, would offer constructive criticism and that it would be made with the intention of improving Government proposals 'if they are capable of improvement.'

Though Fianna Fáil had more deputies than all the other parties put together, Lemass piously promised that 'we who took a primary part in enacting the Constitution under which we work' would not 'complain in the least' if it was used to the detriment of Fianna Fáil. However, in a hint at their long-term strategy of taking out the new coalition by means of its weakest link, Lemass assumed that 'every independent deputy and every member of the smaller parties that have joined Fine Gael in this coalition did what he thinks is right. We will assume that, at any rate, until the contrary is shown.' However, if the opposite was the case, and deputies 'have any explanations or excuses to give, they do not have to give them to us here . . . We do not want to hear them.' Those who had put de Valera out wouldn't be forgiven lightly.

In words that would be echoed twenty-five years later, and in similarly traumatic circumstances for Fianna Fáil, Lemass concluded by saying that he

> heard one deputy saying that the Fianna Fáil Government was handing over a country that is bankrupt. That is not true. You are a getting a country sound in every way—sound nationally, economically and financially . . . We are leaving you this country in good shape . . . Intrinsically the country is all right. That is the way you are getting it. Make sure that you hand it back that way.

The wily Costello declined to respond to the more 'provocative' elements of what had gone before. Instead he welcomed, with fingers crossed, the 'offer of constructive criticism' and noted that 'in the few words I uttered this afternoon, after I had been nominated as Taoiseach, I asked for the patriotic co-operation of deputies on the opposite benches.' After repeating his theme of not being 'in this Government for political purposes' or to 'get any advantage out of political office', Costello sharply dismissed Fianna Fáil's obsession with the nature of the new administration. Lemass could call this 'a coalition, an inter-party Government or anything else—he can call it what he likes'—but they had at least 'shown this country that there can be some Government instead of Fianna Fáil, and that at least is an achievement.'

It was of course a modest enough one, but modest achievement would most certainly be the template for the politics of the 1950s.

Chapter 2

KEEPING THE PAST FOR PRIDE AS MR COSTELLO DECLARES THE REPUBLIC

24 November 1948

The new Government started at quite a lick, for within six months they had done what de Valera had failed to do in sixteen years and cut the last of the ties with the old oppressor. The declaration of the Irish Republic was accompanied by great aspirations that Ireland had finally reached the point where we could 'keep the past for pride'. Though it was increasingly difficult for many to understand why we fought a civil war over issues of sovereignty that de Valera himself had called 'that small difference' and 'that little sentimental thing', we were, alas, still a long way from that point. Instead, the tortuous definition of what being a republic actually meant would consume Irish politics in ways as diverse as section 31 of the Broadcasting Authority Act and Dessie O'Malley's decision to 'stand by the Republic'.

Costello's declaration of the Republic, however, despite the essentially technical nature of the somewhat scattergun process, was a significant moment. It was perhaps all the more important because the honour didn't fall to Fianna Fáil. Though that party wasn't at all impressed by the sight of what Joe Lee called the stealing of its 'Sunday suit of constitutional clothes', the act facilitated a process whereby Fine Gael, which had opposed de Valera's series of constitutional reforms with increasing vehemence in the 1930s, could feel some element of ownership of the institutions of a state that had changed so radically since it had lost power in 1932.

In a three-hour speech, whose length was lamented by quite a few deputies, the Taoiseach began by expressing the 'feelings of pride which animate me in being privileged to sponsor this bill.' This, however, was tempered by humility and 'the certain realisation and knowledge that there are, on every side of this house, people far more worthy.' Fianna Fáil certainly felt that way when

Costello said he hoped that this would usher in 'a new and brighter epoch for the people of the country.' This bill would 'end for ever, in a simple, clear and unequivocal way, this country's long and tragic association with the institution of the British Crown' and 'make it manifest beyond equivocation or subtlety that the national and international status of this country is that of an independent republic.' More important still, it would be 'putting an end to the bitterness and personalities which have poisoned the stream of our national lifeblood during the past twenty-five years.'

Costello stressed that declaring the Republic was not driven by 'nationalistic egoism or isolationism. We are a small nation and we require friends.' This was 'not merely the logical outcome but the inevitable result of a peaceful political evolution that has gone on here in this country over the past twenty-five years.' Indeed, the Taoiseach, perhaps quaintly to modern eyes, noted the strength of our links with England in the form of 'our missionary priests, nuns and brothers' who have 'gone to England and have brought the faith there and are giving no inadequate contribution to the spiritual uplift which is so necessary in the atheistic atmosphere of the world today.'

Costello's central thesis was that the new bill would actually enhance relations with Britain. In breaking 'the last tenuous link with the Crown', far from 'having any feelings of hostility . . . we want to clear away from our past, the past of the country, all obstacles which are a hindrance to the greater and freer development of good relations between our two countries.' As Costello frankly noted, the iconography of the Crown 'entering into the humble homes of Irishmen to arrest them as a prelude to their gibbeting or shooting' hadn't exactly enhanced the profile of the institution, and it was clear, even then, that this was a country that had many miles to go before we could welcome the dear old Queen.

Costello claimed that this legislation would also end the ridiculous situation in which Ireland both was and was not a republic. The uncertainty about this was epitomised by a question-and-answer session between de Valera and James Dillon, which Costello quoted at some length. In it Dillon had asked de Valera, 'Are we a republic or are we not? For nobody seems to know.' After de Valera replied, 'We are, if that is all the deputy wants to know,' Dillon sardonically observed, 'This is a republic. That is the greatest news I heard in a long time. Now we know where we are.'

Of course, by the time de Valera finished explaining that 'the position, as I conceive it to be, is this: we are an independent republic, associated as a matter of our external policy with the states of the British Commonwealth,' and that when it came to the Commonwealth, 'that is a question for which the material necessary for a conclusive answer is not fully available,' everything was a lot more obscure. It was almost as difficult to oppose Dev as it would later be to oppose Bertie.

Costello, however, noted that it was an impossible situation in which, 'nine years after the passing of the External Relations Act of 1936, the material necessary for a conclusive answer as to whether we were or were not a member of the Commonwealth of Nations was not available.'

The new Taoiseach claimed that his decision was also informed by his desire to 'take the gun out of Irish politics' and to get 'some symbol around which our people can rally', but he didn't get a unanimous welcome. Instead the famous independent Dublin TD Alfie Byrne claimed that 'after twenty-six years of an Irish Government' we should not 'take any pride today in proclaiming a republic for only a portion of our country.' Typical of the thinking of the time was his claim that 'in these days of democracy in England, with the Labour Party in power, with the type of people wanting to put them into power,' it was possible, almost immediately, for 'our thirty-two counties' to be united. The problem in the North was confined to 'a dozen, two dozen or five dozen big men' at the top 'anxious to hold their places because they are dug in.'

De Valera, in a typically equivocal way, noted that, 'listening to the first part of the Taoiseach's speech, I could not help thinking how it would have cheered my heart, and cheered the hearts of many of us in these benches, and cheered the hearts of thousands of our people, had that attitude been taken over the past twenty to twenty-five years.' Still, he did 'rejoice that I have seen the day when that attitude could be taken.' His only regret—and with de Valera there was always a quibble—was that 'we are not in a position of declaring on behalf of this assembly a state which could be described fully as a republic for the whole of Ireland'.

It had of course, said Dev, always been Fianna Fáil's intention to end the connection, but it had hesitated lest such an act destroy 'a bridge by which the separated counties might come to union with the rest of Ireland.' After a long history of how, 'having been defeated in our efforts to maintain that Republic by force, we started to try to secure the re-establishment of the Republic by other means', de Valera warned 'the other party' (Fine Gael) that it is sometimes 'much easier to take up a position than to hold it,' and that 'when we pass the bill . . . there is no going back on the Republic.'

Though de Valera made it quite clear to Fine Gael that 'you are not establishing a republic; you are simply declaring that the description of the state shall be a republic,' Seán Dunne of the Labour Party observed that 'the expression "the Republic of Ireland" has a far greater historical significance for our people than any language we could utilise here can express.'

It meant something entirely different to the Protestant Fine Gael TD Maurice E. Dockrell. But now that a republic had been declared Dockrell hoped that peace would come too. 'Heaven knows that in the lifetime of every person in this Dáil there has been a terrible lot of trouble and bloodshed; men have died, men have been wounded.'

The subterranean tensions were epitomised by an astonishing speech from Lemass, who sharply noted that Costello was engaged in a false interpretation of history if he thought that there had been some class of natural evolution whereby the prophecy by Michael Collins that the Treaty would be a stepping-stone had come to pass. Lemass emotionally stated that

> it was nothing of the kind. On behalf of those who fought with me, those friends of mine who died and who were broken or exiled in opposition to the Treaty, I am going to deny that assertion with all the vehemence I can. It is not true. I am not going to support the bill in silence if by doing so I am to be taken as accepting now the very contention I fought against all my life.

The Republic, in short, was still the property of Fianna Fáil, and no coalition would take it away from them.

Lemass noted of the Treaty that it had actually 'died in 1937', rather than with this bill, and he spoke of the personal losses he had experienced, such as how Sergeant O'Brien, 'my friend and comrade in 1916 and 1922, was shot down from behind a hedge.' With a TD hissing, 'You brought a hangman over from England to hang members of the IRA,' and with Lemass snapping at the Labour Party leader, William Norton, 'Who fears to speak of '98?' the ghosts of the Civil War were hovering over the chamber again. Lemass's conclusion was chilly. 'I think the most important feature of these discussions is not so much the bill which is before this house . . . as the fact that a bill with that name and purpose has been introduced here by a coalition Government led by the Fine Gael party.' He gracelessly added that he did 'not want them to make any public act of regret or repentance' for their slowness in reaching this point.

The debate continued to be fiery as the Clann na Poblachta TD Peadar Cowan, who had once attempted to raise an army to cross the border, noted that

> Deputy Lemass talked yesterday about his comrades who died. I had comrades who died. I thought a good deal about those comrades, and I regret that I lived to see a period in our history in which we butchered each other, our comrades and our brothers in the way in which we did butcher them.

Cowan wondered why Lemass had tried to create 'that spirit of bitterness' the previous day, and in truth it is a question that is hard to answer.

In a speech that showed that 'Honest Jack' Lynch had plenty of the true republican blood, the future Fianna Fáil Taoiseach claimed of 1921 that 'the repulsive terms of that Treaty' meant that we were 'nationally static for the ten years that followed the signing of that Treaty.' Lynch, whose mind was never far away from the sports field, recalled of the port in Cóbh and its Union Jack: 'I was as a young boy playing around the shores of Cork Harbour, and I saw the badge of subjection, the Union Jack, flying on part of our own territory to which we were denied admittance.' When de Valera had secured the ports, and the flag was gone, Lynch noted that, 'young as I was, I appreciated the significance of that particular attainment.'

After a further series of snappy exchanges, the Ceann Comhairle intervened to note that 'all sides are entitled to give their views on the historical events of the last twenty years, but in my opinion this house is the worst place to pass judgement on these events.'

This attempt to calm the mood was immediately scuppered by the excitable independent Oliver J. Flanagan, who said of de Valera's views on the prior status of the Republic that, while 'I would be very sorry to be abusive . . . I can say without fear of contradiction that if Deputy de Valera swallowed a nail it would immediately turn into a corkscrew.' Intriguingly, Flanagan also noted that he had

> heard the Civil War being dragged into this debate. I admit I know nothing whatever about the Civil War. I want to know nothing about it, and the majority of the young men in this country want to know nothing about it.

Even if it was an agonisingly slow process, Ireland was changing.

The history of those turbulent earlier years was still whispering when James Connolly's son, Roddy, admitted that this bill 'may not give us everything that we wish or desire. It may not give actuality to that for which Pearse and my father fought and died, but it is another step on that long road towards Irish freedom.'

Meanwhile, Seán MacEntee, Fianna Fáil's decades-long gurrier in chief, had no problem claiming that 'this bill is our triumph; this bill is Fianna Fáil's vindication.' Speaking of Ireland's love affair with the shadow of a gunman, he claimed that the establishment of the Republic meant that anyone who still advocated the use of the gun in politics would be 'an enemy of democracy' and

> unfit to enjoy the rights of a citizen in a democratic state. We must stand firmly on the judgement that such a man is an enemy of the people, and we must make it clear to him that by resorting to the gun in public affairs he has put himself outside the pale of human sympathy and human compassion.

This wasn't just some amiable philosophical dissertation: the treatise quickly segued into an attack on what Frank Aiken had called Fine Gael's 'queer bedfellows'—people such as MacBride, Con Lehane, Jim Larkin Junior, who urged his followers 'to organise in order to establish a workers' republic based on the confiscation of private property', and Peadar Cowan, who had 'declared that he seeks the destruction of capitalism and the establishment of a socialist republic.' Sweetness and light were still conspicuous by their absence.

The thoughtful Labour leader William Norton meanwhile expressed the hope that 'the eradication of domestic political strife will . . . or should enable us to concentrate on . . . national regeneration without dissipating our energies on barren strife over the political status of the nation.'

Strife, however, continued to be the theme of the day as another spat was signalled when cries of 'armchair general' flew across the house. The victim on this occasion, Paddy 'the Bishop' Burke of Fianna Fáil (so named because of the number of funerals he attended), indignantly squawked, 'I was not an armchair soldier: I was a member of the Irish Republican Army,' only to be silenced by the cruel jibe of 'Not when there was any fighting to be done.'

The Fine Gael leader Richard Mulcahy was rather more measured as he observed that

> the Irish people had guns put into their hands in 1913 by the circumstances of that time. It was not because they turned to guns by any national philosophy of theirs or by any particular instinct. They turned to them as a man does who grasps the hands that grip his throat.

And bitter personal experience informed his warning that

> everything that has happened since in our own country and outside has demonstrated to us the miserable futility and incompetence of guns to do anything except to destroy men, their character and their faith.

Ultimately the mood of the Government was summed up by the Minister for External Affairs, Seán MacBride, who had engaged in an extraordinary series of political peregrinations to end up where he now was. MacBride claimed that this bill 'does not declare the Republic of Ireland. The Republic of Ireland was established in our generation in 1916.' It was, however, the moment when we could finally 'inter the history of the last quarter of a century.'

It would take somewhat longer, when it came to that particular virus, for the obsequies to be completed.

Chapter 3

PROTECTING MOTHERS AND CHILDREN? NOT IN OUR REPUBLIC, THANK YOU

12 April 1951

The title of the debate, 'Personal statement by a deputy', suggests an innocuous affair—perhaps an apology for the use of bad language. But the year is 1951, and the personal statement is Noël Browne's resignation over what was the most dramatic political dispute Ireland would see until the Arms Trial. Afterwards, though things would go on pretty much as before for some time, Ireland was never quite the same again.

The Mother and Child Scheme was in its own astonishing way a very modern political crisis—one featuring leaks, surveillance and a war fought within the media, as distinct from on the floor of the Dáil. The magisterial judgement of the *Irish Times* was that its 'most serious revelation . . . is that the Roman Catholic Church would seem to be the effective government of the country.' However, it was far more nuanced than that. The desire, then as now, of the Irish Medical Association to ensure that hospital consultants retained their private practices and kept the taxman out of their offices played as much of a role in the defeat of the scheme as did the bishops.

In truth, even before the furore the Republic of Costello was a curious sort of affair. The poet Austin Clarke, in 'Burial of an Irish President' (the title referring to the refusal of the Catholic Taoiseach and his Government to attend the Protestant funeral ceremony for Douglas Hyde), captured the fearful confessional ethos of the time.

Costello, his Cabinet
In Government cars, hiding
Around the corner, ready
Tall hat in hand, dreading
Our Father in English . . .

Hyde was but a small problem compared with the great unravelling of the Mother and Child Scheme. Whether it was the consequence of bad governance, a power play gone wrong within Clann na Poblachta or the innocence of a radical minister, the one thing it did was to unveil a style of government in which, as the historian Tom Garvin described it, the 'clergy typically used private and secretive channels to get their way.' And though the status of the Church was to abate, Liz O'Donnell's cheeky reference some five decades later to repeated phone calls from All Hallows to Bertie would show just how enduring that invisible power actually was.

In the end, Browne was outflanked on all fronts, but he did secure one pyrrhic victory by means of his evolution into that most useless of things, an Irish icon. Though nothing could have rivalled his pre-emptive disclosures in the *Irish Times* of the secret infighting that had created this crisis, this new status meant that his Dáil speech had its own drama. In it Browne noted that, since becoming Minister for Health,

> I have striven, within the limits of my ability, to improve the health services of the country . . . It is perhaps only human that I should wish to have the honour of continuing the work. However, that is not to be.

He immediately seized the high moral ground—well, that belonging to the left at least—with the ringing declaration that

> to me the provision of a health scheme for the mothers and children of our nation seems to be the foundation stone of any progressive health service . . . It seemed equally important to me that any such scheme, to be effective, and indeed just, should be made available free to all our people.

In an allegation that would be vigorously disputed, Browne claimed that he had been 'led to believe that my insistence on the exclusion of a means test had the full support of my colleagues in the Government.' In any event, the bishops had struck, and Browne's liberal iconography was somewhat compromised by his claim that he, as a Catholic, 'accepts unequivocally and unreservedly the views of the Hierarchy on this matter.' Instead, it being 1951, blame was carefully shifted into safer territory as Browne noted that he had 'not been able to accept the manner in which this matter has been dealt with by my former colleagues' in the Government.

The turbulent minister had already been in conflict with the Irish Medical Association. It was more than adequately represented among the Fine Gael grandees of the Government such as T. F. O'Higgins, who once claimed, from the luxurious environs of the Bar Library, that even establishing a Department of Health was 'expensive, extravagant and unwarranted'.

Ultimately the great public controversy centred on the tangled relationship between Browne, Archbishop John Charles McQuaid and the Taoiseach. In giving a narrative of the events leading up to his resignation, Browne depicted a scene resembling domestic bliss—one in which, all differences having been resolved in the wake of their first meeting, the archbishop and the minister had existed in a state of total harmony. However, in the drama Browne chose to create, this had been poisoned by a scheming Costello, who was little better than the catspaw of the Irish Medical Association.

Browne's subsequent claims were devastating for Costello's reputation. He claimed that he had been ambushed by a shifty Taoiseach who, for motives unknown, and to Browne's 'distress and amazement', had never sent on 'the reply to Their Lordships' letter' expressing the bishops' concerns about his scheme 'that I had prepared and sent to the Taoiseach in the previous November.' There was no better man than Browne to spot a plot, whether one existed or not. So it was that, in explaining his departure, Browne expressed his surprise that Costello had been in constant contact with the bishops without telling him of their unhappiness. He was also puzzled as to why Costello had, 'in the light of this knowledge . . . allowed me to refer in public speeches to the scheme as decided and unchanged public policy.'

In Browne's view there were two possible explanations for the Taoiseach's conduct. It was

> either that he would not oppose the scheme if agreement were reached with the Medical Association on the means test; or that, in the light of his knowledge of the objections still being made by the Hierarchy and withheld from me, he intended that the scheme without a means test must never in fact be implemented.

The inference from Browne's position was clear: the Taoiseach, and the rest of the damned ministers, such as James Dillon and William Norton, had used poor Mother Church as a catspaw to secure the objectives of the consultants. In words that remain fresh today Browne concluded:

> I have not lightly decided to take the course I have taken. I know the consequences which may follow my action. The honesty of my motives will be attacked by able men; my aims will be called into question; ridicule and doubt will be cast upon the wisdom of my insistence in striving to realise the declared objectives of the party to which I belonged.

But he at least could

> lay down my seal of office content that you—members of this house—and

the people who are our masters here, shall judge whether I have striven to honour the trust placed on me.

In his response the Taoiseach was, even by his lugubrious standards, not happy about how he had suffered the usual fate of the individual who endeavours to 'act the role of peacemaker and of friend anxious to help' and who finds 'their efforts repudiated and their actions misconstrued.'

In a forensic dismantling of the claims of his turbulent priest, Costello claimed that, 'throughout the long and agonising months that have just passed, I and three or four of my colleagues gave of our very best, in a sincere desire to help . . . get him out of the difficulties in which he by his own obstinacy had found himself.' Indeed, he noted, 'the last words I addressed to the Minister for Health as he left his cabinet colleagues last Friday' made it clear that 'we still were willing to help him and did not want to turn the corkscrew on him.' Costello sounded more than a little like a peeved spouse when he noted that 'my attitude during all those frightful months received the thanks embodied in the document read here today by Deputy Dr Browne.'

Costello emphatically denied Browne's central contention that he hadn't been informed of the bishops' unease. The unhappy Taoiseach noted that

> some time after we assumed office—I have not got the habit of making notes or memoranda; I have much too much to do, so I am not in a position to say on what date—I first became aware of the fact that the Hierarchy of this country had made representations to my predecessor privately. I emphasise the word 'privately' because I intend to refer to that aspect of the matter later.

Costello noted that he had 'given a copy of that correspondence to Deputy Dr Browne some time subsequently', and he attacked the 'underlying and vicious suggestion in all this controversy that I and my colleagues in the Government roped in—if I may use that vulgar expression—the Hierarchy in order to get us out of the difficulty of being ensnared in a scheme we did not like.'

Amidst all this chaos the one consolation for Costello was the courteous and 'kindly' behaviour of His Grace the Archbishop of Dublin. Costello said his close engagement with this affair had begun when he attended 'the Archbishop's House on 12th October of last year' and was told that he 'had just had, the day before, an incredible interview with the then Minister for Health'. Costello added:

> May I say . . . in the context of a wider issue on this matter, that all this matter was intended to be private and to be adjusted behind closed doors . . . It would have been dealt with in that way had there been any reasonable

person, other than the former Minister for Health, engaged in the negotiations at that time.

Browne, 'erroneously as it now appears', might have believed that he had satisfied His Grace and Their Lordships in all respects on the Mother and Child Scheme. But Costello claimed that McQuaid

> told me that, at that interview, the Minister for Health brushed aside all suggestions about the invalidity of the means test and the free-for-all scheme, and would consider nothing but the question of education, on which he said, 'You have a point there,' and that he would consider it. The minister himself terminated the interview and walked out.

Costello recalled that he had asked the archbishop, who wasn't used to such treatment, if he would 'permit me to try to adjust the matter with my colleague' and had 'offered myself for the sacrifice, which I am called on to make today.' The Taoiseach had afterwards told Browne that the archbishop had assured him that, 'in order that there should be no suggestion that they were dealing harshly with Dr Browne, going beyond their functions or interfering in the political affairs of the country in any way . . . this matter could be dealt with quietly and privately.' Such indeed, Costello noted, was the gentle kindness of McQuaid that he had brought Browne 'into his own private room, before he met the other two members of the Hierarchy, in order to assure him of his kindliness and interest in him, and to assure him that what the bishops were doing was in his own interest.'

This wasn't the only example of paternalism. Costello claimed that 'no picture that I can present to the house, in words or otherwise, could tell what I and my colleagues the Tánaiste, Mr Dillon and Dr [T. F.] O'Higgins have gone through to settle this . . . disedifying dispute between the Minister for Health and the medical profession.' In truth, Costello himself wasn't averse to a bit of reinvention: he claimed that the medical profession had been 'maligned and slandered and libelled in every disreputable way' by claims that it had 'been standing between the people and this scheme.'

The truth, according to Costello, was that 'every time there was any suggestion of an attempt to meet the then Minister for Health, to forget the past and the controversies, the people who said they were willing to come in and consult were the medical profession, and they were turned down every time with contumely by the then minister.' Eventually push had come to shove, and Costello had been forced to tell his errant minister he would not 'belong to any Government for one moment that was in favour of the socialisation of medicine.'

The breakdown between the minister and the Government began from that moment to accelerate. An exasperated Costello noted that the Department of Health had then published a brochure entitled *Mother and Child: What the New Service Means to Every Family*. The astonished Costello said it was 'never sent to us as a cabinet. That was the way in which we got that document—the alleged scheme, a booklet which the then Minister for Health "is about to introduce".' The appalled Taoiseach noted that then, 'somewhere about that time—I think it was the 8th of March—an advertisement of a lurid character appeared in the newspapers' about the scheme.

In its wake, Costello had then received the dreaded letter from Archbishop's House expressing McQuaid's surprise that he had read 'in the daily Press of the sudden determination of the Minister for Health to implement the mother and child health service, in the manner in which he conceives the service.' Costello noted that the archbishop was happy to 'take this occasion of expressing again to you, on behalf of the Hierarchy and on my own behalf, my grateful appreciation of the immediate understanding and co-operation I have on every occasion received from you, as Taoiseach, in all that concerns the provision of a sane and legitimate mother and child health service.'

Browne, in contrast, when asked, had said, 'I am not going to do anything about that letter. There is nothing in it. It does not require an answer. The whole thing is all nonsense. There is nothing in the archbishop's allegation.'

Relations, Costello admitted, had deteriorated further when Browne had gone to him asking for a 'cabinet meeting . . . to get . . . £30,000. I said it was an extraordinary proceeding and asked, "What do you want it for?"' Costello recalled that Browne had told him:

> If I get the £30,000 I will have the doctors killed on Sunday. I will finish the controversy on Sunday. It will be finished for all time, if I get the £30,000. The private medical practitioners are meeting on Sunday, and I believe that if I get the £30,000 the controversy will be at an end. The doctors will be killed and beaten.

Browne was talking to the wrong man, for at this point Costello stated:

> I took my stand—the stand that I am now accused of having taken all the time, and of having taken surreptitiously. I said that I thought all this trouble with the doctors was coming to a disreputable head. I said . . . whatever about fighting the doctors, I am not going to fight the bishops; and whatever about fighting the bishops, I am not going to fight the doctors and the bishops. It may come to a point where either you or I will leave the cabinet on this, unless we can settle the matter with the bishops.

Then, a clearly exasperated Costello noted that 'on Holy Thursday'—a day on which the 'Archbishop of Dublin had been up at 4:30 a.m.'—McQuaid had, 'while consecrating the Holy Oils . . . received a message from the Minister for Health that he wanted to see him immediately.' The pious Costello added that, 'in view of the underlying suggestions running through the minister's indictments and letters about His Grace the Archbishop, I want again to put this in as further evidence of the extraordinary kindness and consideration of His Grace towards Dr Browne' that he 'saw him that day, which is the busiest day in the year for a bishop.'

Subsequently Costello noted that 'Dr Browne rang me and told me he had been with His Grace the Archbishop of Dublin' and had said he 'agreed with His Grace that the matters arising out of the Mother and Child Scheme should be adjudicated upon by the Hierarchy.'

In a moment echoing de Valera's prophecy about the reputation of Michael Collins, Costello observed of Browne's response to that judgement that: 'no matter what I do I shall never catch up with him to the end of my public life.'

Costello could condemn 'the infinite capacity of Dr Browne for self-deception' or condemn him for breaking his pledge to accept the views of the Church; but the resigning minister had 'put across by propaganda, on the unfortunate people of the country, the idea that they will get something for nothing, and that every woman who is going to have a child can go to the finest specialist in Dublin and get first-class treatment free of charge,' and Costello was the villain who had thwarted this.

The summing up was harsh by Costello's standards.

> I want to say here that if Deputy MacBride had not taken that course, I myself would, under the Constitution, have requested Deputy Dr Browne to give me his resignation . . . I had formed in my own mind, having regard to my experience over the last six months and the history of the affairs . . . the firm conviction that Deputy Dr Browne was not competent or capable to fulfil the duties of the Department of Health. He was incapable of negotiation; he was obstinate at times and vacillating at other times; he was quite incapable of knowing what his decision would be today, or, if he made a decision today, it would remain until tomorrow. It has been said that he is inexperienced, but I regret my view is that temperamentally he is unfitted for the post of cabinet minister.

Happily, one special relationship did survive. Costello cited a subsequent letter sent to 'My Lord Archbishop' stating that, having 'on the occasion of your visit to me on the 5th instant informed Your Grace of my own acceptance of the decision' after their meeting, the Government had expressed its 'complete willingness' to 'defer to the judgement so given by the Hierarchy.' Costello then referred to McQuaid's 'deep appreciation of the generous loyalty shown by you and by your colleagues in graciously deferring to the judgement of the Hierarchy', and he expressed his concern that in the wake of Browne's actions it was 'inevitable' that there 'will be suggestions made as to the intervention of the Church authorities in state affairs.'

Mr Costello's ecclesiastical *bona fides* were still sound, but nothing captured the extraordinary bitterness of the subsequent debate better than the claim by the outspoken former Clann TD Peadar Cowan that the furore occurred because Browne was more popular than MacBride, so 'he must be downed, and he must be damned.' Cowan said he felt 'compelled to say these things and to make no bones about the fact that I consider the Minister for External Affairs [MacBride] to be one of the most dangerous characters in the country . . . I can speak with some experience. I was number 1 to be executed by him.'

Fianna Fáil meanwhile played the wisest game of all. Seán Flanagan, quelling his own restive TDs, said of the dispute, 'Let it be between them now, and let us keep out. Our scalps are fairly safe while they are at each other.' And de Valera dismissed the entire debacle with the scathing 'I think we have heard enough.'

Mr Costello's troubles, in contrast, were still not over, for the first communication poor Costello received after his speech was a complaint from McQuaid demanding an immediate response to the cheek of the Irish News Agency in asking His Grace for a thousand-word article on the Mother and Child Scheme. Costello simply put his head in his hands and wailed, 'Dear God, this is the end.'

In fact, it was only the beginning.

Chapter 4 ～

THE DUKE OF PLAZA TORO RETURNS, LEADING FROM BEHIND

13 June 1951

It was perhaps typical of Irish politics that, while the Mother and Child Scheme had inflicted grievous damage on the coalition, its collapse was actually brought about by the far more earthy issue of the price of milk. In the subsequent election the closeness of the result indicated that, despite a somewhat embittered end, the Government hadn't been entirely unsuccessful. A new spirit of Keynesianism had informed fiscal policy; Marshall Aid had begun, if not to flow, at least to trickle into the country; and the establishment of the IDA had shown receptivity to new ideas. Fianna Fáil, in contrast, had been so bereft of policy that Lemass later admitted, somewhat shamefacedly, that it had gone to the country essentially with its 1948 manifesto. De Valera also had been a curious sort of opposition leader. His first response to ejection from office was to go on a world tour to put the case against partition. Oddly enough, the Chief soon learnt that the world was more preoccupied with other issues.

When it came to lesser political mortals, the most compelling example of the standard of debate was the tug of war between Fianna Fáil and Fine Gael about whether the national anthem should say 'Fianna Fáil' or 'Laochra Fáil'. It was eventually settled in favour of 'Fianna Fáil' after 1957, when that party secured an unbroken sixteen-year run in office, at the conclusion of which no-one particularly cared about the issue.

Ironically, after the election, had the independents been handled with greater care Costello might have prevailed. The situation was so finely balanced—Fine Gael having provided a Ceann Comhairle from their own ranks—that Costello lost the vote for Taoiseach only by a margin of two, 74 to 72. But the lack of real hunger for office, which was so characteristic of Fine Gael's Law Library political dilettantes, meant that power was handed over on a silver platter to the avaricious Fianna Fáil tribe.

It was characteristic of the time that, before the vote for the Taoiseach's office, the first issue raised was the death of the Papal Nuncio. After the obsequies concluded, Richard Mulcahy, nominating Costello for re-election, claimed on behalf of Fine Gael that 'we promised that we would bring a new spirit back to Irish politics. That promise has been very adequately fulfilled.' It was, given the fractious nature of the break-up of the Government, arguably an optimistic position. Mulcahy, though, claimed that Costello had

> brought back to our country that spirit of unity, that spirit of harmony, that spirit of strength that was eternally our strength in our struggle for our independence. Nothing was more indicative of the man than that there should come to him in February 1948 the leader of Clann na Poblachta and the leader of the Labour Party to ask him to surrender all his own private interests . . . and ask him, 'Will you surrender your person, your business and all your other interests, change the whole course and form of your life, and accept the leadership of an Irish Government to bring a number of Irish parties together to form a Government?'

Seán Lemass, in contrast, claimed that it was de Valera who was the outstanding figure in Irish political life. But it was hard to avoid the impression that at this stage of de Valera's career 'the whole story of Deputy de Valera's life, as battalion commandant in the Irish Volunteers before and during 1916, as the man elected President of the Republic in 1919 and national leader in the eventful years that followed' was wearing a bit thin.

It was typical of the cross-party sense of despair that much of the debate was dominated by the desire for a national government. Seán MacBride, whose intrigues with Noël Browne had played a central role in busting up the previous coalition, issued the first appeal.

Sadly, though the cantankerous independent James Cogan also appealed for unity, the sentiment appeared to be skin deep, as Cogan followed this up with the claim that 'the Minister for Posts and Telegraphs [James Everett] on a number of occasions in my constituency proved beyond all shadow of a doubt that the Labour Party is closely associated with international communism.'

James Everett was actually more associated with jobbery, but the subsequent exchanges are evidence of the bitter nature of 1950s politics, with Everett shouting at Cogan, 'They gave you your answer: the Broy Harriers' (a nickname for the Special Branch of the Garda Síochána, under Ned Broy, noted for their harassment first of the Blueshirts and then of the IRA). Everett then asked, 'What about the daughter of one of the deputies opposite getting a job? What about Mr Lemass's brother—£3,000 a year?'

We swiftly disappeared further into surrealism as the new Labour Party TD Seán Keane began his speech by recalling that, 'on the 6th or 7th of January 1937, I was in charge of 250 men to go out to fight with General Franco in Spain.'

The Ceann Comhairle understandably warned, 'We cannot go back upon history of that kind.'

One of the more powerful speeches came from the Labour Party leader, William Norton, whose reputation has never really recovered from Noël Browne's livid character assassination in his autobiography, *Against the Tide*. Norton's defence of the outgoing Government provides us with a more accurate portrait of his political persona. He claimed that 'for the past thirty years no Government has even taken office in this country under more favourable circumstances', for 'we have brought stability to the nation, and we have given our people a standard of living incomparably better than they had in 1947.' He contended that one of the Government's critical first acts 'was to repeal the penal taxes which the present Government imposed in 1947 on cigarettes, on tobacco, on beer and on cinema seats. We gave back to the people £6 million per annum by the repeal of these taxes.' There were 'more people today in industrial employment in this country than at any time in the past thirty years', and the Government had also 'introduced the Social Welfare Bill, which not only modified the means test but increased old-age pensions, blind pensions, widows' and orphans' non-contributory pensions.' Even agriculture, he claimed, had prospered so well that 'you can get as much today for a rabbit as you could get for a calf when Fianna Fáil were in office.'

In contrast, despite the claims by Lemass that 'Fianna Fáil had a cut-and-dried scheme on social security in the Department of Social Welfare,' when Norton had 'got officials to search the records from top to bottom . . . the only thing I could find in the department was a document the size of a quarter of a foolscap sheet of paper' on which was written 'about twenty words not connected with social security at all.' That, he said, showed 'the abiding care and the deep thought which our predecessors had given to the problem of social security.'

Norton then trained his sights on the spectacle of Peadar Cowan telling Dev 'the reason he was voting for Fianna Fáil was as a protest against the Irish bishops' interference in politics.' This, Norton suggested, was somewhat ironic, given that 'Cowan a few years ago was frequently criticised—and, indeed, on many occasions, blackguarded—by Deputy MacEntee for being the tsar-like chief of the Vanguard organisation, which Deputy MacEntee wrote down as the wildest and most irresponsible communistic organisation in Europe.' Norton added that, 'in propping up the Government', Cowan had 'demoted himself from being the vanguard of the people to being the mudguard of Fianna Fáil.'

Citing de Valera's previous critique in 1948 of 'mixum-gatherum Governments', Norton told the returned Chief that 'he has got a collection of every kind now, political flotsam and jetsam to try to keep Fianna Fáil in office, and I am telling you that I wish him the best of luck with some of them. I would not have the support of some of the gentlemen at any price.'

Amidst sharp exchanges between Cowan (who had compared himself to James Connolly) and MacBride, who snapped, 'For goodness' sake, do not class yourself with James Connolly', the independent TD Jack McQuillan offered the most logical analysis of the electoral result, observing that an uneasy people had decided that 'what they would really like is a caretaker Government.'

James Dillon castigated the Fianna Fáil platform of 'Trust Dev' and 'Give us a majority Fianna Fáil Government', saying that 'now Deputy Lemass with that superb and brazen aplomb, with which I am only too familiar, and which I have long admired as leaving Burmese brass in the shade, boasts of the fact that, like the Duke of Plaza Toro, he led his forces from behind.'

Dillon tore into the situation where 'Deputy de Valera fights a general election, and when he has been defeated produces his programme', for which Fianna Fáil had simply robbed the Government's clothes. Fianna Fáil, according to Dillon, had engaged in 'striptease politics, as they divested themselves of every rag of decency when they embarked on their campaign.' Their former 'raiment was old-fashioned. It was a bit shabby. It was the 1948 design, but at least it covered their nakedness.' But Fianna Fáil having 'passed the post limping and naked', then came 'the bargain sale. Today, Deputy de Valera is the Annie Oakley of Irish politics: "Anything you can do I can do better".'

Though Dillon claimed that this 'degrades Irish politics; it degrades us all that a party can come into this house . . . on a programme . . . that it was not fit to produce before the campaign began,' he reserved his most bitter critique for Noël Browne. In a prophetic speech he warned about

> the devastating reverberation of the tale he purported to tell all over the world wherever there are enemies of Ireland . . . The echoes have only begun to roll, and not all the eloquence of every deputy can catch up with the mighty army of lies which is marching behind that standard . . . to prove that in Ireland it was true what Salisbury, what Balfour, what Carson said: that home rule was Rome rule.

In a scenario such as this he had been 'aghast' to hear Browne say, 'It is all over, so far as I am concerned,' and Dillon correctly predicted that 'it will not be all over in the lifetime of the youngest man in this Dáil.'

In the aftermath of the election result Costello claimed that, in spite of his defeat, he had 'no doubt that the vast majority of the electors desired an inter-party Government. I have equally no doubt that some of the independent deputies who voted against the inter-party Government were voting against the very people who elected them to this Dáil.' The more ambitious Fine Gael TDS, if there were any, wouldn't have been too impressed with Costello's proud declaration that, when it came to the independents, 'nobody got any offer or any guarantee from me.' It is unlikely that they would have been too consoled either by Costello's decision, after the result, to

> register the protest here against the action of these people who, I believe, have acted contrary to the mandate of their electorates. They have put the Government in a very difficult position, a position in which the Taoiseach was elected by the slenderest majority in the history of this house, a majority which probably would not have been secured had we not felt it our duty to do what perhaps we might not have done, to nominate a Ceann Comhairle.

The likely fate of those independent TDS was best summed up by Dillon, who noted of one who had compared de Valera in 1948 to King Herod seeking 'to destroy an Infant rival' and who had called MacEntee a 'senile delinquent' that 'he is not the first simple, kindly creature who has walked into a parlour and found there nothing so exotic . . . as King Herod, neither a Tetrarch nor a chief priest—nothing but a hairy spider.' But, Dillon chillingly added, in joining forces with de Valera the innocent might suffer the fate of the 'young lady from Riga who went out for a ride on a tiger—I know the poem goes on that they both came back from the ride with the lady inside and a smile on the face of the tiger.'

But in spite of Dillon's eloquence, or in some cases perhaps because of it, the electorate had chosen to go for a ride on what was by then a rather moth-eaten tiger, and to let Dev step in for what many believed would be a final curtain call.

Chapter 5 ～

SUFFER THE LITTLE CHILDREN . . . IN BLIND INDIFFERENCE

23 April 1954

God was in his Heaven, de Valera was back in power, and on September Sundays, as part of de Valera's bucolic vision, you could see the Artane Boys' Band march before each all-Ireland. Of course, like so many other elements of de Valera's Ireland, Artane was a multilayered place. Beyond the hagiography, the journalist and author Gene Kerrigan claimed that Artane was a 'byword for fear' in working-class Dublin in the 1950s, a place where Christian Brothers, condemned to a life of boredom and celibacy, took out their frustrations on young working-class boys who were guilty of nothing more than being a social nuisance. In a country in which—like somewhat more refined Nazis—priests, judges and Government officials regarded orphaned and indigent pupils as inferior beings suitable only for menial employment, the treatment of these boys rarely surfaced.

It wasn't completely hidden, though. A Dáil debate in 1947 had revealed that a nineteen-year-old boarded out from an industrial school to a farmer had been forced to sleep on a manure cart. This had been treated as entirely normal, and the inconsequential matter of the abuse of children lay dormant until the radical TD Peadar Cowan, who was described memorably by Seán Lemass as being 'as cute as a pet fox', raised the issue of a boy who had been injured in St Joseph's Industrial School at Artane. The debate consisted essentially of two statements: one by Cowan—whose liberal views led to him being compared by Fianna Fáil's considerably less liberal Seán MacEntee to a 'Red Pope', a 'crawling communist' and a 'sort of abortion'—and another by the Fianna Fáil Minister for Education, Seán Moylan, who was yet another old Civil War hero.

Cowan began by noting that 'the boy concerned is aged fourteen-and-a-half years. He has been in Artane Industrial School for one-and-a-half years, and during his period there his conduct has been satisfactory.' However, on the 14th of the month

> he was punished for some boyish altercation with another boy. Apparently, as I am informed, before the punishment was inflicted the doors were locked, the windows closed; and the punishment, which was the normal punishment, was inflicted in the presence of all his classmates. The punishment, I am informed, consisted of a number of slaps to the hand . . . but on the completion of that punishment the boy was ordered to submit to further punishment with the edge of the strap, and he refused to accept that punishment.

In what was a cruel age, nothing untoward had occurred up to that point. But as the situation escalated, a second Christian Brother was sent for, whereupon the boy 'ran from the place in which he was being punished, lifted a sweeping brush, which was apparently standing in a corner, and held it up as a protection.' The Christian Brother who had arrived saw the brush, 'struck him in the head, injuring him, struck him in the back, injuring him, struck him on the arm, and broke his arm.'

The assault was followed by an astonishing series of events in which it took two days for the boy to be admitted to hospital and to have his arm set. According to Cowan, the boy's mother, who hadn't been informed about this assault for a number of days, had, on hearing of her child's fate, attempted to see the superior of the house. Having first been refused, she went to see Cowan.

Cowan noted that 'she came to me about half past eight yesterday morning. I communicated by telephone with the superior, and she was then allowed to see her boy. She was shocked at the state in which she found him.' A perturbed Cowan added, 'Yesterday was the 22nd, the incident occurred on the 14th, and eight days afterwards, on the 22nd, she saw the boy.'

He defended his decision to raise the case on the basis that 'these boys, who are sent to these schools by the courts, are all the responsibility of the Minister for Education, and the Minister for Education, as I understand it, must answer to this house and to the country for the conditions under which the boys sent there by the courts are kept.'

In a prescient observation Cowan told the Dáil that the Christian Brother 'who injured the boy was barely past twenty-one years of age, not much older than the little boy who was injured in this fashion,' and he warned the minister that 'the country will want an assurance from him that punishment, if it is to be inflicted on those sent to industrial schools, will be inflicted by some person of experience and responsibility. If punishment were to be imposed in a fit of hot temper it would be exceptionally bad, and in fact in this case it could be dangerous.'

In a sign of the times, however, even Cowan regretted mentioning the incident. A neighbour of the school, he believed that the boys he saw were exceptionally fit, well clothed and happy. While he was 'personally satisfied that it was an isolated incident', the fact that it had occurred showed, he claimed, that the department and the minister 'should have the closest supervision of schools such as this, where children, many of them without parents at all, are sent to be brought up.'

In truth, if Cowan thought the Government would respond positively to his warning about the need to 'zealously guard and protect children' he was wasting his sweetness on the desert air. Moylan, the ascetic Minister for Education, stated that the seedy events were an isolated incident, warning parents that 'any guarantee I give them of full protection for their children is no licence to any of the children to do what they like.' He added that, when it came to our industrial schools, 'there is a very consistent system of inspection', and he stressed that he had personally 'visited practically all of them' and made 'personal and consistent inquiry as to what is happening in them.' However, though he admitted that 'the schools are deficient in many things', the problem with fulfilling the promise of the Constitution to treat all the children of the nation equally was that this 'will cost a great deal more money from the state than the relatively small amount that is paid now.'

By admittedly modern standards, Moylan was somewhat offhand about the breaking of a child's arm by an adult Christian Brother. He stated that 'accidents will happen in the best-regulated families, and in this family there are about eight hundred boys.' He cleverly plunged a dagger into the reputation of the children in his supposed care with the observation that 'many of them were sent to Artane because of the difficulties of their character and because of a good deal of mischievousness of conduct.' The minister did admit that 'the unfortunate background' of many of these boys and of their incarceration might be 'possibly due to evil social conditions'. But this merely meant that deputies should 'realise how careful the handling of them as a group must be.' Significantly, Moylan was anxious to note again that, while the schools were very successful, 'it would be very difficult to improve the conditions under which the schools operate, certainly without substantial subvention from the state.'

Moylan even concluded on a rhetorical note. Ignoring the minor issue of a fourteen-year-old child with a broken arm, the fiscally parsimonious minister of a state—and of a political party—that was even more parsimonious in the virtues of charity claimed that he could not 'conceive any deliberate ill-treatment of boys by a community motivated by the ideals of its founder.' Equally, he could not 'conceive any sadism emanating from men who were trained to a life of sacrifice and of austerity.'

In fact the Ryan Commission into child abuse later unveiled a series of radically different facts about the very same case. The minister might have believed that Christian Brothers were incapable of acts of sadism, but at the commission the brother who inflicted the injuries admitted that 'I lost my temper, and in the spur of the moment I caught the brush and hit the boy. But how often or where I hit him I can't say for definite.'

The commission's report noted that the attack left the boy, Thomas, with 'lacerations to his arm and head, in addition to the fracture that was later diagnosed.' The second Christian Brother, who also testified at the commission, admitted that he had 'seen a boy hit several times with a brush, causing visible injuries to his head and arm' but 'didn't realise there was any harm done . . . at the time until some time afterwards.' It was an admission that rather contradicted the claims that violence wasn't a feature of life in Artane.

The report noted of the minister's claims of there being a regular regime of inspections that there was 'no evidence that the inspections conducted on the Department's behalf included an examination of the use of corporal punishment.' Typical of the mores of the time, the Inspector of Industrial Schools, having subsequently been informed of the episode, suggested in the mildest of terms that the department's circular on 'Discipline and Punishment in Certified Schools' might be 'brought to the notice of the School Staff from time to time'.

It was an affair that, in truth, had few heroes. The press, when it came to this 'school for delinquents', unquestioningly reported the view of the teachers that 'the story had been exaggerated'.

Ultimately the absence of any change in the treatment of children was epitomised by the response of Honest Jack Lynch some years later to a query by Noël Browne about the fate of a child forcibly removed from his father to an industrial school, against the wishes of both, because of non-attendance at Mass. The response of the department—that the minister couldn't intervene in the matter—shouldn't surprise us. Like the rest of his type, Honest Jack knew that interfering in sensitive matters like this would gain him no votes in convents.

Chapter 6 ∿

DEV STEPS OUT, COSTELLO
STEPS IN AGAIN

2 June 1954

By 1954 it was time to put them out again, for the return of de Valera had provided us with one of the most disastrous Governments in the history of the state. The expansionist instincts of Seán Lemass had been foiled by the deeply conservative Seán MacEntee, who had noted in 1952 that Irish finances were 'difficult almost to the point of despair'. De Valera, in his concessionary speech, would claim that the country was 'in a most favourable situation', but it was still reeling from the budgetary 'butchering of the taxpayers' of 1952 and the subsequent deflationary crusade.

There was, sadly, scant evidence of any other crusades. In 1952, for example, the Dáil returned from its Christmas break but, finding that there was no legislation to deal with, promptly adjourned again. In a startling example of the failure of the Government in 1951–4, within Europe only Ireland and occupied Austria had failed to increase agricultural production. This, however, was only one of a multitude of failings. It was bad enough that, when compared with its successful Northern neighbours, the Republic still resembled a vast, run-down sort of farm. But the most wounding consequence for Fianna Fáil of the economic failure of the Free State was summed up by Joe Lee's elegant observation that 'the laughter of de Valera's comely maidens was now being heard in the nursing homes and the typing pools of England.'

Meanwhile the lack of any suggestions as to how they might return was typified by the claim of de Valera's confidant Erskine Childers that 'unemployment was only solved in dictatorships'.

The mood of the country during that period was captured by an IBEC report that noted:

Paradoxically with the actively voiced ambition for economic betterment there runs an undercurrent of pessimism and a lack of confidence in the prospects of achieving the prescribed aims. The declarations of expansive proposals are frequently qualified by expressions of a conflicting anti-materialism and a philosophy of an asceticism that opposes material aspirations.

The return of J. A. Costello offered little evidence that any of this would change in the near future.

Instead, all attention was cast back to an idealised past. Richard Mulcahy again stepped aside and asked the Dáil to select Costello, who again reluctantly accepted the 'chalice' of national leadership. Far from looking to the future, Mulcahy, the Civil War veteran, attempted to evoke the spirit in which we, 'in our days, being called into politics as young men, were fortunate in that we had minds like that of Griffith, with a purity of outlook and a purity of pen, and characters of steel like Pearse and Connolly and Clarke'. A country desperately attempting to determine if it had a future was instead referred to Griffith's belief, in the first issue of *Nationality* in June 1915, that 'the Irish who have survived 700 years of atrocities that are not fiction and kept their ideals through it all to be, in essence, one of the greatest peoples who have appeared on the earth.' Mulcahy then stated that

> there is not a single one of our people and not a single deputy here who does not subscribe to Griffith's declaration of faith. We picked up the spirit of that faith in our days, we were inspired to follow men . . . who, in an action of faith, broke through the political difficulties of that time, not caring what might happen to them and caring only that the spirit of the race would be unified and strengthened and kept alive to meet whatever difficulties the country might face at that time, and difficulties it faced.

Though Mulcahy claimed that in Costello's previous Government 'there was a very considerable lightening of the political atmosphere and very great political achievement,' the mood of national despair was accurately captured by Seán MacBride, who claimed that 'the best type of Government which would serve the interests of the nation in the present situation is a Government that would be representative of all the principal parties.' The reason for this was the utter failure of the new state to secure 'four main objectives to which, at least, lip service would be paid by all parties and all deputies in this house.' These were partition, unemployment, emigration and, typically for the time, 'the task of saving the Gaeltacht, which is rapidly dying, and without which the efforts that have been made to preserve the language will be utterly wasted.' MacBride claimed that 'before the men who are responsible for the setting up of this state pass away it would be possible to give a better example. Many of us are growing old. Many of the members of this house who are here today will probably not be in the next Dáil.'

Referring to a speech by Mulcahy in 1948 in which he had said that 'some of us can see the hand of God tracing a new chapter in the history of our country,' MacBride hoped that

the hand of God will in the next few years trace a new line for the development of our political institutions. It is my hope that men on both sides of this house who have in the past rendered valuable service to this nation, who have been responsible for the setting up of the institutions of the state, will realise their responsibility and will be prepared to come together, if for no other reason than to give the rising generation the hope of a spirit of tolerance and an inheritance of political example.

It was a view that was echoed by Jack McQuillan, who attacked the amount of time spent in the Dáil on 'cod motions' and 'scalphunting'. In language that has a modern resonance, he observed:

I do not know how many corners we have turned in the last thirty years, but we are still as far away from prosperity as we were when we first started out . . . I would like to see in this state, in the autumn of their lives, Deputy de Valera, Deputy Mulcahy, Deputy Mac Eoin and Deputy Aiken—all those men on both sides of the house in Fianna Fáil and Fine Gael—on one side of the house and members of one party, because there is no fundamental difference between them except a difference based on the bitterness of the Civil War.

McQuillan claimed that they had all done 'marvellous things for the people of this country prior to 1922'—and one has to say that thirty years was a bit of a lacuna, to put it mildly—but de Valera wasn't at all enthusiastic about the notion of an all-party Government, which would inevitably lead to a 'stifling of opinion'. Dev scornfully noted that someone had 'suggested that it would be a grand thing for the nation if the new Minister for Education and Deputy Mac Eoin, the new Minister for Defence, and a number of us all got together as a Government. Do you not know that we would be laughed at from one end of the country to the other?' The ageing Chief warned that 'this talk about national government is nonsense' and that 'such a Government would not be good for the country in normal times.' He believed that 'the present times are normal. I believe, considering our past, that there is as little bitterness in this country as in any country that has passed through a similar set of circumstances'. He gave the example of being in America in 1919,

very many years after the Civil War. I happened to be down in the capital of Virginia. I was at a lunch at which there was a judge of the Federal

Court, who was sitting at the table with me, and he struck the table and said, 'I hate these damn Yankees yet.' That was quite a number of years after the Civil War, which ended in 1865.

The exchanges then began to get somewhat salty. De Valera's observation that he opposed coalition 'because I believe that, in general, they are bad, and I will give my reasons' was met by the sharp response that it was 'because it put you out.' De Valera piously replied, 'I can bear these things just as well as most people. We have been here before.'

Dev then treated us to an example of his subtle, but still lethal, political style. He noted of the role of the Labour Party that he did not think 'the country will be served by going to the extent of extreme socialism.' He recalled how he 'happened to be passing Kilmainham Jail recently, and I saw the stoutness of the walls. I remembered some of the remarks made by . . . the minister in charge of industry and commerce [William Norton] about the people who should be put behind the stoutest prison walls the state could provide.' That wasn't the end of it, either, as Dev stated that one of the things that 'groups which have advanced socialist views aim at is to get hold of the Department of Justice, the police and so forth.'

The Government deputies were less than impressed with de Valera's attempt 'to try to drive a wedge between the Labour Party and the other parties in the Government' by trying to 'engender a feeling of apprehension on the part of business interests because of the fact that Deputy Norton had expressed certain views in regard to profiteers.' It was also, to put it at its mildest, something of an exaggeration to suggest that the new Labour Party Minister for Justice, James Everett, whose main claim to fame was a failed effort at jobbery when it came to a postmaster's job in Baltinglass, had Trotskyite leanings.

The Taoiseach issued a cold rejoinder to de Valera's abstruse musings. He had, thankfully,

> no intention whatever of following the leader of the opposition into theoretical considerations as to whether or not coalition Governments or inter-party Governments provide good government for the people whom they purport to represent. We are here on these benches tonight because the Irish people by a majority vote have put us here.

Costello claimed that from the beginning of the election he had made it clear that

> in so far as I was personally concerned, and so far as the party that I represented was concerned, we were stating to the people that we desired

to have an inter-party Government . . . that the condition of the country was such . . . as to demand that all or as many as possible representatives of the Irish people should come together and pool their resources.

This, he somewhat idealistically claimed, would even have been the case 'if Fine Gael were returned to this house with an overall majority.'

In an echo of an earlier age, Costello once again claimed that Fine Gael had told the people that 'neither I nor any of my colleagues, nor any member of the Fine Gael Party, desired office. We told them, above all, that we made no promises.' But circumstances had 'put myself forward to the people as one who possibly could form that Government. I did so reluctantly but entirely from a sense of duty and responsibility.'

Costello noted of de Valera's speech that 'the leader of the opposition has told the house tonight in great detail of all the advantages that we are now entering into.' The problem with this, he declared, was why the 'present opposition' was not 'returned by the electorate, if that were so?' This was all the more surprising given that 'every device that could be operated by the opposition by—will Deputy Lemass permit me to quote his letter looking for funds?—"modern electioneering methods" was put into the election campaign in order to get votes and get back.' This was done by means of a policy of 'lying propaganda'. Costello warned that, while he agreed with 'Deputy de Valera as to the necessity in modern democratic conditions for an opposition in modern politics,' the country would not 'stand for . . . Fianna Fáil's obstruction to the march of progress of the nation.'

In a rare confession of political failure Costello admitted that

> this country has suffered in the last six years. Many people have suffered unnecessary hardships because of the political instability of both Governments, the inter-party Government and the last Government. What is wanted . . . [is] a Government that would be stable—a Government that would capture the confidence of the people through the fact that it's going to last and be stable.

The *Irish Times,* meanwhile, simply declared of de Valera that 'the time of his useful service has come to an end.'

Chapter 7 ⌇

'NATIONAL PROGRESS HAS HALTED': LEMASS ADDRESSES THE STATE OF THE NATION

13 December 1956

Costello's aspiration to end the erosion of national confidence wouldn't be fulfilled. Instead, by the close of 1956 the state and its woebegone Taoiseach were being forced to confront their political failings in the starkest of terms. Initially Costello's Government had displayed some reformist instincts. But in a familiar pattern of bad luck it had been undone by the economic contraction that followed the Suez Crisis. The iron conservatism of the Minister for Finance, Gerard Sweetman of Fine Gael—who imposed 'swingeing cuts in public expenditure' in the only country in western Europe in which, from 1955 to 1957, the volume of goods consumed actually fell—depressed the economy at the precise moment when a stimulus was needed.

It wasn't as though there had been any shortage of depression. The travails of a lost decade are eloquently summed up by a passage from a local paper in Co. Mayo, quoted in Breandán Ó hEithir's *Begrudger's Guide to Irish Politics*. The paper noted with muted indignation of the following year, 1957, that it 'is gone and may all our bad luck go with it. It was a gloomy and depressing year . . . Roughly an average of 60,000 were unemployed every week, while emigration took as big a toll as ever on the cream of the youth.'

Back in December 1956, at the debate on the Christmas adjournment, the mood was equally stark. The Government, courtesy of a renewed border crisis, had lost its majority, and Fianna Fáil was experiencing its own division, between the ageing adherents of austerity and the younger 'musketeer' advocates for Keynes. There was no better evidence of the palsied nature of the party, however, than the response of de Valera to an initiative led by Noël Browne (yes, that one) that supported free second-level education. The wily de Valera accepted the principle in total—subject to 'one small addendum' of 'when financial considerations permit'. Browne soon resigned from Fianna Fáil, and few could blame him.

The disarray of Fianna Fáil may actually have served to intensify the acerbic nature of the analysis by Seán Lemass of the state of the nation. He admitted that there was not one 'responsible deputy on either side of the house who is not apprehensive of the economic and social conditions which may prevail . . . when it reassembles here in February next.' The year 1956 would be 'recorded in history as one of the worst years which this state has experienced since it was established, with the exception only of some of the war years.' Speaking of a steep decline in 'the confidence of the public in the country's future prospects', he warned that, 'in the past, no matter how adverse the circumstances, there was some progress to record.' Now, however, 'all the economic indicators tell us that national progress has halted and indeed that the country is losing ground in important directions.'

In a cold survey of the political realities, Lemass noted that, as the Government 'will remain in office at least until February the 13th', the only thing this 'final discussion' could do was to 'make an effort to ensure that they will not merely sit down and do nothing during that period'. But while he hoped that they could 'find within themselves the capacity to exertion', Lemass wasn't optimistic, seeing as the response to the 'unforeseen' balance of payments crisis had been one of panic and of the introduction of 'a policy of restriction, a policy designed to lower the living standards of our people . . . through special taxes designed for that purpose' to deflate the economy. We would see that again some six decades later, and the results have been alarmingly similar.

In an analysis that would be hotly contested even by his own party, Lemass claimed that 'the great need of our economy is to secure an expansion in overall production.' Though the economic doctors were differing, there could be no denying that the state was in a mess. Lemass starkly noted that, 'for the first time, apart from the war years, the Minister for Industry and Commerce has to record a serious diminution in the number of workers employed in industry.' Inevitably this meant that unemployment, 'as shown in the number of workers on the live register, is higher now than it has been at this time of the year for over fifteen years' and that emigration 'is proceeding at an unprecedented rate.' The collapse, meanwhile, in economic sentiment meant that 'there is no business concern . . . which could hope now to raise capital by public subscription through the stock market, and, indeed, no company would attempt it.'

Even the Government was struggling to raise funds, though the failure of a recent loan had not been 'due to the terms of the loan' but to 'the disappearance of public confidence in this Government' over its 'maladministering' of 'the affairs of the country.' It was a thoroughly modern economic crisis in other ways too, as Lemass noted that the 'the curtailment of investment activity . . . accompanied by the effects of the credit squeeze . . . is bringing the level of business activity down continuously.' This would not improve, either, so long as the coalition 'aimed deliberately at promoting unemployment, at forcing down living standards in order to keep the national accounts in balance.' This might balance the books, but it would lead only to 'falling production, falling employment, a serious deficit in international payments on current account, a drying up of capital, of credit, a restriction of business activity of all kinds.'

In a scathing attack on the Government's response to the crisis, Lemass cited a recent speech by the Taoiseach in which Costello had 'put all the goods in the shop window'. Lemass, though, wasn't impressed by the 'proposal to establish an agricultural council to advise the Minister for Agriculture' and an 'industrial council to advise the Minister for Industry and Commerce' or by the fact that 'there is also to be a capital investment council', one of whose members was 'on record as saying that emigration—the fact that emigration is possible—should be a matter for rejoicing.'

While Lemass couldn't be criticised for his observation that 'there is no worthy national aim to be realised by bringing about a lowering of the standard of living of our people,' his own solution, that 'a general election is the first essential step to the initiation of any programme of national recovery,' was less than convincing. It might have been 'futile for the Government to think, in present circumstances, that they can do anything other than preside over a further deterioration,' but there was more than a slight element of whistling past the graveyard in his claim that 'the mere prospect of a new policy, the chance of more effective administration, would . . . produce, by itself, an immediate revival in business activities.' Lemass didn't expand on his interesting theory that the return of the 76-year-old half-blind de Valera would 'influence the decisions of business boards and managements all over the country to expand rather than to curtail the scope of their activities'—and perhaps that was understandable.

In a sparsely attended debate, the support provided by the first Government speaker—the minor backbench Labour Party TD Dan Desmond—for the coalition was equivocal. Desmond was at his happiest in attacking the admission by Lemass, at the most recent Fianna Fáil ard-fheis, at which the party was thinking of securing power 'in terms of two or three months', that Fianna Fáil had 'no wish to produce a half-baked policy or one which could not be properly checked officially.' A scornful Desmond said, 'Apparently, after all the years that he has been a member of the Government, Deputy Lemass in 1956 is afraid of producing his party's policy, which he says is, at the present time, only half baked,' and some weight was carried by his query as to whether we should 'listen to the so-called sincere pleading of

Deputy Lemass for an election when he has only a half-baked policy.' Little, it appeared, had changed since 1951, when Fianna Fáil had gone to the country essentially on the basis of its 1948 manifesto.

But in an indication of growing coalition tensions, Desmond also said of the Labour Party that 'we are not smiling at the position; we are not saying that everything in the garden is lovely. Very often we are saying the reverse, and we make no secret of the fact.' It was clear that Labour had been sickened by the era of coalition and was steeling itself for the virtuous age of isolationism. According to Desmond, 'we are convinced that part of our present trouble is that to a certain degree we are following a policy which we ourselves in opposition condemned in 1952, a policy of restriction, a policy in which the budget of 1952 showed to have dire results,' and he warned that any continuation of 'the policy of 1951 and 1954, which to us was a wrong policy . . . could not have our support if it were to continue in the 1957 to 58 period.'

Ultimately the most pessimistic element of Desmond's speech was the warning that 'the only thing that may help democracy for the next few years is the fact that up to the present time there is no-one on the horizon who could take over this country as a dictator.' However, had such a person been available 'we could throw our hats to the wind for the next twelve months preaching about democracy, when we are not prepared to utilise democracy . . . to provide for the people and for the economic security which should be theirs.'

The new Fianna Fáil TD Neil Blaney, whose own ambivalence about democratic norms would wreak future havoc on his party, displayed typical Fianna Fáil pragmatism when he told Desmond that 'half a loaf at any time is better than no bread. The fact is that if we have only a half-baked policy . . . on the other side of the house, including himself and his party, have no policy whatsoever.' In spite of the harsh nature of the times, Blaney had little sympathy for Costello. When Fianna Fáil had been imposing MacEntee's austerity policies, the then opposition had claimed that Fianna Fáil was acting in this way because 'we thought the people were living too well, that they were eating too much and drinking too much.' It was an accusation Fianna Fáil had never faced before.

Blaney was undoubtedly being polemical when he claimed that 'we are now heading more quickly than ever for the break-up of this state as a unit of any significance than . . . during the previous coalition'. But his portrait of a 'western seaboard' in which 'I see every day and every week . . . houses . . . built under a Fianna Fáil Government . . . [in which] the windows are being shuttered up . . . never to reopen' was bitterly realistic. And an increasing number of voters were sharing his distaste for a Government 'with its head in the clouds, telling us that this is no fault of theirs, that they are doing as well as any other Government ever did, that they are really in difficulties and that they cannot be blamed.'

The little-known Tadhg Manley captured the doleful mood in Fine Gael as he noted that this was a Dáil that had 'gone completely away from the standard of the parliament we read about in our youth, the standard of Grattan's Parliament here in Dublin in 1778.'

After Manley asked what was an increasingly common question—'whether we are capable of conducting our own affairs along realistic lines in accordance with the people's wishes'—two old adversaries got to grips with each other. Seán MacBride claimed that Seán MacEntee was 'one of the most disheartening things in our public life.' MacEntee then snapped, 'Go on, Uriah Heep.' After the abuse ended, MacBride responded to Blaney's query as to 'why we supported the present Government if we did not agree with its policies,' answering, 'We know that the alternative to Deputy Sweetman as Minister for Finance is Deputy MacEntee, and we know that Deputy MacEntee's policies will be far worse than Deputy Sweetman's.'

An obviously disenchanted Taoiseach didn't exactly lift the mood when, in language that intriguingly resembles that of Brian Cowen, he noted that, while 'the year 1956 presented this Government with difficulties and problems which faced no other Irish Government,' these were not 'due to anything that we did or omitted to do, or that we failed or neglected to have done.' Costello then slammed a 'hypocritical' opposition who,

> far from giving one single piece of help to the Government or to the country in the nation's difficulties . . . have set themselves out in every possible way, at every time, and in every direction, not merely to embarrass the Government, but to prevent the Government or the country from taking, and submitting to, the necessary steps to retrieve the economic and financial ills that were affecting this country.

This wouldn't be the last time such comments would be made about Fianna Fáil.

In spite of such difficulties, however, Costello claimed that at least the Government could say, 'and I believe the country understands it now, that . . . we as a Government, an inter-party Government . . . were strong enough in times of stress and trial to . . . take unpopular measures . . . in the national interest.' It was thin enough gruel, but did Fianna Fáil have anything better? The Taoiseach certainly didn't think so. In critiquing the 'slighting references' made by Lemass to the speech he made, he noted that the Government at least had 'a policy'. In contrast, the Taoiseach was curious about the fate of 'the proposals for spending £90 million to £100 million that were outlined by Deputy Lemass last year. Nobody knows where they are to get that money. Everybody knows that the Tory finance policy of Deputy MacEntee is opposed to that policy.'

In an unrelentingly downbeat address, Costello claimed that

> we have done our job . . . We have no illusions that everything is grand . . .
> We believe we have done a hard, and a thankless, but a necessary job. We
> face the future not with any degree of complacency but knowing that we
> have even more formidable difficulties . . . We are going to do that job in
> our own time, and . . . when we have had time to bring our policy into
> operation we shall face the country with confidence, knowing that Fianna
> Fáil will never disgrace these benches here again.

It all ended on a fittingly bitter note, with Lemass snarling, 'That is the way the
Taoiseach asks for co-operation.' Costello cuttingly replied, 'I have long since
ceased to hope for it.' Whatever Costello's views were on their co-operative
instincts, his expectations about the continuing exile of Fianna Fáil from
power were not to be fulfilled.

Instead, months later, when three of Fine Gael's leading lights journeyed up
to the Áras to return their ministerial seals, the gloomy mood was captured in
an exchange after James Dillon had said he 'was never in a public house in my
life except my own in Ballaghaderreen.' After Costello remarked that he had
only once been in a pub, the third Fine Gael member, Paddy Lindsay,
exploded, 'I know now why we are going in this direction today.' In truth,
though there were plenty of other reasons for de Valera's victory, Lindsay
wasn't too far wrong.

Chapter 8 ∼

HOPING FOR AN 'UPSURGE OF PATRIOTISM': MR LEMASS IS CHOSEN

23 June 1959

It came as a shock to some, but in 1959 the Irish political system learnt that de Valera was actually mortal. The Chief's period of 'useful service', which had stretched across four decades, was finally over. Though he had secured the insurance of being stowed away in the Park for the next fourteen years, even for de Valera it had been a messy exit, as he flitted from the Dáil chamber chased by Noël Browne and Jack McQuillan over his lucrative takeover of the Irish Press Group by stealth.

De Valera might have claimed in 1958 that 'Ireland's sun was only rising', but he had left a wretched legacy. Lemass would have to deal with a sclerotic civil service and a party and, more importantly still, a Government whose defining ethos was one of suspicion when it came to modernity. The dream of an Arcadia that could remain safely cut off from the world had turned into a Frankenstein's monster, which, as Tom Garvin noted, was 'increasingly held to be undesirable, unfair and unendurable.'

The proof of this proposition was that since independence a quarter of the country's people had fled a society of demoralised bachelors and spinsters. Yet in spite of these failures the first two years of de Valera's last Government had been dominated by an attempt to change the electoral system by getting rid of PR. It wasn't good enough, and Lemass himself admitted before his election that Fianna Fáil has 'accepted the conclusion that the economic development proposals which it initiated twenty-six years ago . . . have not proved to be sufficient to bring about all the economic and social progress which we desired and which we believed can be accomplished.'

All these factors meant that there was a distinct absence of warmth in response to the new dispensation. Referring to the Government's curious obsession with PR, the Fine Gael leader, J. A. Costello, claimed that his opposition to Lemass was not based on

> the personality of the Taoiseach designate but on the fact that he and the Government who have resigned, and who are now in office awaiting re-election, have been guilty in recent times of grave dereliction of public duty and gross breach of the confidence that was imposed in them by the electorate on the occasion of the last general election.

Costello said that, were 'the circumstances . . . different from what they actually are, we possibly could find it in our hearts to have some sympathy for the person who is now—for whatever length of time remains to the life of the Government—appointed here today or tomorrow.' However, the first unique circumstance that had to be confronted was that, normally, any new Taoiseach would have 'the comfort and support of the fact that he has recently secured a victory in the polls' and comes 'fresh from the people with a clear mandate.' In this case, however, the Government had 'just come from experiencing a very severe rebuff from a big majority of the Irish people.' It was deserved, in Costello's view, because of the dereliction of duty that saw, 'for nine months now, the country given over to academic and philosophical discussions of the various electoral systems and the advantages and disadvantages of electoral systems.'

Dev might have been trying to pull a bit of a stroke, but the claim by Dan Desmond of the Labour Party that abolishing PR was an attempt to 'to put back the hands of the clock, to introduce into public life here a system that in the early years of this country brought bloodshed, hatred and bitterness into the hearts of Irishmen' did appear to be a tad hysterical. It wasn't exceptional, unfortunately, as Joe Blowick claimed that 'the illegal bid for dictatorship had been blown sky high by the people.'

Noël Browne, in contrast, was somewhat more conciliatory. He observed that 'one is so overwhelmed by the mediocrity of most of his cabinet colleagues that it would appear to me to be clear that the Government had little alternative but to put forward Deputy Lemass.' Browne's support, however, was qualified by the undeniable fact that Lemass had 'left us with a near-constant 10 per cent unemployed and has led to the best part of three-quarters of a million of our choice young people getting out of the country.' Browne hoped that

> Deputy Lemass will be honest enough and, I hope, shrewd enough to understand that that is the real measure of his failure, and the failure of the test he has asked us from time to time to apply: the failure to give employment to those who need it. In that context his handling of the creation of an Irish industrial arm has failed signally.

While there was an element of hope in Lemass's new freedom from 'the conservatism of his leader . . . and the jealousy of his colleagues,' Browne honestly believed that Fianna Fáil was 'in government for the last time.'

James Dillon, in contrast, simply called Lemass a fraud, one who in 1957 'plastered the country with posters calling on the women of Ireland to vote for him so he could get their husbands jobs.' Now, however, a mere two years later, they resemble 'a jittery crowd of frightened men . . . Look at them: a combination of Stygian gloom, interrupted occasionally by hysterical outbursts. They have got the wind up.'

Others appeared to be in a similar condition. According to the independent TD Frank Sherwin, 'history has proved that when the big chief goes everything flops. When O'Connell went, the Repeal movement flopped. When Parnell went, his movement flopped. Even when Cromwell died, his son got panicky and handed back full control to the generals.'

Oliver J. Flanagan, never a man to leave a thought unspoken on a momentous occasion, claimed of the future national treasure Lemass that, when it came to his record, 'we must associate him with failure, graft and dishonesty.' Unsurprisingly this sparked what the record cautiously refers to as 'protestations'; but an unrepentant Oliver J claimed that 'he has exercised political Fianna Fáil jobbery, and he is carrying it out in Bord na Móna, where I have knowledge of it . . . We all remember the railway shares with which he was associated, and we all remember the Locke Tribunal.'

In truth, Oliver J would have been wise to forget that particular debacle, but he wanted to 'give the house another reason why Deputy Lemass should not be elected Taoiseach.' Only a few weeks ago, Flanagan claimed, Lemass had written 'a blackmailing letter to people—company directors and others—associated with his department. He put the gun to their heads and asked them for money to fight an election.'

After Flanagan claimed he had the book with the names and addresses of the directors—unsurprisingly, it never actually surfaced—Donogh O'Malley, who would in time have many a tussle with Oliver J, asked the Leas-Cheann Comhairle, 'On a point of order, sir, are you going to allow Deputy Oliver J. Flanagan to continue in that slanderous vein?'

The Leas-Cheann Comhairle, who was making the best of a bad lot, had precisely that intention, though Oliver J was doing little to help him via claims that 'the most damaging part of all was for any man about to be prime minister in three weeks to put the name of his son-in-law [Charles Haughey] at the bottom of the letter, a deputy of this house, and say, "If you do not send the money to me, send the money to him".'

Whatever about Oliver J, Brendan Corish's claim for Lemass—'When I think of him I think of Sir Anthony Eden, who was not recognised until relatively late in life'—though understandable, was somewhat less than prescient.

The welcome mat continued to be noticeable only for its absence as M. J. O'Higgins of Fine Gael tutted dolefully about how we had 'two or three words in Irish from Deputy MacEntee and another couple of words in Irish from Deputy Dr Ryan when proposing Deputy Lemass as Taoiseach.' Neither of them, O'Higgins said, 'made any reference to the work Deputy Lemass will do as Taoiseach . . . We have no idea whatever what policy Deputy Lemass, as Taoiseach, with a new Government, proposes to follow.'

The mood didn't improve in the wake of the announcement by Lemass of his new Government. He claimed that the amount of work faced by the Government meant that 'the only practical course is to make the minimum of changes.'

But a disappointed Costello noted of the bright new Government of all the Civil War ancients that there was nothing here to 'dissipate the extraordinary cloud of dullness that has hung over the Fianna Fáil Government for many years past.' Costello also offered a cutting analysis of the position Lemass found himself in. He was 'something like a prisoner at a Russian trial confessing in public his faults. He confesses that his policy of self-sufficiency, his policy of high tariffs and quotas, has not resulted in any real prosperity in the country or any hope for economic prosperity.'

Dillon came back for a second bite of the cherry, somewhat sorrowfully claiming that after twenty-five years of Lemass's 'policy of economic development' we were 'on the industrial side . . . an underdeveloped country' comparable to Greece, Iceland and Turkey.

Frank Sherwin colourfully summed up the deteriorating morale among those who had lived outside of de Valera's charmed circle of Government colleagues. His doleful claim was that 'I am sure some of the backbenchers of his party . . . and some good men I know, have gone on the beer—to put it straight—they got so tired waiting for an opportunity.'

Lemass, however, was quick to hit back at his critics, reminding the Dáil that the reason the day's proceedings were necessary at all was that 'the previous Taoiseach, Éamon de Valera, has been elected Uachtarán na hÉireann by popular vote.' Lemass, reasonably enough, found it 'difficult to follow the reasoning which interprets this event as implying some undermining of public confidence in the Government.' The new Taoiseach welcomed Costello's offer of constructive opposition, though he sardonically noted that 'his assurances appeared to have come wrapped in a rather strange package.' Unlike some of his dainty colleagues, Lemass admitted that, 'personally, I have a liking for the rough and tumble of the party conflict, and indeed I think it does not do any harm to the national interest.' It was, after all, generally 'through the disputation of political parties that the people become aware of the political issues that are under consideration here.'

Lemass noted of policy issues that 'the best time for that' might be 'in the

Taoiseach's estimates next month'. However, he did tell the TDs that 'there is no need for deputies to seek to impress on this Government the urgency and the importance of getting under way development projects that will give employment and improved conditions.'

Unsurprisingly, he dismissed the prospect of a general election on the grounds that it would be unfair to the country and the Government. In an oblique reference to what would be a U-turn on economic policy, the new Taoiseach noted that the Government, having 'in the past eight months or so published a programme of economic expansion as an official white paper' that had won expressions of approval from 'organisations representing all economic interests', might be better served by implementing it than by talking about it.

Towards the close of his speech, Lemass, a politician who was far more idealistic than his reputation suggested, offered the Dáil a rare insight into his personal political philosophy. 'I believe that national progress of any kind depends largely upon an upsurge of patriotism—a revival of patriotism, if you will—directed towards constructive purposes.' Unlike the school of rhetoricians whom Liam Cosgrave summarily dismissed as 'dying for Ireland again', Lemass described his idea of patriotism as 'a combination of love of country, pride in its history, traditions and culture, and a determination to add to its prestige and achievement.'

It was a remarkably clear and level-headed vision when compared with the ornate speechifying that typified so many newly elected Taoiseach's proclamations of intent. But simplicity is often one of the principal signifiers of genius.

AFTER THE LOST DECADE NEW HOPE BLOSSOMS . . . BUT OLD PROBLEMS SCOWL

Chapter 9 ∽

A TURN TO THE LEFT: LEMASS LEADS ON

23 April 1963

Possibly the best measure of Lemass's achievement is that he left the country in a very different state from the one he found it in, where, according to the historian Diarmaid Ferriter, 'the language of malaise' was endemic in public discourse. This shouldn't come as a surprise, as Ireland in 1959 was a country that wasn't working, in every sense of the word. Between 1951 and 1961 more than 412,000 people emigrated, and this at a time when employment had fallen by 38,000. Another poignant indicator of the stultified nature of the Ireland that de Valera's parsimonious caution had shaped was that 64 per cent of its population was single. It was the highest percentage of unmarried women in the western world, and few of these singletons were living in sin, either. Indeed, such was the level of desperation about the vanishing Irish that at one point a tax on bachelors was proposed.

The situation was so grim in 1957 that Ken Whitaker, Ireland's good civil servant, had written the provocatively titled paper 'Has Ireland a Future?' and warned that people 'are falling into a mood of despondency. After thirty-five years of native government, can it be, they are asking, that economic independence achieved with such sacrifice must wither away?' That was about to change, as Lemass embraced Whitaker's opposition to the dangers of 'un-progressive isolation' and to an economy centred on tariffs and self-sustainability. He did so with such enthusiasm, Whitaker noted (with either great innocence or subtlety), that 'it was a very pleasant surprise when the Fianna Fáil Government committed so much to self-sufficiency and protection abandoned it all so readily.'

The embrace of modernity and foreign investment made for some change from the famous visit of an IMF delegation in 1958, described in John Horgan's biography of Lemass, during which it was treated by de Valera to a latter-day version of the St Patrick's Day 'comely maidens' speech of 1943. After de

Valera's departure one of the members of the group had said circumspectly to Whitaker, 'He's a strange man, your PM.'

The economic renaissance that occurred during Lemass's reign as Taoiseach was critical, but while he disguised his ambitions behind a veneer of bluff pragmatism his achievements were as much in the arena of national morale as in mere economic statistics. Lemass essentially went to war with the post-colonial lassitude of a state that was so comfortable with underachievement that the main opposition party, much to the contempt of Lemass, cared little about whether they were in government or in opposition.

It wasn't a perfect journey, though, and one of Lemass's prime concerns was to ensure that the Government and the state maintained a sense of impetus. Nothing embodied this more than the budget of 1963. It occurred at a moment when Lemass was coming under pressure. Growth had fallen off, and the spirit of 'nationalism and idealism' that Lemass had hoped to inculcate in the governance of the country was, according to John Horgan, 'becoming lethally vulnerable to the claims of special interests and the industrially powerful on both sides of the negotiating table.' When it came to a budget that would pass by only one vote, the omens were not good. In 1960 the Government had introduced the delights of PAYE to the masses. Now they were planning to introduce a newfangled turnover tax that would eventually evolve into the modern-day version of VAT.

Such a development certainly put Fine Gael on the offensive, and their testy spokesperson on finance, Gerard Sweetman, noted that 'there are two things which always seem to me to be typical of the Fianna Fáil party: one is the brazenness of their bluff, and the other, the excellence of their propaganda.' According to Sweetman, however, nothing could disguise the fact that in this budget 'they have not merely raided the till but they have taken the whole till away.'

For once, after the recent years of prosperity, Fine Gael was in a position to make hay. New statistics, Sweetman warned, had revealed that, 'in spite of all the ballyhoo, in spite of all the propaganda, and in spite of all the promises by Fianna Fáil, between 1956 and 1962 . . . there are today, as we stand here, 58,500 fewer persons employed in Ireland than there were six years ago.' He was well entitled to ask:

> Where are the 100,000 jobs the Taoiseach promised? Where was the great plan the Taoiseach promised he had only to take out of a drawer and put into operation . . . Where are the placards Fianna Fáil had about wives getting their husbands back to work?

In a cutting critique, Sweetman observed that all Fianna Fáil was creating was new taxes and jobs for themselves.

Last year and the year before, people got from the Minister for Finance a new form of taxation in PAYE. This year they have got another new form of tax . . . a turnover tax. I think most of them will go home tonight and tomorrow wondering what new tax Fianna Fáil are going to think up for them next year.

Worse still, Fianna Fáil, 'instead of taxing perfumes, furs, expensive motor cars and jewellery—as was announced by the Minister for Lands, Brian Lenihan— is taxing bread, butter, sugar, tea and milk and all the necessaries of life.'

After Sweetman noted with confidence that 'these are the obsequies of Fianna Fáil', James Dillon, leader of Fine Gael, contentedly claimed that Fianna Fáil now resembled the gambler 'who has plunged pretty heavily already and determines he is now prepared to let the tail go with the hide in one mighty effort.' He asked where the consistency was in a situation in which,

having gone on record in 1961 as saying that a purchase tax, or a substantial increase in direct taxation—such as provided for here in the extravagant increase in the corporation profits tax—was inimical to expansion, we find ourselves in 1963 . . . levying the very two taxes which it was stated only two years ago were absolutely fatal to any prospect of achieving that objective which we have internationally committed ourselves to seek.

Dillon compared the Government to 'the man who sold his soul for a penny roll and a lump of hairy bacon.' But if the opposition believed, or at least hoped, that the impetus of the Lemass revolution had been halted, they were to be disappointed by his speech.

Lemass made it quite clear that 'this budget rests on the proposition that economic and social progress require increased Government spending.' He warned that 'the stimulation of higher production, the realisation of higher levels of employment, the extension of health, education and social welfare services, the provision of more houses, the improvement of communications and similar public services which make for better living in town and country, all require to be financed in whole or part through the budget.' It was, he observed with some distaste, a fact that Dillon had 'ostentatiously avoided in the whole of his speech.'

Lemass then noted that a crucial benefit of the budget was that it would 'help to clarify the really fundamental differences in approach to national problems between the Fine Gael and Fianna Fáil parties, about which there may have been some deliberately fostered ambiguity in the past.' The Fine Gael approach, as disclosed in Dillon's speech that afternoon, Lemass said, 'is negative, deflationary, timorous, political in the extreme. The Fianna Fáil attitude is, and I hope will always remain, positive, constructive and national.'

Lemass was in quite the Scandinavian mood as he observed that it was 'noteworthy that in the wealthier countries the proportion of the national income taken for public purposes is higher than in the less well off countries.' This was 'understandable', because a country can

> give itself better public services only to the extent that the total national income provides a margin over and above what is necessary to maintain reasonable living standards. As we get better off, we can spend more—we can spend more relatively as well as absolutely—for desirable public purposes, and it will be the policy of this Government to do so.

In a rare direct statement—well, rare for Irish politics, at least—Lemass noted that

> it is just foolish to fulminate against taxation and to demand at the same time more spending for better public services. Nobody likes taxation, and nobody is expected to like it.

Far from losing his bearings, Lemass was about to engage in an equally critical shift in political direction to his abandonment of the protectionist economic policy of the 50s. In a piece of political scene-setting that would forge the template for an extraordinary efflorescence of new initiatives, such as free education, Lemass told the house that he believed 'the time has come when national policy should take a shift to the left.'

The shadows of MacEntee and the conservative old guard were finally being cast aside. For Lemass this shift meant, firstly,

> more positive measures than have heretofore been attempted ... to ensure the effective translation of the benefits of economic progress into the improvement of social conditions and specifically an equitable wage structure, wider educational opportunities, the extension of the health services and of our systems of protection against the hazards of old age, illness and unemployment.

Secondly, this move would involve

> more direct Government intervention when necessary to keep the national economy on an even keel while maintaining the pace of our economic advance; thirdly, the maintenance of state investment activity at the highest possible level, having regard to available resources; and, fourthly, the more detailed planning of our economic activities so as to ensure the flow of resources in the directions where prospects are best, if necessary

diverting them from sectors where prospects are poorest.

He signalled the direction in which he was looking by expressing his desire to draw

> the attention of deputies to the statement made by the Minister for Education . . . when he said that he intends shortly to make a statement regarding Government policy in respect of the development and strengthening of the country's educational facilities.

Lemass added that he did not wish to 'anticipate that statement; but what I do wish to do is to congratulate the Labour Party on having produced a policy in that respect.' Such a move, he warned, was all the more necessary because, 'in the world of tomorrow, economic progress in this country, as in others, will depend more upon the education, training and skill of our people than on muscle power.' He warned that the 'time is not far distant when the unskilled labourer will be in diminishing demand, and it is not too soon to start preparing the next generation of our people for this situation.'

The old man in a hurry was also in a pretty tart mood when it came to complaining businessmen, and he felt the best response to increased taxation was to 'maximise efficiency'. Better still, those companies worried about higher taxes might even 'try to expand their export sales, to divert more of their products into exports, if they can do so, and in that way escape the effect of the tax rise altogether.' After a bullish Lemass stated that the Government 'framed this budget in the conviction that there are great and exciting prizes to be won for this country, provided we go after them boldly and intelligently,' he was momentarily slowed by a sardonic quip of 'What, again?' from the new Labour Party leader, Brendan Corish.

The Taoiseach, though, was in no mood to be stopped, and ministers were advised to curtail their summer holidays, for this was 'not a time for rest but for exertion; this is not a time for retrenchment but expansion; not a time for timidity but courage.' In a warning that retains its resonance four decades later, Lemass said:

> We have experienced in recent years all the excitement of a vigorous growth and all the stimulus of new hopes . . . Some of our national critics used to say that we as a people always proceeded by spurts and stops, that we lack the stamina for a sustained effort. We can prove to them how wrong they are by the manner in which we face up to the opportunities which now face us.

In the long run, of course, national progress would stall—not least because of the fleshier desires of his son-in-law, Charles Haughey. For now, though, Lemass was still prepared to lead on as he sought the new big idea that would take the country forwards.

Chapter 10 ～

IN THE 'AFFLUENT SOCIETY' EVEN THE UNDESERVING POOR DESERVE JUSTICE

12 October 1966

As Ireland prepared to celebrate the fiftieth anniversary of the 1916 Rising, the official line was that we had finally become an 'affluent society'. But even in the 1960s, amidst the modest prosperity of the new ballroom culture of Cloudlands and Dreamlands, and the rather less bashful Taca variant, we were a long way away from being the perfect country. Seán Lemass had somewhat frantically announced the need for a shift to more left-wing politics in 1963, but the old nineteenth-century Poor Law attitudes were still clinging on tightly. The mohair suits might have been shining, but the staple diet in a large number of working-class estates was still tea and bread. Thousands of children were still incarcerated in industrial schools, and the Department of Health was busy ignoring reports about the maltreatment of patients in psychiatric hospitals.

The dispute that evolved within the Dáil over yet another example of the less than equal state of the nation was all the more intriguing because of the personnel involved. James Dillon was the recently retired Fine Gael leader, whose time in office had been marked by serious tensions between himself, the last great scion of the Irish parliamentary tradition, and the radical 'Just Society' wing of the party. Brian Lenihan (senior), in contrast, was a progressive, 'No problem', modernising Minister for Justice, seen as being on the somewhat shallow Keynesian wing of Fianna Fáil.

In this debate both sides found themselves in a surprising place after Dillon rose, in the wake of a newspaper report on a court case, as an advocate in the 'grave case of a citizen of this state who is described as homeless and friendless, hungry and sick, physically and mentally.' He admitted that he didn't know the man or 'his attendant circumstances', and he acknowledged that there were outstanding charges in other courts. However, he said these were peripheral matters when set against the judge's claim, in sending the man to Mountjoy, that 'our society cares for this sort in the same way as we did a hundred years ago.'

Dillon was soon in full rhetorical flow and claimed that 'I want to avail of the house to challenge that statement. I deny it.' He added that the judge had said that

> the man has been very seriously ill for a considerable time, and he has pleaded guilty to breaking and entering a hotel by opening an unlocked door and stealing ten shillings from one of the rooms. He did not touch any other property in the hotel, and the money he took was spent on food.

In what was certainly a poignant tale, the investigating officer, Dillon said, had accepted that

> the man needed the money for food. He has no friends or relatives, save for one who lives a hundred miles from here, and with whom the defendant has not been in communication for two years . . . Gardaí are satisfied that this man is not physically ill but, to some extent, mentally ill.

He noted that, ultimately, the most critical aspect of the case had been the judge's own admission that 'the state of our society does not provide for the defendant.' Dillon wanted to 'deny it', as he 'would be ashamed to be a member of the house if that were true.' A somewhat optimistic Dillon claimed that

> we do not deal with problems of this kind today as they were dealt with a hundred years ago. For one thing, we have a sovereign parliament, which protects our people, and we are not living under an alien administration.

This meant that the Minister for Justice is

> answerable to us and not to the British House of Commons . . . Because there are 144 of us here, this homeless man has 144 friends, because we represent the Irish people.

Such an outwardly benign situation meant that,

> since this is evidently a case where the prerogative can be exercised and the man released from jail, I want to put the case that we cannot rest easily in this house if we believe that there is a man in jail who was mentally ill

when the act complained of was perpetrated.

In an intriguingly progressive analysis of poverty, Dillon said:

> The undeserving poor are entitled to justice . . . We are not living under
> Queen Victoria, and I am putting it to the minister that if there is a man
> of unsound mind, however undeserving, in jail for breaking and entering
> a house to get ten shillings to buy food because he was hungry and
> homeless and friendless . . . we do not believe that this society to which we
> belong . . . this affluent society, does not cater for the likes of him.

Despite his status as a less-than-closet opponent of the Just Society, there were
strong elements of that philosophy in Dillon's warning that

> there is no one of us who might not sink into the gutter in our time. But
> if any one of us did sink to the level of abandonment . . . he would have
> friends and relations and people who would be there with counsel and
> solutions and undertakings and explanations.

In contrast, Dillon noted that 'the reason this man is in Mountjoy is that he
has no relatives and no friends and no-one to speak for him'. But 'whatever
offence he committed, if his mind was sick, it is not appropriate that, because
he was poor and homeless and friendless, we should shovel him into
Mountjoy.' Instead, we should be able to proudly say that 'here in Ireland,
under our own Government, we do make provision not only for the deserving
but for the undeserving poor.'

As was his wont, Brian Lenihan attempted to smooth any unhappiness over
with the emollient observation that 'Deputy Dillon is certainly to be admired
in his pursuit of the interest of the individual, but on this occasion I think he
has just not got hold of the facts.' Lenihan then told the Dáil that he had taken
a personal interest in the case and could 'assure the deputy that all the lay,
medical and psychiatric advice is that this man is being very well looked after'.
In an inadvertent admission about the Irish psychiatric services, Lenihan
claimed that 'he is probably being much better looked after in that respect
than he would be outside.'

Dillon at this point interjected, 'But he is in jail.'

This small consideration had no effect on the sanguinity of Lenihan, who
assured

> the deputy that this word 'jail', which he uses in such a manner, with a
> Victorian connotation, is not the manner in which we use the term today.
> We happen to have evolved here, under successive Governments, a

humane administration of justice. As far as anybody in this sort of condition in jail today is concerned, he is better off than he would be in most of the hospitals in the country.

It didn't exactly say much for the condition of the hospitals either, but the minister wasn't to be moved. The interjections started to become rough at this point, with Dillon snapping, 'That is insane,' and Lenihan urging, 'Now let us get back to the facts and away from the hysterical bluff'.

Lenihan agreed that there was 'a sacred obligation residing in any Minister for Justice to exercise the prerogative of mercy', but in this case Dillon was 'bluffing' and 'acting in a hysterical and hypocritical fashion'. Showing that he could wield the knife with the best of them, Lenihan added that 'the deputy is using the word "jail" in the Victorian sense, and he is as outdated as Charles Dickens.'

The incandescent minister repeated the view of the prison psychiatrists that 'the man is much better left alone' and added: 'Deputy Dillon is doing no service to this man's future. He is merely making use of this man's case across the floor of the house for the purpose of his own advertisement.'

But ultimately the most acute query of all came from a little-known Fine Gael deputy, Fintan Coogan (senior), who asked, 'What about when he comes out?'

Answer from the minister there came none, for, like that of many others in Fianna Fáil, Lenihan's radicalism was somewhat skin-deep. This was epitomised by his subsequent visit to the industrial school at Artane: within minutes he had said to his driver, 'Get me out of this fucking place.' It was a liberty the children he was supposed to protect did not have.

Chapter 11 ∽

THE RELUCTANT TAOISEACH TAKES TO THE PITCH

10 November 1966

Though it didn't look that way at the time, when Lemass decided it was time to end his quasi-monarchical status as the old Taoiseach of a young Government the ease of the transition was surprising. As the unwanted handing over neared, Charles Haughey was for some the great hope; for others he was a creeping nightmare. Patrick Hillery summed up the majority view on Haughey's move for power in his typically understated fashion: 'People did not think much of what was offering.' Others were less subtle, and party veterans such as Oscar Traynor and Gerald Boland openly feared that Haughey would yet drag the party into the mire: already by 1966 he kept horses and rode to hounds, was photographed wearing a top hat and had developed very public expensive tastes.

The most acute summary, in contrast, of the character of Jack Lynch—or certainly of how he was perceived by the liberal intelligentsia—came from the great satirist Breandán Ó hEithir, who made the claim, somewhat tongue in cheek, that it was 'simply not true that Jack Lynch did not have a vision of Ireland, just as de Valera and Seán Lemass did.' Lynch's Ireland, however,

> revolved around the Munster final . . . Drink would be consumed in manly moderation before and after the Great Event, and songs would be sung in orderly but forthright fashion. 'The Banks', 'The Boul' Thady Quill' and 'An Poc ar Buile' would make the rafters ring, but any troublemaker who struck up 'We Shot 'Em in Pairs Comin' Down the Stairs' would be immediately handed over to an understanding constabulary. ('Just a few thumps, sergeant. He can't hold it.')

Lynch certainly played up his apolitical status when it suited him. No other politician would ever have claimed that when he was 'first asked to stand I did toss a coin as to whether I would or would not stand', though he was also anxious to make it clear that the coin wasn't tossed as a choice between Fianna Fáil and Fine Gael but rather as to whether he would stand at all.

Lynch was also a genuinely reluctant convert to ministerial life. Noel Whelan in his history of Fianna Fáil notes that it took de Valera three meetings to persuade Lynch to take a Government position. When Lynch admitted that his wife wouldn't like it, the aged Chief, in a rare display of humanity, replied, 'We all have trouble with our wives.'

That wasn't to be the end of the trouble with the wives: Lynch's wife was later opposed to his taking the Taoiseach's post, and George Colley's wife wasn't willing to allow her husband to withdraw. As he tried to sort the debacle out, an astonished Lemass asked, 'What kind of people have I got when one man has to get his wife's permission to run, and the other has to get his wife's permission to withdraw?'

Within the Dáil, Lynch's accession was a frosty affair. The Fine Gael TD Gerard Sweetman warned that

> the election of 1965 was fought on the slogan of 'Let Lemass lead on.' Now that Deputy Lemass has decided not to lead the Fianna Fáil party . . . it is proper that the only way in honour of dealing with this would be for the Fianna Fáil party to go to the country and ask the people to decide what they want to do, now that their slogan is no longer operative.

Oddly enough Fianna Fáil wasn't at all keen to take that road. In what would become a continuing theme, Sweetman also warned that Lynch's leadership was the starting-gun for the most 'disreputable battle of the knives the country has seen.' This was a 'battle of the knives that has not yet ended', for the mysterious 'they' will 'go on sharpening their knives, and their tomahawks, for poor Deputy Lynch.'

The Labour Party, meanwhile, entertainingly proposed Brendan Corish for the role. Though the party was somewhat short of the numbers required, the colourful Seán Dunne claimed that this wasn't a fruitless exercise. The party was instead

> engaging by our actions in a solemn declaration of intent . . . Every day that passes adds to the mass of evidence of growing support for the Labour Party. The youth especially, clear of mind and eye, repelled by the political cynicism which they see in Civil War parties, are looking in growing numbers to the ideals of Connolly and Larkin.

In the somewhat cynical environs of the Dáil the Labour Party candidacy was proposed and disposed of without too much fuss, while the outwardly tranquil mood of the Fianna Fáil TDS was summed up by a comment of 'Another all-Ireland, Jack' after the formality of the vote was over.

Lynch's acceptance speech was pithy. He deeply appreciated 'the honour that has been conferred on me. All I shall say now is that I shall endeavour to fulfil my duties as Taoiseach to the best of my ability.' The quiet man concluded by noting that 'no man left a greater mark on the progress of the nation than Seán Lemass. As I said already, he has set the highest of standards because these are the only standards he knew.'

The Fine Gael leader, Liam Cosgrave, was somewhat less impressed with the standard of Lynch and of his not-so-new Government, claiming that 'it has been apparent for a long, long time that ministers have been vying with one another in looking for preferment and advancement' and that Government policy 'has been largely made and wholly implemented by civil servants.' He added that

> one immediate change that had to be made was that, whatever else was done with Deputy Haughey, he had to get out of Agriculture, because with him farming was a late vocation. Like a politician in another country who was, I understand, baptised and vaccinated on the same day, neither of them took. Not since the days of landlordism has there been so much resentment and bitterness in rural Ireland.

Cosgrave, who possessed a unique capacity for putting the interests of the country above those of his own party, was even less impressed by the statement from the retiring Lemass that the 'one consideration that is important above all others, so far as I am concerned, is the success of the Fianna Fáil party in the next and subsequent general elections.' For Cosgrave that was 'surely a false foundation on which to build democracy,' and he was to be proved correct.

A touch of humour managed to enter the proceedings when Cosgrave noted of the 'insatiable lust in Fianna Fáil for place, power and profit' that 'so bad was it recently, before the conflict was resolved, and so far had the situation developed, that one Fianna Fáil deputy, who shall be nameless, was found to be canvassing for both Deputy Haughey and Deputy Colley.'

Cosgrave, a wise observer of the power games in Leinster House, claimed that the Government had been 'too anxious to protest unity and too anxious to show amity and benevolence in photographs between the incoming Taoiseach and Deputy Colley. Everybody knows the present Taoiseach would not harm a fly and that any dispute was not between him and Deputy Colley.'

He drily noted of the far-from-young ranks of Fianna Fáil that 'the remark Deputy Lemass made recently about not wishing to become a historical relic certainly was hard on some of his colleagues: some of them nearly had to be carried out.'

The new Labour Party leader, Brendan Corish, expressed the hope that 'we may see some significance in this new era in that for the first time in thirty-five years there sits in the seat of the Taoiseach a person who was not actively engaged, nor could he be, in the events of 1922 or the five, six or seven turbulent years that followed.'

Corish's earthy colleague Jimmy Tully was more dismissive. While 'we all agree in the house that Deputy Jack Lynch is a very nice fellow . . . I should like to point out that the political scrapheap of this country is littered with very nice fellows.'

Seán Dunne, also of the Labour Party, was even crueller, chuckling that 'it is often said of the equine or canine species that they won pulling up. Here we have the case of a winner who was backing away.' Fianna Fáil's sensitivity about the 'reluctant Taoiseach' status of Lynch meant that it was in no humour to tolerate Dunne's claim that 'the position of Taoiseach has become "the Corkman's burden".'

But after Hillery snapped at Dunne, 'The Abbey only opened in time for you', it was ultimately Fine Gael's great old stager, Dillon, who stole the show. He claimed that

> the people ought to know what brought Deputy Lynch to where he is now. Sixty years ago the Marquis of Salisbury was Prime Minister of England. He was an old man, but he got an *idée fixe* in his mind that he wanted his nephew Arthur Balfour to succeed him. I want to submit that it is common knowledge in this country that six years ago there was an ageing prime minister in Ireland who got an *idée fixe* in his mind that he wanted his son-in-law to succeed him, Haughey.

Dillon claimed he had seen the entire scene

> unfold here in Leinster House. I saw Deputy Haughey and his Camorra, Deputy Lenihan, Minister for Justice, Deputy O'Malley, Minister for Education, and Deputy Blaney, the Minister for Local Government . . . walk through the corridors of the house telling some of the younger members of the Fianna Fáil party, 'Vote for Charlie, because if you vote for Charlie and George Colley is elected, he is not vindictive; but if you vote for George and Charlie gets elected, he will follow you to the death.' I saw some young, inexperienced members of Fianna Fáil quail at that.

It hadn't worked, however, and Dillon had witnessed the moment of recognition. He recalled seeing Haughey's face, white as parchment, and I said, 'Haughey is gone down the sink.' Remember when he failed to land his fish last Wednesday night? He will never land it. He is finished. He stinks politically, of course.

That wasn't to say that Lynch was secure either. Instead, in a piece of prophecy that was as accurate as it was dramatic, Dillon asked,

What is a *via media* [middle way] in politics? . . . Oh, yes; it is something. It is expendable. As soon as the knives have been sharpened . . . they hope . . . to send that decent man to the Park . . . But do not imagine for a moment that it is not going on now. There is not an hour, or a day, or a week, until they break his heart, that the clash of knives will not be heard in the corridors of Fianna Fáil.

It had begun to get cantankerous, and the Ceann Comhairle warned the TDS that it was 'not in order to refer to members of the house as imbeciles.' One Fianna Fáil minister was told that he was the 'Minister for Codology', and the arrival in the chamber of Martin Corry, a corrupt, abusive veteran Fianna Fáil TD, meant that the debate would become even sharper. As Corry tore into an opposition of 'laddy-o-lee lawyers', and as he claimed that the only thing the 'muck and filth' scattered around the house was fit for was to 'manure a couple of acres of spuds', it was clear that, despite Corish's optimism, Civil War politics was dying hard.

In his response the reluctant Taoiseach unveiled some of the steel he disguised so well. There was a discreet dart at Haughey in the warning that 'material progress alone would be barren indeed if it were not accompanied by the moral and intellectual development of all the individuals comprising our community.' A strong fiscal conservatism was evident in Lynch's view that 'there can be no such thing as free education: the community must be prepared to pay one way or the other.' There was a return to the themes of de Valera in the reminder to the Dáil that 'the Government defined the national aim as being to restore the Irish language as a general medium of communication.'

Above all, what Honest Jack now wanted, as we carefully resumed our way on 'the road back to the rate of economic progress we received between 1958 and 1965', was 'a better team spirit'. Rather like Bertie Ahern's subsequent 'people before politics' philosophy, Lynch believed that 'politics is about more than enacting legislation and drawing up programmes': it was also 'a question of evoking the great personal qualities that are deeply rooted in our Christian belief', and we must 'set our hearts and minds to it steadily'.

The new man also had words for the opposition. He treated 'with the contempt they deserve the lurid fantasies of knives and tomahawks painted by

Deputy Dillon,' and he claimed that it was 'a source of comfort to me . . . that members of the Fine Gael party have descended to the level of personal abuse to attack the Government.' In Lynch's view it was 'only when men are good men and are adequate to the tasks to which they have set their hands that enemies resort to such low tactics.'

As for the calls for a dissolution of the Dáil, well, in Lynch's view the opposition would be better advised to 'save their graveyard whistles for the time when they are really passing graveyards', as, far from being 'a reluctant Taoiseach', he intended to be 'a vigorous and progressive one'.

It would turn out that he had no choice in the matter.

Chapter 12

'SO CHARMING AS TO BE DANGEROUS'

30 November 1966

One 'teammate' Honest Jack would be marking very closely in his new role as captain was his radical Minister for Education, Donogh O'Malley. As with so many other things, the massive education reforms in Europe after 1945 passed Ireland by. Instead, the main objective of the system inherited from the British continued to be the creation of priests, bureaucrats and patriots. Nothing summed up the prevalence of this view more than the belief of Tom Derrig, de Valera's Minister for Education up to 1948, that 'education beyond the elemental level destroyed children's ancestral cultures.'

Of course, another factor informed this less than elegant pessimism. Tom Garvin noted that, in a nation whose destiny was to farm, the establishment feared that education would produce only 'troublemakers, political cranks and fanatics'. This spirit was best captured by the Fine Gael Minister for Education, Richard Mulcahy, who noted that the 'advance of knowledge had led to endless destruction and misery.'

However, as it became increasingly evident that an education system that hadn't fundamentally changed since independence wouldn't develop the work force that was needed to drive the new economy, Lemass encouraged bright new ministers such as Paddy Hillery to begin the process of widening the provision of education. As trouble from the Church was either ignored or sidestepped between 1958 and 1968, the number of children in secondary education rose from 96,058 to 116,859.

It was a slow revolution, but the process accelerated swiftly when O'Malley discovered a study commissioned by Hillery that revealed that free secondary education would be much cheaper than previously thought. Intriguingly, the appointment of O'Malley to Education had terrified Fianna Fáil as much as the opposition. When O'Malley was a young TD it had taken the combined forces of Lemass and de Valera to impose some control on the wildest of the new Fianna Fáil musketeers, and his arrival into Education was accompanied by sulphurous murmurs from his colleagues that he had left the Department of Health 'gravely insolvent'. But perhaps Lemass—who had let it be known in 1964 that 'education policy would be settled in the manner of Tone'—felt that there was 'a need . . . to shake up the conservative educational establishment.'

Lemass certainly got what he wanted in spades when, on 10 September 1966, without any warning to his Government colleagues, O'Malley chose the less than salubrious territory of a meeting of the National Union of Journalists in Dún Laoghaire to announce the imminent provision of a scheme of free second-level education. Whether O'Malley's dramatic declaration occurred on the basis of a nod and a wink from Lemass or was an exercise in kite-flying that went out of control will never be fully resolved. However, the fact that the scheme went ahead in spite of the fury of the conservative Minister for Finance, Lynch, provides us with a partial answer.

Lest we cloak O'Malley with too much saintliness, there was a strong element of political cuteness surrounding the declaration, for Fianna Fáil was a past master at delaying revolutionary decisions until the point at which they appear entirely conventional.

A Fine Gael party that had been dominated by the economic conservative Gerard Sweetman might have fought this tooth and nail, but in a country becoming embarrassed by its backwardness Fine Gael had, ever so cautiously, embraced the ethos of the Just Society and was preparing to launch its own reforms.

O'Malley's Government travails may explain why his performance in outlining the realities of his scheme was, in the wake of his first euphoric announcement, rather sheepish. In a speech that appeared to be aimed as much at his own colleagues as at the opposition, he reminded the TDs of 'the Government's decision to raise the school-leaving age to fifteen by 1970 and of my own policy, and that of my predecessors in office, Deputy Dr Hillery and Deputy Colley, to provide . . . a post-primary course covering three years.'

O'Malley appeared to be looking as much at enemies behind him when he claimed that 'a series of reports has highlighted the extent to which ability to pay has governed the rates of participation in post-primary education.' He observed that there was 'a growing awareness among the public generally of the handicaps arising in later life from the lack of an adequate education. There is, accordingly, widespread and growing pressure for post-primary education facilities to be brought in.'

The main obstacles to this for a student from a lower-income family were 'the inability of his parents to pay the school fees demanded, their inability to meet the costs of schoolbooks and requisites, the need for an additional breadwinner in the family, the absence of motivation in the family environment, and the cost of transport in rural areas.' Interestingly, the most critical difficulty of all was the need for a free school transport system.

This, O'Malley admitted, meant that his new scheme had exchequer implications. However, in language that was intriguingly similar to that used by Lemass, he warned that 'every worthwhile development in the social and economic advancement of any nation calls for some sacrifice on the part of those best able to bear it.'

Those with a keen political sense could clearly see that O'Malley was feeling the chilly breath of the new Taoiseach, Honest Jack, and the equally cold breath of Ken Whitaker, the revered secretary of the Department of Finance, when a somewhat muted minister admitted that he could not 'place any utopian scheme before the house.'

Paddy Lindsay of Fine Gael, a pompous, overbearing, west of Ireland barrister, was certainly unimpressed. He claimed that the proposals had not been a Government policy 'and cannot be construed as such.' It was instead a 'makeshift document rushed out over the weekend in order to combat the publication of the Dublin Fine Gael policy.' The Fine Gael Law Library man said that, far from being 'the real Messianic force of our time in relation to preaching the gospel of free education,' O'Malley had only come up with 'the dampest squib which has ever been presented in this house.' Lindsay wondered:

> What are the people going to think? Will they not describe this minister, who showed bravery on the 10th of September at 7:30 p.m. in the Royal Marine Hotel, Dún Laoghaire, that is not matched in this document on 30th November—less than two months later—in the words of Disraeli in 'Endymion', as a 'figure flitting across the stage', as a 'transient and embarrassed phantom'?

After Lindsay noted the contrast between then and today, when the 'minister was very nice and quiet when he was delivering his speech', O'Malley couldn't refrain from saying, 'I love the Disraeli bit.' Lindsay modestly noted that 'it is a good bit' and expressed the hope that 'the minister is not now going to break forth from the chains that were binding him while he was reading this and become the charming extrovert he usually is, so charming as to be dangerous.'

Ultimately, however, there was a general acceptance that the time for free second-level education had come. Tom O'Higgins, who was a somewhat more progressive creature—in Fine Gael terms, at least—noted that 'more and more in recent years people have come to accept the fact that a small country such as ours, if it is to survive in the world that surrounds it, must provide a level of education for its citizens at least as high, if not higher, than other countries.' He noted with some justification that Fianna Fáil had in this regard 'allowed the years to slip by . . . where discussions consisted of . . . a series of slogans and clichés about the importance of principles which they rarely understood, and all the time our young people were emigrating to accept menial employment in other lands.'

Though supportive, O'Higgins was still somewhat dubious about the *bona fides* of the scheme. He warned that 'the Minister for Education is well known to ride his tongue on a long rein . . . He is well known for speaking first and thinking afterwards', and there was more than a touch of the hurt feelings in his observation about the place chosen for O'Malley's announcement: 'I suppose that, in a minister's life, journalists are very important.'

The absence of cheers eventually provoked O'Malley to sardonically ask, 'Is there not any little bit of good in my proposal?'

O'Higgins wasn't biting and instead said, 'I doubt it. I shall examine it very carefully, and by the time I have finished we shall see.' For now, though, in his view it was 'a mere crust to the people', one with which O'Malley was hoping to 'make a name for himself and his party' with the 'little bit of money' he had found.

The disputations O'Malley had had with Lynch, who had suffered from conniptions over the decision, explained O'Malley's exclamation '"A little bit of money"—I wish you would tell the Minister for Finance that.'

After a satisfied Dillon exclaimed, 'Now the cat has leaped out of the bag,' O'Higgins, speaking out of both sides of his mouth, expressed his 'greatest sympathy with the Minister for Education for his troubles in the last couple of months.'

An unperturbed O'Malley simply noted that 'I am always in trouble,' but he got scant consolation from the Fine Gael tag-team.

O'Higgins noted that 'you are in right trouble now,' and Dillon sagely observed, 'These are the fruits of being bust.' Though Fine Gael continued to niggle, the objections verged on the ridiculous, with O'Higgins warning of the 'the danger . . . that such a scheme could convert our educational system overnight into one divided on a class basis between free schools and fee-paying schools.'

Tom O'Donnell, also of Fine Gael, meanwhile expressed his concern that 'the need for an additional breadwinner is very often a serious and a big obstacle, particularly in the case of the working man who has a large family of six to eight children.'

David Andrews of Fianna Fáil was more ebullient.

This estimate is a historic document. No matter what is said, it is the beginning. Let me say about it, and the Fine Gael and Labour documents, that it opens, as President Johnson is wont to say, a consensus. It is a beginning.

Frank Cluskey of the Labour Party was somewhat more generous than Fine Gael, not that this was hard, and noted that the minister

> has been open to certain amount of attack by opposition speakers, including members of my own party, regarding his announcement at some function—I think it was a journalists' function in Dún Laoghaire— of this new plan to provide what he described as free education. I believe the minister was sincere. I believe he was concerned enough to put himself out on a limb. Whatever else may be said about the minister, I think it should be acknowledged that he knows how to deal with his colleagues in the Government. It is my opinion that this announcement was made by the minister in the full realisation that, once he had made it, his colleagues would find it very difficult not to implement it. The minister is entitled to credit . . . [for] being somewhat unique in his progressiveness amongst his colleagues. If this is the only way to advance . . . to put the Government on the spot in order to advance somewhat, I am prepared to give him full credit for his courage in doing so.

O'Malley didn't live to see if his vision would be fulfilled by far less courageous colleagues. His early death meant that, in a very different way, he did become a 'figure flitting across the stage' of history. His legacy, though, was certainly not transient.

Chapter 13

THE REVENUE ARE NOT THE ENEMY: MR HAUGHEY'S FIRST BUDGET

11 April 1967

T he fantastical nature of Charles Haughey's career was epitomised by his status as the only Irish political leader to have had their political obituary delivered as part of the warm-up speech at an ard-fheis at a time when they still led the party. In 1991, in her 'time for you to be going now' speech, Máire Geoghegan-Quinn told the faithful that 'there will never be a time like it again—never such excitement, never such achievement, never such heartache, never such happiness—as the time they will talk of as the Haughey era.'

Back in 1967 the man who would glide through the imagination of his people like a well-fed shark had a long road to travel. Amidst all the opinion, analysis and condemnation, perhaps the key to the motives that drove him was his simple observation that 'most people lead absolutely miserable lives.' It was a fate that Ireland's very own Great Gatsby, who had experienced a hungry upbringing, was absolutely determined not to share. Unhappily this same determination terrified the ascetic old aristocrats of both Fianna Fáil and Fine Gael, though even their worst suspicions couldn't have imagined just how much damage Haughey's egotistic rapacity would do to his party, to the state and ultimately to himself.

Of course when it came to those living the 'miserable lives', the Haughey soap opera, with all its contradictions, was a constant source of fascination and, for many, aspiration. Ironically, given the post of Minister for Finance he had just secured, Haughey had made his fortune in an accountancy practice that specialised in tax avoidance. From that, it was believed, had come the Gandon mansion, the high living, the riding to hounds, the stud farm in Co. Meath, one of the Blasket Islands and all the rest of the activities that so scandalised those frugal Fianna Fáil veteran republicans.

Though his gilded rise had suffered a setback in the Fianna Fáil leadership contest, the portfolio he had secured was, for Haughey, a more than adequate consolation. There he could preen, prowl and wait, as he was a man who would only have to get lucky once.

He was also a minister who would take his own road. According to Haughey, under temperate Jack the 'the dominant note of financial policy' might have been 'one of caution'. But for the man who would invent the economics of 'boom and bloom', in 1967 the major economic incentive, unsurprisingly, was 'to step up investment so as to re-establish the growth rates experienced in the earlier years of the decade'. The new man therefore noted that 'the circumstances of this year point to the need for continued cautious reflation of the economy.' Like any good child of Lemass, Haughey claimed that 'social investment in housing, education and hospitals would continue to be a necessary prerequisite for a full and balanced economic development.' It would not, of course, in any way harm Fianna Fáil's friends in Taca either.

Haughey was also particularly intent on fulfilling the educational objectives of his musketeer colleague O'Malley, stating that 'for the development of Ireland's full potential there is no more fundamental or important investment than education.' Important new plans for post-primary education were therefore afoot in the form of a scheme for the provision of free school buses and for the assistance of talented students in securing access to higher education.

Haughey admitted that 'we have had in recent years to keep on raising taxation in order to cover the cost of the additional services and aids demanded by various sections of the community.' Happily, though, the public had, 'with some grumbling, accepted that these expenditures were desirable on social or economic grounds'—and now it was payback time.

In particular he noted that there was a 'growing consciousness in our community of the problems of the old, and a good deal of voluntary personal service is being devoted to their welfare.' Haughey noted that, 'for their part, the Government have been considering particularly the difficult circumstances of old people who live alone . . . We have decided to give this group additional help by way of free electricity and transport.'

The Fianna Fáil backbenchers were already counting the new votes as the mansion-owning Haughey expressed the saintly hope that this would end the situation where 'the electricity bill can be a worry when resources are limited.' The even better news for our pensioners was that 'a scheme is being worked out in consultation with CIE whereby old-age and blind pensioners will be able to travel free of charge in CIE buses and trains during periods when traffic is not heavy.'

This was followed by the sight—truly delightful to modern eyes—of a moral lecture by Haughey about the importance of compliance with the taxation system. The Minister for Finance noted that 'nobody enjoys paying income tax, and some tend to dramatise the collection of tax properly due as a struggle between the citizens and the Revenue.' Haughey stated that, 'firstly, the officers of the Revenue Commissioners have instructions to draw the attention of taxpayers to any reliefs to which they appear to be clearly entitled.' However, he was even more anxious to note that 'there is no such entity as "the Revenue" in the sense of an enemy of the citizen. Every good citizen ought to pay his tax, and there must be effective means of dealing with deliberate evasion or refusal to pay.'

More than a few eyebrows in certain circles must have been raised at Haughey's pious claim that 'tax when one person escapes paying is not conveniently wiped out but is shifted onto the shoulders of his fellow-citizens.' This unfortunate state of affairs meant that, according to the minister, there should be no escape from the responsibility of taxpayers to be compliant. Conveniently forgetting his financial adviser Des Traynor, Haughey stressed the importance of 'a general obligation in every person carrying on a trade profession or profit-making activity of any kind to keep correct records of his basic business and professional transactions.'

The bright new minister also expressed unhappiness at the fact 'there is considerably greater freedom of entry here into the business of banking than is allowed in other countries.' On the recommendation of the Central Bank, Haughey now proposed 'to seek the approval of the Government shortly for the introduction of legislation to control, through the agency of the Central Bank, the establishment of such institutions and to keep their operations under review so as to provide greater protection for people depositing funds with them.' The unfortunate depositors with Matt and Patrick Gallagher's bank must have wondered where that legislation disappeared to. Haughey, in contrast, snaffled £300,000 from Patrick Gallagher after he became Taoiseach.

In what was a rare enough occasion for a budget, or any other speech, the Minister for Finance concluded with a dissertation on the importance of 'culture and leisure'. According to the aspirant Taoiseach, 'in modern society, as income standards rise, there is a compelling social necessity to devote increasing attention to the problems of leisure.' He claimed that good cultural and recreational facilities are 'now accepted as an obligation by enlightened governments everywhere', adding that it would be 'unthinkable to abandon people to the monotony of a working life unrelieved by the stimulus of cultural and intellectual activity.'

The unease within Fine Gael was captured in a claim by its spokesperson, Tom O'Higgins, that 'it must indeed be a great relief to Fianna Fáil deputies that they at last have a budget they can applaud.' He mischievously added, 'Indeed, at least one deputy, the Taoiseach, sitting beside the Minister for

Finance, must have reflected on the implied criticism contained in the minister's statement of the budget introduced last year and previous years.' O'Higgins did his best to disparage the dramatic statements about free electricity. 'The poor old couple and the poor old person about to get some concession in relation to travelling and electric light cannot have it given now.' Instead it was being 'postponed until August, when the nights are short and there will not be a shilling saved on the electric light.' It was, however, an intervention that carried little weight.

The debate was enlivened by a brief exchange over cigarette duty, in which Haughey's comment that he didn't smoke cigarettes provoked Fine Gael's none-too-proletarian Gerard Sweetman into making the sharp comment that Haughey was more 'in the cigar class'.

The increase in excise duty on beer inspired James Dillon to ask, 'How much of this particular commodity was consumed at the last dinner given by the members of Taca? And might I further enquire whether it was the draught or bottled variety?'

An unperturbed Lynch simply replied, 'A good few pints, if the deputy wants to know, and we are well able to drink them.' It had been 'Murphy, Beamish and Guinness, in that order.'

'It is a comfort that they were getting something for their hundred pounds,' Dillon returned. 'I was afraid that it was pure benevolence.'

But it wasn't all sweetness and light. During one sharp exchange Richie Ryan of Fine Gael told Haughey that his 'propaganda' damaged the 'dignity of the house'.

Haughey snarled, 'You are only a gutty,' adding that Ryan and his party were 'only a bunch of twisters.'

The Fine Gael leader, Liam Cosgrave, in typically understated style, drily observed that 'the really best part of the minister's speech was kept for towards the end. I have no doubt this was the part the commentator on the "Irish Press" was referring to when he said that the minister's speech had the hallmark of class'. Cosgrave felt that this was obviously a reference to 'the part dealing with culture' and that Haughey had obviously been told:

'Say something about culture' . . . It sounds well even if you do not mean to do anything about it. A reference to culture is always impressive. I have always had the impression that culture and Fianna Fáil, if not mutually exclusive . . . is certainly a forced marriage. It sounds well. You get a certain amount of plaudits for it.

Jack Lynch wasn't experiencing a happy time either. Jimmy Tully, one of the more forceful Labour Party frontbenchers, complimented 'the Minister for Finance on the slick way he prepared and put across his budget. Last night on television he was slick also'. But Tully was terribly disappointed 'that when the Taoiseach stood up to speak on the budget there were seated behind him the miserable number of twenty deputies of his party.' He noted that he had 'been in the house since 1954, and it was always traditional that when the Taoiseach came in to comment on the budget the back-room boys are whipped up and carted in to be seated behind him.' Tully therefore was all the more surprised that 'the necessary discipline was not invoked today when the Cork Taoiseach stood up to speak.'

Lynch defensively replied that it was 'an expansionist, reflationary budget—a budget which reflects the need of the occasion', and he sharply told Tully to stop 'trying to damn me with decency'. Whatever about poor Jack, it wasn't a tactic any of them would try on Haughey any time soon.

Chapter 14 ∾

HOT DAMES ON COLD SLABS: THE BEGINNING OF THE END OF THE AGE OF CENSORSHIP

10 May 1967

O ne of the defining features of our new state had been a binge of censoriousness that included the Censorship of Films Act (1923); the Intoxicating Liquor Act (1924), which tackled opening hours; the Intoxicating Liquor Act (1927), which reduced the number of pubs; the abolition of divorce in 1925; and a spanking new Censorship of Publications Act (1929).

The former excommunicants of Fianna Fáil were equally anxious to display their Catholic *bona fides*: in 1933 they had placed a tax on imported daily newspapers, in 1935 the Criminal Law Amendment Act saved us from the dangers posed by contraceptives, and the Public Dance Halls Act (1935) curbed the menace of country dances.

Such was the nervousness of the age in relation to morality in literature that on one notorious occasion a Seanad debate on the issue wasn't recorded lest any innocents be corrupted by the transcripts. Little changed in the 1950s, when, in what was acknowledged to be a uniquely squalid affair—even by Irish standards—the authorities of the state in effect conspired to destroy the Pike Theatre for the sin of simulating the dropping of a condom during a performance of Tennessee Williams's *Rose Tattoo*. Amidst the usual riots, the owner was charged with 'producing for gain an indecent and profane performance'; but what he was actually guilty of was annoying Archbishop John Charles McQuaid.

In the period 1950–55 the Censorship of Publications Board banned an average of two books a day by such authors as Graham Greene, Frank O'Connor, John Steinbeck, George Orwell, Austin Clarke, Brendan Behan,

Honoré de Balzac, Samuel Beckett, André Gide, Marcel Proust, Ernest Hemingway, Norman Mailer and Dylan Thomas, and the 1958 Dublin Theatre Festival was cancelled by order of the ubiquitous Archbishop McQuaid, who was, perhaps wisely, opposed to the dramatising of *Ulysses*.

Behind the scenes, however, things were subtly changing. From the 1950s an increasing number of letters from McQuaid to Lemass were greeted by the response: 'His Grace's letter does not call for a reply.' Even the Department of Justice was starting to take the view that certain Catholic organisations were attempting to force on the population 'a standard of propriety that exists nowhere else in the world.'

In political terms the evolution of a more liberal mood was epitomised by the radical nature of Lemass's final Government. A new generation had inherited the reins of power, and to such an extent that Frank Aiken and Seán Lemass were now the last members of the 1932 government in office. Lemass had even attempted to persuade the by now venerable MacEntee to retire from the Dáil, only to be told that he was 'no spring chicken' himself.

In a new Government of rakish *bons vivants* like Charles Haughey and liberals like Donogh O'Malley and Brian Lenihan, the situation where the archbishop said No, and where no-one got to hear Molly Bloom say Yes, was, even for Fianna Fáil, becoming embarrassing. What was needed was an Irish solution to an Irish problem, and Lenihan was the perfect man for that.

Introducing his bill, a wary Lenihan told the Dáil that it has 'two very specific and limited objectives'. As he noted that, 'first, it proposes to limit to twenty years the life of any prohibition order made on the grounds that a book is indecent or obscene', it was clear that no-one was going too swiftly in the direction of the liberal Republic. This caution informed Lenihan's promise that the bill would therefore still preserve 'the powers of the Censorship of Publications Board to make a fresh prohibition order' in respect of any banned book. Critically, though, the new regime would also 'remove the time limit of one year on the right to take an appeal against any prohibition order in respect of a book.'

Having gone through the basics, an uneasy minister noted that 'indecency, obscenity and censorship are words that provide a perennial source of controversy' and that 'no fundamental change in the system would find favour.' However, Lenihan admitted that it was possible 'to produce a sizeable list of books that, as the law stands at the moment, are prohibited for all time and which have achieved recognition among responsible people here and abroad as being important works of literature.'

It was, in short, time to stop embarrassing ourselves in front of the neighbours. According to Lenihan, 'a good proportion of these very books are by Irish authors, some of whom are regarded as being amongst the finest writers in any language.'

In Lenihan's charitable view, to put it mildly, one important cause of the difficulty was that the Censorship of Publications Board was trying to 'bring to bear on each publication that comes before them what they believe to be the judgement of the average, mature and responsible adult of their time.' The problem with this, Lenihan claimed, was that 'the views of that character type, the average man of sound judgement . . . do not necessarily remain the same from generation to generation.' Some would have argued that the opposite was the cause of the difficulty; but while it might have been stating the obvious to say that a decision made in the 1930s 'would not necessarily meet the same measure of approval' in today's world, it was a statement that had been beyond the capacity of all previous ministers.

Lenihan also noted that the 'fantastic and unparalleled social and technological changes' that had taken place in the last forty-odd years meant that there had been 'a quite definite change in the general tolerance of outspokenness in literary productions.' In a display of modesty that was rare enough by Irish standards, he did not 'propose to speak on the moral problems associated with the freedom generally exercised with writers nowadays, nor am I competent to do so.' But, he noted, 'I think it startlingly clear that, under the law as it is, some books stand banned for all time that would not be banned nowadays.'

Of course, many books banned twenty years ago would still be banned today. But Lenihan, probably accurately, surmised, 'I have no doubt that they are of such limited merit as to be most unlikely to be found in circulation twenty years after publication.' When it came to the better class of book, though, Lenihan—speaking in his capacity as the nation's probation officer for literature—felt that these deserved 'to be given a fresh start after the lapse of a reasonable length of time.' Though Lenihan was open to changes on the twenty-year rule, the cautious minister also went to some pains to note that there would be no 'erosion of the censorship system.'

After Lenihan congratulated the Censorship of Publications Board, whose 'task has never been a pleasant one' but who have 'served the country well', M. J. O'Higgins of Fine Gael summed up the apprehension over this delicate issue in his claim that there should be free expression of the TDs' views, since Fine Gael didn't regard 'a bill of this type' as one that should be 'debated from a purely party—a political—point of view.' O'Higgins did manage to summon up sufficient courage to agree that 'it is appropriate that the house should now, after a lapse of something over twenty years, consider again the question of censorship.' He even called for some further liberalism, suggesting that the board should 'always have within their membership, for example, some reputable critic, or some publisher or literary journalist.'

O'Higgins also suggested that the minister should consider the subtle but important change from the 1929 act, in a section of which, when it came to prohibition, 'one of the matters about which the board required to be satisfied was not simply that that there was something indecent or obscene in the book, but that the book was in its general tendency indecent or obscene.'

Surprisingly Lenihan received scant enough support from the Labour Party ranks, where a proletarian suspicion of long words still lingered. The normally liberal Seán Dunne appreciated 'very well that the temptation must have been very great for the practising politician to let the dog sleep on', and he felt that Oscar Wilde's remark in the preface to *The Picture of Dorian Gray* ('There is no such thing as a moral or an immoral book. Books are well written, or badly written.') represented 'the extreme of literary arrogance, which is unacceptable to the average person.'

Dunne didn't go so far as to set his star by the former Labour Party minister James Everett, whose template for matters cultural was the man resting on his settle bed in Co. Wicklow. But it was a close enough thing, with Dunne admitting that when it came to censorship he was 'inclined to the belief that the use of what might nowadays be described as "picturesque language"— but what those of us of middle age were brought up to regard as dirty words— is prompted . . . mainly by the desire to achieve certain publicity.'

In what many authors would have seen at the time as something of a contradiction in terms, Dunne claimed that it was a well-known fact that one of the best methods of promoting the sale of a book was to procure its banning in the greatest number of countries. Dunne, however, raised another intriguing point. 'What will our position be if we enter the Common Market?'

Brian Lenihan looked at that sleeping dog, observed that it was 'a big question' and passed gingerly by.

Meanwhile, David Andrews of Fianna Fáil happily returned us to basics, warning that the censorship laws were often used by certain novelists who would 'come to Dublin Airport with their saucy publications under their arms, and a conveniently placed photographer would take a snapshot which would appear in the various journals throughout the world.' Andrews did concede that it was unfortunate that several winners of the Nobel Prize were banned; but there were 'authors of other books herein which consist of nothing but muck and trash.' Andrews cited the title of one of these books, *Hot Dames on Cold Slabs*, 'which is by a man by the name of Michael Storme.' It appeared to be the case, in the world of David at least, that if a couple of Nobel Prize-winning authors had to be banned it was a risk worth taking if the country was saved from hot dames on cold slabs.

Such was the sensitivity of the affair that there were even proposals that appeals against censorship decisions could be made to the high court *in camera*. The squabbles continued into May, when Seán Moore of Fianna Fáil contended that 'if a book was indecent twenty years ago it is still indecent twenty years afterwards. It is just pandering to so-called liberal thought . . .

that can do no good.' Moore claimed that 'it is well known, particularly on the Continent, that one set of particular publishers may produce a book, being on the outside something from the New Testament, but inside you find it is a pornographic book.' He asked the minister if the innocent Irish citizens had any safeguards against such nefarious acts.

After Lenihan admitted that this was a task beyond even his capacity, Jimmy Tully archly warned against the continuing dangers of too much 'raw material' in literature. He didn't define what he meant by 'raw material', and perhaps that's just as well.

Lenihan attempted to calm things down by noting that the whole issue of censorship was 'an eternal subject, which has exercised many minds over many years—the minds of St Paul, Milton and deputies—but, to put the matter in perspective . . . what we are doing in this bill and in the amendments is rationalising censorship.'

It was a brave ambition, but trouble quickly broke out again when the mischievous Dunne raised the fact of the scabrous Irish poem *Cúirt an Mheán Oíche* having being banned in English but not in Irish. As the Fianna Fáil arch-conservative Seán Moore asked if Dunne was a 'liberal', and as Dunne referred to 'Pharisees', the gentle revolution was struggling to get off the ground.

Amidst the exchanges, with Moore snapping that he 'knew the Pharisees who sit in this house, and they are not on these benches,' and with Dunne philosophically observing that 'we were all born with the stain of Original Sin', Tully reintroduced some pragmatism to the debate. He was concerned that 'the tendency of the Department of Justice has been not to appoint young people to the board, and some of the members have not survived for twelve years.'

Lenihan, meanwhile, scurried out of the house a sadder, but not necessarily a wiser, man. Still, he had at least avoided being drowned by a moral furore, and, by Irish standards, this was a result.

Chapter 15 ∾

OLIVER J. FLANAGAN'S FISHY TALE

8 November 1967

It was late 1967, and the eternal Irish verities were being nudged by the winds of change to such an extent that a woman on 'The Late Late Show' could just about safely say—so long as she was married, of course—that she had done without the comfort of a nightie on her wedding night. The careers of the Three Musketeers—Charles Haughey, Donogh O'Malley and Brian Lenihan—whom Seán Lemass had favoured in the belief that young men, rather than an old Taoiseach, were needed to run a new country, were still relatively unblemished. But as the zephyr of sixties liberalism warmed the chilly state monolith that de Valera had built, when it came to literature and morals the redoubtable Oliver J. Flanagan, who was both a Knight of St Columbanus and a Knight of St Gregory the Great, wasn't about to leave the pass undefended.

Oliver J had a track record in such affairs, but not even the despairing, anarchic spirit of the recently deceased Flann O'Brien could have invented the farce in which the Dáil would experience two furores about the potential of a short story involving a trout in a jug of water to foster a culture of sexual immorality. Oliver J had initially gone on the offensive with a Dáil question as to whether the Minister for Education considered 'suitable for children of thirteen the textbook "An Anthology of Short Stories", which, Oliver coyly noted, 'contains on several pages certain words and phrases.'

An unimpressed Donogh O'Malley issued a tart reply.

As regards the three expressions supplied with the deputy's question, I am satisfied that only people of very delicate sensibility indeed would object to the third of the expressions, and I rely on the good sense of teachers to point out to their pupils that, while the other two expressions form an integral part of the text of what is one of the great short stories of the world, they should not include these expressions in their own vocabulary.

Flanagan asked, 'Is that the end of the reply?' and was sharply told, 'Sin deireadh.'

Sadly it wasn't, for Fine Gael's great conservative controversialist told O'Malley, 'Well, I will break into English.' He asked O'Malley if he was happy with quotations such as that 'on page 194': 'The capitalists pay the priests to tell us about the next world so that you won't notice what the bastards are up to—' With O'Malley snapping, 'What are they up to?' and Oliver J tutting about the prevalence of words like 'bastard' and 'bugger', the Ceann Comhairle anxiously fretted about the advisability of 'having a debate on this question.'

O'Malley, though, had a Fine Gael ignoramus in his sights and told Flanagan that he was 'quoting from one of the greatest short stories, "Eve of Destruction".' (In fact it was from 'Guests of the Nation' by Frank O'Connor.) James Dillon tried in vain to salvage Oliver J by asking O'Malley, 'By whom?' but his query was drowned out by a rare breakout of the cultural wing of Fianna Fáil as Charles Haughey wailed that if Flanagan's template for cultural excellence was followed 'you would have to abolish Ovid and Horace.'

Our friend 'interruptions' appeared on the records as a result of a query by the salty future Labour Party leader Frank Cluskey about whether it was possible for a child of thirteen not to have heard such language. An undaunted Flanagan claimed that this was 'a serious matter', and Haughey wondered if Oliver J was also plotting to abolish Shakespeare and the Bible as well as Ovid and Horace. In fairness to O'Malley, he attempted to suggest to Flanagan that 'the purpose of education is to educate,' but Oliver J was having none of this educating them 'in bad language . . . We were taught "Thou shalt not take the name of the Lord thy God in vain".'

It all ended somewhat querulously. O'Malley snapped, 'It is not for me to refer to Blessed Oliver or anything like that.' Flanagan promised that he would be raising the issue again.

True enough, a week later our man Flanagan was back and was in no humour to be trifled with. He demanded that the Minister for Education treat it 'as a serious matter and one of very great concern to many parents' and that he take steps 'to have books used in schools . . . with a better standard of language and expression which will meet with the approval of children and parents.' There were, Flanagan claimed, 'very many short stories which could be used for children for reading and studying in which the language would be on a par with the standard of language used in the homes of decent children.' The idealised Irish family, which must have been exhausted by the frequency of its appearances on the public stage, then made its inevitable entry in the form of the claim that 'it is typical of Irish parents that they see that their children use a very high standard of language.'

By now the laughter had already begun, but an undaunted Flanagan snapped that 'it is all very well for Fianna Fáil deputies to laugh at this, but there are many parents who do not laugh at the use of language which is foreign to their homes.' The anxious arbiter of standards once again directed the minister's attention to the infamous quotation about the capitalists and the priests and warned that 'that type of language might be expected in a low-class pitch-and-toss school but should not be contained in a book for young children, many of whom are in the first years of preparation for, perhaps, a religious life.'

As he moved on to another quotation from the same story—'Just as a man makes a home of a bleeding place, some bastard at headquarters thinks you're too cushy and shunts you off'—an irate Flanagan again noticed that this was 'a cause of laughter to the Fianna Fáil party, but it is no cause of laughter to parents.'

The onslaught on bad language—'Ah, for Christ's sake', 'poor bugger' and other expressions that would 'cause horror in any well-conducted and properly supervised home'—continued as Flanagan noted that 'again we see, on page 202, "then, by God".' O'Malley was then sharply told that one of the most important roles of teachers was that of conveying 'a proper understanding of Our Maker, of the Almighty, and children have been taught to use these expressions only in prayer and with great reservation.'

The worst, however, was yet to come. Our man quoted from Seán Ó Faoláin's story 'The Trout', in which the central character

> leaped up and looked out the window, and somehow it was not so lightsome now that she saw the dim mountains far away and the black firs against the breathing land and heard a dog say, bark-bark. Quietly she lifted the ewer of water and climbed out the window and scuttled along the cool but cruel gravel down the maw of the tunnel. Her pyjamas were very short so that when she splashed water it wet her ankles. She peered into the tunnel. Something alive rustled inside there. She raced in, and up and down she raced, and flurried, and cried aloud, 'Oh, Gosh, I can't find it,' and then at last she did. Kneeling down in the damp she put her hand into the slimy hole. When the body lashed they were both mad with fright. But she gripped him and shoved him into the ewer and raced, with her teeth ground, out to the other end of the tunnel and down the steep paths to the river's edge.

Flanagan tutted about the 'most suggestive' language and noted that the anthology might well have been approved by the senior inspector of O'Malley's department, which included in its membership Reverend Father Veale of Gonzaga and Reverend Mother Enda of Eccles Street. But, Flanagan said, 'with very great respect, it is the minister himself who is responsible to the house, not Father Veale or Mother Enda or the other members of the committee.' Of course, lest he be seen to be attacking any princes of the Church, Flanagan noted that 'they are very distinguished educationalists, and I would receive with admiration and sincerity any recommendation they make, but they are not responsible to the house.'

The less than happy minister assured Flanagan 'that there is no necessity for him to exhort me to treat this question seriously. I am well aware of my responsibilities.' He noted, however, that 'the modern short story . . . has become a highly sophisticated art form' and coldly asked if Flanagan had 'read the whole of the story'. When Flanagan confidently claimed, 'From cover to cover,' O'Malley gave Flanagan a second chance, stating that Flanagan certainly 'must not have read the story from which he quoted the extract.'

Oliver J asked, '"The Trout"?'

'Yes,' O'Malley helpfully answered.

Oliver J, unwisely so, perhaps, was decisive in his reply. 'Very suggestive. I did not like it.'

The opportunity had arrived and O'Malley struck back with a chuckle of 'the saying *Honi soit qui mal y pense* [Evil to him who evil thinks] was never so appropriate as it is tonight. Does the deputy, if he has read the story, realise that it is his own vivid and excitable imagination—'

Oliver J desperately interjected with the timeless constituency politician's plea of 'No, parents have written to me.'

O'Malley wasn't to be stopped. 'If he had read the story he would see this young girl is going into the tunnel to catch a trout and not to catch anything else. If these ideas which the deputy is putting into Irish minds, which no doubt, as on the last occasion, will be widely published in tomorrow's papers, are all he can find in Seán Ó Faoláin's "The Trout", which has been described also as the finest short story of Ó Faoláin, then I can only say, "God help us".'

A wry O'Malley noted that 'it is a very lucky thing that Ó Faoláin and O'Connor cannot combine to write a story on proceedings here tonight,' and he sharply commented that 'I know that Deputy Flanagan possibly has ambitions in another sphere, and that perhaps he hopes one day to be leader of the Knights.' In O'Malley's view, while Deputy Flanagan was 'quite entitled to aspire to such a great office . . . anyone using the Catholic Church for his own material or other advancement makes me vomit.'

The debate is as good an example as can be found of how formidable a politician O'Malley was at the peak of his powers. But a few months later he was deceased, and with him went a little, if not most, of the radical spirit of the musketeers.

ENTER HAUGHEY AFTER JACK SECURES TOO MUCH OF THE LOVE OF THE PEOPLE

THE ARMS CRISIS: A STATE AND A PARTY CONFRONT THE ENEMY WITHIN

6–8 May 1970

It all started off so innocently on a Tuesday afternoon in 1970. There was something of Beckett in the exchange between Liam Cosgrave and Jack Lynch about the resignation of the Minister for Justice, Micheál Ó Móráin. Cosgrave asked Honest Jack, 'Can the Taoiseach say if this is the only resignation we can expect?'

Jack replied, 'I do not know what the deputy is referring to.'

Obscurity continued to be the order of the day as Cosgrave asked, 'Is it only the tip of the iceberg?'

A cautious Lynch asked, 'Would the deputy like to enlarge on what he has in mind?'

Instead, Cosgrave cryptically noted that Lynch could 'deal with the situation'.

Lynch replied, 'I can assure the deputy I am in complete control of whatever situation may arise.'

Cosgrave merely muttered that 'smiles are very noticeable by their absence,' and there, for now, the matter lay.

However, if Lynch thought Cosgrave was fishing without a hook that sleepy afternoon, he was wrong: Cosgrave's line was hooked and baited.

The return of the Northern spectre after the long cold war had already been the catalyst for one of the most elemental crises both in Fianna Fáil and in the Irish state as the hope of the 60s was quashed by more fundamental political verities. Such was the seriousness with which the deterioration in the North in 1969 was viewed that there had been nine Government meetings in ten days.

During that time Lynch's status as a temporary little leader was tested to the full. He struggled against the irredentist tendencies of Neil Blaney, Charlie

Haughey, Micheál Ó Móráin and the irascible Kevin Boland. Though Lynch regained a parlous element of control with the aid of such allies as the Minister for Foreign Affairs, Paddy Hillery—who would later famously tell a Fianna Fáil ard-fheis mob that 'ye can have Boland, but ye can't have Fianna Fáil'— his position wasn't helped by his British allies, who fobbed the Government off with a junior minister when they raised concerns about the North.

As the northern crisis escalated, rumours began to circle that elements of the Government were using a relief fund for nationalists in the North to purchase arms for the newly formed Provisional IRA. It was a horrendously complex affair best summed up by the observation that, 'just as Lynch had determined a policy of suppressing the IRA . . . key ministers had embarked on a policy of supporting and rearming them.' Lynch's response to the situation, when he was finally informed, wasn't helped by his perilous position or by the fact that his Minister for Justice had a very public drinking problem.

The Taoiseach eventually moved against Ó Móráin. But he wavered over the appropriate response to the powerful Blaney and Haughey. On 20 April the secretary of the Department of Justice, Peter Berry, had told Lynch the details of the plot, and a week later Lynch requested the resignation of Haughey and Blaney. They refused, the Government was told of the affair, and there, astonishingly, the matter rested, until a leak to the Fine Gael leader, Liam Cosgrave, put a rocket under everyone.

Stephen Collins, in his history of the Cosgrave dynasty, captures the sombre mood of the Fine Gael leader after Lynch had said that no further Government resignations were in the offing. In the Fine Gael rooms Cosgrave had asked a gathering of party elders—Tom O'Higgins and his brother M. J. O'Higgins, Mark Clinton and Jim Dooge—for their advice lest the story was 'a plant to make me go over the top.' Clinton told him it was 'of such national importance' that the 'only thing is to go to the Taoiseach, and go to him tonight.' On his return, Cosgrave 'sort of stood in the door and closed the door behind him and then he looked up and then he looked at us and said, "It's all true".'

The following morning the nation awoke to the most dramatic evisceration of a Government that Irish politics had seen, with Lynch dismissing his Minister for Finance (and putative successor) Charles Haughey. Another aspirant leader, Neil Blaney, had been sacked, and a third senior baron, Kevin Boland, who had once notoriously scrunched up a note sent to him by Lynch in the Dáil chamber and thrown it to the ground in full view of the opposition, had resigned.

As Lynch struggled to retain the support of his party—and of the Government, for Fianna Fáil had a razor-thin majority—the Dáil, other than for a brief and testy order of business, didn't sit on Wednesday. But when it reconvened the following day, while Lynch had regained some faltering control of his party and cabinet, on the floor of the Dáil all hell broke loose thanks to a thunderous speech by Cosgrave. After a brief reprise of Lynch's gnomic replies to Cosgrave's cryptic queries the previous Tuesday, Cosgrave told the Dáil:

> At approximately eight o'clock on Tuesday night I went to the Taoiseach's room and gave him the facts that I have related to the house. By ten o'clock two ministers had been dismissed, or an attempt had been made to dismiss them, and at approximately the same time a third had resigned.

An appalled Cosgrave said it was time for 'the house and the country to decide, once and for all, if we can believe anything from any Fianna Fáil minister or deputy.' He noted that 'the real facts were suppressed from the house elected to serve the people until I felt it my duty to disclose the facts as I knew them.' This was

> the greatest scandal that has hit this state since we won independence. I am not given to verbal exaggeration. In fact, some of my friends in the press have probably thought that I have been unduly mild in my remarks during my political career.

Nothing, however, could disguise the fact that 'a deliberate and calculated attempt was made to conceal the facts from this house' by a party that had been concealing from itself 'the plots, the intrigues, the subterfuges' surrounding an attempt by elements of the Government to import arms for use in the territories of a neighbouring state by an illegal terrorist organisation.

In a situation such as this we could perhaps forgive Cosgrave for the slightly politicised claim that 'for the second time in the past half century, in our long and chequered history, this country and our people may thank God that they have this party to maintain and defend and assert the people's rights.' He noted with some justification that 'only for this party there could be a real danger of civil war, civil war of the worst kind, of a religious character,' and he stated clearly that 'this Taoiseach and this Government must now resign and dissolve this Dáil and let the people elect a Government in whom they can have confidence and who will guarantee their lives and liberties . . . and show to the world that this country, this state established by Griffith and Collins, is fit to and will govern itself.'

Kevin Boland had absolutely no intention of apologising for anything. Instead he thundered about how 'the position is that two members of the Government have been dealt with on a *lettre de cachet* [sealed order] basis, the penalty in this case being dismissal from the Government rather than incarceration in a modern Bastille.' This, he claimed, was 'a violation of human rights . . . inconsistent with the dignity of a free man.' He added that he did not accept that it was 'reasonable to expect ministers of a Government to serve under the condition that if Mr Peter Berry says a thing, you did it,' and he called Cosgrave's 'informer' a 'man of no honour'.

The future Chief Justice Tom O'Higgins said he did not know 'what the result might have been if Deputy Cosgrave had not gone to the Taoiseach and if the Taoiseach did not learn as he did that a tip-off had been given.' In truth, some forty years later we're not sure either. O'Higgins did admit that

> there are decent men in Fianna Fáil, honest men in Fianna Fáil . . . but they have allowed something rotten to happen: they have allowed a canker to grow which has nearly destroyed the credit of Fianna Fáil in the country. Maybe it was a hopeless effort to mix two brands and two ideals, to mix the captive republicanism of the past . . . with the modern, mohaired approach of others; but, whatever it may be, this mixing of water and wine did not produce a good bottle.

The more combative Fine Gael frontbencher Richie Ryan simply claimed that 'it is no longer possible to believe daylight from the Taoiseach. We now know that he tried to cover up treason.' Understandably, this met with vigorous protestations from Lynch, but an unperturbed Ryan noted that the Minister for Finance was 'allowed to continue to prepare his budget speech . . . at a time when the Taoiseach knew that the same man was endeavouring by force of arms, or by association with people who were prepared to use force of arms, to pervert the whole destiny of this country.' The question of what Jack actually knew would never be fully resolved, but Ryan was sure that he had put 'party interests' over the 'national interest'. The doubting Taoiseach had procrastinated over Haughey and Blaney because, according to Ryan,

> he feared them; he feared their wrath; he feared the number of supporters they might have in the cabinet; he feared the number of supporters they might have in the Fianna Fáil party; he feared their associates outside; he feared the IRA . . . and was hoping that this dreadful thing, this nightmare, would dissolve, or that somebody else would find a solution without confronting him.

The Labour Party's intelligentsia were equally unimpressed with Honest Jack. David Thornley, in a prophetic speech, said 'it would be a national tragedy if a picture was to emerge from this of a nice, kindly, absent-minded Taoiseach who had facts brought to his attention and then behaved with strong, ruthless moral integrity.' This, he said, was more than 'a little rumble in the intestines of the body politic', for there had in fact been 'an extremely effective junta in the cabinet which, effectively some people say, ran the cabinet over the heads of the Taoiseach.' By now the rumours were so devastating that Thornley even asked if Haughey had really fallen off a horse—this was the reason given by Lynch—or if had he been 'assaulted by members of an illegal organisation.' Other, more scabrous rumours were also circulating; but they, unfortunately, didn't reach the floor of the Dáil.

Conor Cruise O'Brien lashed at the danger caused by 'the emotionalism and the confusion, the bungling and duplicity of the Taoiseach's party'. He noted that Lynch might say of Blaney et al. that 'they are able and dedicated and brilliant', but, for Cruise O'Brien, 'they have dedicated their ability and brilliance to mischief.' He noted that it was 'rather hard in the circumstances of May 1970, as we move into one of the most tense and dangerous summers in this island, to forgive someone who rakes up emotions of an old civil war.' Of the Fianna Fáil applause for Blaney, who said he was leading a Fianna Fáil advance, Cruise O'Brien said 'it will be an advance of Gadarene swine towards the gulf of civil war they are heading for.'

As the hour grew later, and as drink entered the arena, the old school of Civil War politics made a return. One Fine Gael TD alleged that he had heard a former Fianna Fáil deputy

> boast recently about how they got into power. It was no news to me, for I was well aware of it. He said, 'I went into my local booth in the morning, and I asked the presiding officer how many votes were cast, and he said, "Ten." I got the block . . . and put them in. "Come out now," says I, "and I will stand you a drink. Your job is done".'

Amidst shouts of 'there are whores on your side' and 'shut up, you Donegal East smuggler,' Michael O'Leary of the Labour Party, subsequently of Fine Gael, temporarily restored things to a more elevated plane by noting that the affair had all the elements of a Greek tragedy. He warned, though, that one consequence of this was that 'every decision this Government will take in its remaining days will be subservient to that need of this Taoiseach for permanent popularity at all costs.' O'Leary slammed 'the sedulous fostering of that image of being everyone's uncle . . . that public sentiment which will say, "Poor Jack, surrounded by all those rough thugs, Blaney, Boland and Haughey".' He said of the new entries, 'Do not tell me that this children's cabinet will be any match for a party which allows Boland, Blaney and Haughey to roam amongst the party faithful'.

Despite talk of plots to kill the Taoiseach, Garret FitzGerald warned that 'no man will destroy the peace of our country, no matter how he plots, and, by God, the plotting has started already.' He told Lynch that 'the leader of a government must, above all, act decisively. He must not dither . . . He must grasp the nettle the first time the issue comes before him.' It was advice that Garret wouldn't quite follow subsequently, but FitzGerald's well-disguised cunning was revealed as he stripped away the alibis of the Fianna Fáil plotters. He noted that their denials were most interesting, for

> we all, as politicians, know the art of the denial of what was not said, the art of saying that one did not do something which is not in fact the crime one committed. These men apparently denied to the Taoiseach that they had instigated this. I was not aware that anybody suggested they did instigate it. They were asked by an illegal organisation to facilitate the passage of arms. The IRA were the instigators: they were the facilitators.

FitzGerald could fret all he wanted over Blaney's 'Hitler-like ability to stir a mob' or note of Lynch's claim of having requested resignations on 29 April that 'we have to face the fact—it is a miserable fact to face, and I have difficulty facing the Taoiseach when saying it—that that statement is not true.' But Honest Jack wouldn't be diverted from his intention to play the victim.

When he finally spoke, Lynch unctuously noted that 'it matters not that the opposition, and Fine Gael in particular, used this situation for their political advantage.' He would rise above that, and he had, in fairness, been faced with a unique situation when it came to conducting investigations and making decisions. The description of his confrontation with Haughey resembled a scene from a Jacobean drama, with Lynch claiming that Haughey had been in 'a very weak state: he was unable to articulate, and his breathing came heavily. His hand was in a sling; his face was swollen.' And the Minister for Justice 'had entered hospital some days previously.' According to Lynch,

> one can understand that, during the two weeks while I was reviewing and sifting information and interviewing people, those two weeks were not easy ones for me. Much less easy, of course, was the decision I took. I think it is not unreasonable that I thought long and considered much the action I was to take.

Lynch noted that he, Blaney and Boland 'had grown to political maturity together', and, in what retrospectively appears to be an astonishing confession, he admitted that his hand had been stayed by the absence of a family tradition in the War of Independence. In words that showed how thin the veneer of modernity was that covered the old Civil War divides, he confessed that 'it made the task all the less easy that I realised that my family had not the same tradition of service.' And there was also the concern about 'the effect it was likely to have on the political future of able and brilliant men.'

In what would be his most serious political error, Lynch said of Haughey that 'his political future was, and I hope could yet be, particularly bright.' Lynch admitted that when Cosgrave came to him 'I acted quickly then, but I had already made up my mind.' And he defended himself against accusations of lethargy by saying that if he followed up every rumour he 'would not be here today but in some kind of institution.' It was unlikely, though, that the hard men in Fianna Fáil were impressed by Cork's dear boy when he added, 'I know little about guns. In fact, I get sick in my stomach when I think of guns in the hands of immature, unauthorised or irresponsible people.'

As for Fine Gael's leader, Cosgrave, one vignette captures well his nature, when, during one point in the furore, Fianna Fáil squealed, 'Take him out.' Cosgrave looked over coldly and told his fretful backbenchers to be quiet. 'Do not worry: I will not be silenced by anyone.' It was leadership in the raw, and the mob on the Fianna Fáil benches knew it.

Lynch survived and for a while even prospered, but it can be argued that in a very real sense Fianna Fáil never fully recovered from the trauma of senior members of its elite engaging in treasonable activities against the state, or from a Taoiseach being initially unwilling to dig these 'mongrel foxes' out. Lynch had sown the dragon's teeth, but it would take a further four decades for the harvest of that irresponsibility to be reaped.

Chapter 17 ∾

JACK'S 'EXERCISE IN PERSUASION'

21 March 1972

Ayear has passed, and it is as if what P. J. Mara would later dismiss as 'that old Arms Trial shite' had never happened. Jack is still in power and, with the tomahawks for now decommissioned, is eyeing up the possibility of an astonishing third election victory in a row. For now, though, the priority is to secure Seán Lemass's final dream: ending what Ken Whitaker had called the dangers of 'un-progressive isolation'.

As far back as 1962 Lemass had warned that staying outside Europe would 'condemn us in perpetuity to a position of economic inferiority, leave us a beggar amongst the nations, seeking to maintain a dying economy on the crumbs of charity from our wealthy neighbours.' Lynch himself had embraced the concept of union with Europe to such an extent that he was almost lyrical in his support for the idea that Ireland would 'finally, like Robinson Crusoe, come off the island.'

It had been a difficult journey, and nothing summed up Ireland's peripheral status more than the keeping by the EC mandarins of our carefully crafted application in a drawer on the grounds that until Britain joined there was no point in considering our application. However, the departure of the de Gaulle *Non* meant that Ireland was poised for a final break with de Valera's dream of insular self-sufficiency. The imperatives of the market had trumped the old dreams of cosy homesteads.

In the Dáil debate the canny Lynch was in typically cautious form. He made it clear that the 'obligations do not entail any military or defence commitments.' With an eye to the Labour Party in particular, he sharply refuted 'the claim made by some that we could have obtained a much more favourable deal and even that we could have negotiated changes in community rules.' These people, he said, 'chose to ignore the fact that these policies and rules were worked out by the present member-states after years of arduous and prolonged bargaining.'

The many vested interests who were fearful about the dismantling of the final remnants of protectionism were also assured by Lynch that 'the timetable for the gradual removal of protection will give industry an adequate breathing space for making the necessary adjustment to . . . free trade.' Old tariffs certainly died hard, and it is typical of the very different nature of the Irish economy then that assurances were provided for a 'greatly extended transitional period . . . for the motor industry and . . . the steel industry'. Coincidentally, both had a substantial presence in Cork.

Lynch was even more anxious to make it clear that 'membership will give our farmers the greatest opportunity they have ever had to increase their product and income'. While the EEC 'offered us the first real prospect since independence of achieving full employment and ending involuntary emigration', it posed challenges too, and Lynch stated that the central issue facing the voters was 'one of confidence in the capacity of our people to make a success of membership.'

The observation that 80 per cent of our agricultural exports went to Britain moved the debate on to 'sovereignty and the political future of the country.' In language that would also become familiar, Lynch slammed the 'half-baked', wilder flights of 'anti-Common Market oratory', including 'emotive expressions such as "rich man's club", "neo-colonialism", "capitalist plot" and so on.'

Lynch dismissed the claims that within the EEC 'we would be stripped of our sovereignty, our resources exploited by half-baked Europeans hungry for profits while we remain helpless in the face of decisions taken in the interests of larger and more powerful member-states.' Tellingly, he asked, if this was the world we existed in, was it reasonable to expect that outside the EEC, 'on the other hand . . . these same countries would suddenly become filled with sweet reason and light'? The Taoiseach dragged up another old crowd-pleaser, warning that it would also be tightening partition if we stayed out, for 'surely it is self-evident that . . . we would be conferring on the border the status of frontier, both economic and political, between ourselves and the rest of Europe.'

Lynch's capacity for using irredentist nationalism in the service of the European ideal was another example of his political subtlety. The conclusion of his speech on the virtues of European union was, however, more emotionally engaged than was normal. He made the profound—by Jack's standards—statement that it was 'a salutary exercise to reflect on the kind of Europe—even the kind of world—we would have today if the European statesmen in the seat of power at the beginning of the century had been endowed with the same vision, the same dedication to peace.' Our attitude to European unity, according to Lynch's philippic, should be that 'it is conceivable that Europe and the world would have been spared two devastating wars, that we would not have had the division of Europe into two blocs, and that we would be nearer to a solution of the problems of the developing world' if it had come earlier.

On this, as on so many issues at that time, a buoyant Labour Party was inclined to take its own road. Justin Keating warned that 'our state of economic development renders full membership exceedingly dangerous.' Joining the EEC, he claimed, was 'an exercise in persuasion rather than in serious economics,' for we were 'in fact economically a colony of the United Kingdom. We do not have control of our own financial institutions; we never have had. We do not have control of our own currency.'

Few, however, were in the mood to listen to complexities about the dangers to our sovereignty posed by 'free trade in goods' and, worse still, 'free outflow of capital' when there grants to be secured for farmers. Though the Labour Party spokesperson also raised the dangers of harmonising wage rates and social services, which would come back to bite subsequent Governments, Keating was anxious to note that he wasn't a natural Eurosceptic. He did 'not find membership of the EEC unthinkable.' The EEC, he said, 'may develop into something reasonable, or it may develop into something loathsome.'

The Fine Gael leader, Liam Cosgrave, was certainly not a natural Europhile. He noted of Europe that his support for the union was informed essentially by his status as 'a pragmatic politician'. He felt that the Common Market 'is now a fact of life. It is an institution of six countries which came together with the intention of unifying Europe for developing aims and objectives to which most deputies here subscribe.' He added that there was little point in Ireland avoiding that reality.

Reality was to become an increasingly alien concept when it came to the rest of the debate—one that acted as a mirror to the continuing intellectual squalor of Irish politics. It was bad enough that such was the absence of interest in this critical development that TDs had to be officially summoned to fill the empty benches on several occasions. But the level of the discussion was captured in an astonishing battle in which the speech of the Labour Party frontbencher Jimmy Tully was repeatedly interrupted by the independent TD Joe Lenehan, who appeared to have arrived in the chamber in a tired and emotional state.

As the barracking began Tully attempted to dismiss his nemesis with the observation that 'it is too bad that a deputy who has not been seen for three months in this house should come in now and attempt to interrupt the debate. I would ask the deputy to go back to where he has been all evening'.

Lenehan was not for leaving easily, answering that he had 'as much right as a big, fatheaded "gobbaloon", wherever you come from. I am not sure. You have no more rights than I have.'

Tully snapped that it was 'absolutely ridiculous that this sort of thing should be allowed, that somebody should go down to the bar for three or four hours and then come up here and try to upset the business of the house.'

Undeterred, Lenehan told Tully, 'I was not born in the bog like you were: I was reared,' and then disappeared from the pages of history.

Things didn't exactly improve as the Fine Gael TD Paddy Donegan colourfully claimed that Ireland's sovereignty was

> like the girl who got married. You might say she lost her virginity, but if she did she gained something very much more important and more enlivening for herself in this world, and that was she became a married woman who raised a family.

It was all too much for Conor Cruise O'Brien, who warned, 'There are ladies in the gallery,' though one presumes that if they were married the women wouldn't have been too distressed. Cruise O'Brien, meanwhile, felt that the key to the Labour Party's somewhat surprising position is

> related to a metaphor used by a member of the British Labour Party shadow cabinet opposing Britain's entry, not on ideological or absolutist grounds, but on the grounds that he did not think Britain could stand the shock. Speaking of the blast of full Common Market competition, his point was that a cold shower may be bracing and a tonic for a healthy man, but if your organism is not in very good shape it could kill you.

His warning codicil was that

> the British economy may be a relatively sick economy in comparison with the advanced industrial countries, but compared with our economy Britain is an Olympic runner. If Britain cannot face that cold shower, are we really so ready for it?

It was bad enough, mused Cruise O'Brien, that the Irish voter had been deceived, but the Government had also presented to Europe

> a sick, backward economy, which is what we have, and what they know we have, as a fully developed economy.

After George Colley claimed that 'our tariff-free access to the expanded Community market will be a very powerful inducement indeed, especially to industrialists who are located outside the enlarged Community,' Oliver J. Flanagan was inevitably having no truck with any of this optimism. He warned the deputies of a town near Amsterdam where, during a visit by friends of his,

> there was no-one to be seen on the streets at 10:30 p.m. . . . . The people were all in their homes either in bed or watching television. When they went for refreshments there were only two people present at 9:30 p.m. On the other hand, at 5 a.m. they were wakened up by the people going to work and were told in their hotel that it was time to come down to breakfast. By 7 a.m. women were returning home from having completed their shopping.

Flanagan asked:

> Would life be worth living if Ireland adopted these standards? There is a typical Irish way of life. I hope it never changes. We may be described as easygoing, but a little satisfies us. If we continentalise ourselves the good old restful Irish way of life may be disturbed, and I would not like to see that happening.

Garret FitzGerald attempted, bravely, to raise the tone of things. He attacked the apparent view of some that

> an important and significant point on the question of entry . . . was that the people in Europe get up earlier than we do and we would not be up to dealing with them because of the early hour at which they rose. When this is the common theme of several speeches against, and this is the level at which the matter is discussed, one despairs of having a serious discussion of this whole matter.

Despite the unavailing efforts of Garret, serious discussions on Europe—and on plenty of other issues, for that matter—would, alas, continue to be a rarity.

Chapter 18 ∾

THE ORIGINAL QUIET MAN COMES TO POWER

14 March 1973

Within Fine Gael, by 1972 the glory of the Arms Crisis debate had been largely forgotten. Instead, as the election neared, even Labour Party figures were being told by Garret FitzGerald that 'we must get rid of Liam, we must get rid of Liam, you know.' The intensity of the plotting was summed up by Richie Ryan, who was to be a Minister for Finance under Liam Cosgrave and a backbencher under FitzGerald and who told the journalist and author Stephen Collins that on one occasion Garret left a meeting 'in his usual hurry' with a 'huge bundle of papers' but left one paper behind with a tot suggesting that in any leadership battle Cosgrave would be ahead on the first count but that Garret would win on transfers from other candidates.

There were certainly few obvious similarities between FitzGerald, a liberal trapped in a Blueshirt party, and Cosgrave, who told opponents of the American bombing of Vietnam that they were allowing their 'humanitarian instincts to lead them to become communist dupes.' Things came to a head at the ard-fheis in May 1972, when, fortified by a generous couple of whiskeys from his friend Liam Burke, Cosgrave compared his critics to 'mongrel foxes' who for now might have 'gone to ground', but he would 'dig them out, and the pack will chop them when they get them.'

But by December 1972 the liberal mongrel foxes, far from having gone to ground, had turned on the Blueshirt hounds. In the Dáil, Cosgrave was preparing to defy his party and vote for Jack Lynch's hardline proposals to abolish jury trials for IRA membership. Cosgrave's decision meant that his leadership of Fine Gael would be untenable. But then, as he was left totally isolated in the Fine Gael party rooms, a series of explosions rattled the very windows of the Dáil.

Though the Dublin bombs—and, more critically still, his response—saved Cosgrave's leadership, the fractured state of Fine Gael, together with the absence of clarity over a likely alliance with the Labour Party, was all too tempting for Lynch, who called a snap election for 5 February. On one level the very fact that Lynch was still in the political game was a miracle, given what had happened during the Arms Trial. But while it appeared that Lynch had restored the old orthodoxies of hearth, homestead and hurling, Ireland was a changing country.

The Fianna Fáil old guard, such as Seán MacEntee, might once have railed about how the Labour Party of Brendan Corish and Jimmy Tully stood for 'the red flames of burning homesteads in Meath', but the retirement in 1971 of the toxic duo of Éamon de Valera and Archbishop McQuaid was the clearest example of how the times were finally a-changing.

This extended to the cold war between Fine Gael and the Labour Party, who for the first time since 1957 offered the electorate a real alternative by going to the country on a joint platform. A crucial factor had been the realisation by two ageing leaders that it would be better to stick together than to hang separately. However, in a damn close-run race, Fianna Fáil also reaped the whirlwind of the Arms Trial. While Lynch had appeared to escape unscathed, Corish had been sufficiently unnerved by the affair to decide that Fianna Fáil wouldn't get a free run at power again.

In keeping with the low-key style of Cosgrave, whose defining political trait was a dislike of 'codology' and fancy sentiment, nominations for Taoiseach were proposed and seconded on both sides, and that was that. Things soon livened up after a Cosgrave-inspired break to ensure that the deputies could enjoy 'a little sustenance'. Lynch, while 'formally opposing the nomination just made by the Taoiseach', wanted to extend to him 'our congratulations on his appointment and wish him well in a general way', since the way of the world meant that they could not be expected to 'wish him well in a narrow, political way'.

The inevitable sporting metaphor wasn't long in coming, as Lynch congratulated the 'individual ministers who have passed the post'. However, the canny Lynch, who knew well the dangers posed by those behind him, also took 'advantage of this occasion to congratulate my own party on the magnificent results achieved . . . returning as we did sixty-nine deputies and achieving a higher poll.'

Lynch noted that 'we are now, as we have always been, implacably opposed to a coalition form of government for this country.' But on this occasion the people at least 'knew in advance that an alternative coalition Government was available.'

In another classic example of his political capacity for playing the injured pet, Lynch indulged in the usual promise—'We intend to be a fair, constructive, vigilant and disciplined opposition'—even though poor Jack hadn't enjoyed 'that latter quality in the opposition that faced us.'

The most intriguing feature of Lynch's concession speech was his decision to use it as an opportunity for marking out the potential for a radical new Northern policy. He claimed that 'the publication in some days' time ... of the British White Paper on Northern Ireland' meant that the Government was taking over 'at a time of great opportunity, notwithstanding three-and-a-half or four years of much political difficulty.'

In a statement that wasn't at all to the liking of the many surviving republican irredentists in his party, Lynch used the nomination of Cosgrave to ask unionists to 'accept that the aims of those who plant bombs, who kill and maim and destroy in the name of Irish unity—these are not our aims and do not have our consent.'

Lynch's subsequent analysis would inform the Belfast Agreement of more than thirty years later. The Gordian knot posed by Ulster was that

> each community now fears that whatever settlement is reached will establish it as a . . . permanently disadvantaged minority . . . One community fears that any settlement will re-establish it as a permanent and alienated minority in Northern Ireland; the other that it will be sold out and submerged against its will in an Irish republic.

He added that it should be clear

> at least that there is simply no hope of creating now, after fifty years of failure, a new and stable Northern Ireland in which the present minority will accept that status permanently and abandon their aspirations. It should also be clear that there can be no hope of stability or peace in any settlement which would try to impose a united Ireland—a settlement under which the present unionist community in the North would become, or feel themselves to be, a disadvantaged and dissident minority.

It was time, therefore, given these realities, for both sides to move on and resolve 'this dark cloud' that has 'overshadowed much of our thinking and actions in recent years.'

The Government benches only began to get restive when Lynch piously referred to the 'solid foundations' that Fianna Fáil had laid in government. Honest Jack noted that when Fianna Fáil took office in 1957 'emigration was at an appalling level of 60,000 ... there were almost 100,000 people unemployed, and the economic collapse was so severe there was widespread despondency and even despair for the future of our country.' Now, 'for the first time since the Famine, there is a steady increase in population; living standards have improved by more than two-thirds'.

The industrial base had been 'transformed from an unhealthy dependence on a heavily protected home market into a competitive export-oriented sector that can look forward with confidence, along with the equally dynamic and expanding agricultural sector, to the challenge and opportunity of participation in the new Europe'. Lynch noted that it was now 'twenty-five years and twenty-five days since the first coalition took office in the country. It was my first day coming into Dáil Éireann, and I remember well the words with which my predecessor finished his speech on this motion.'

When the less than impressed—for it had been a lengthy speech—Labour Party leader, Brendan Corish, sighed, 'We have it off by heart,' Lynch cited the warning in 1948 of the late Seán Lemass: 'We are leaving you this country in good shape . . . Make sure that you hand it back that way.'

The new Taoiseach, Cosgrave, was equally unimpressed and claimed: 'I think the real reason the country is all right is that it has got rid of a Fianna Fáil Government.' In spite of this abrasive beginning, his acceptance speech stressed 'the issue of co-operation . . . The Government was formed in a spirit of co-operation, and I believe that that spirit of co-operation will influence their work and guide their activities.' He promised to 'seek the co-operation of groups of citizens in the community who have come together to further a particular environment in dealing with their social ills' and also to seek the co-operation of trade unions, employers and farmers' groups.

Cosgrave might have been following a furrow that had already been well ploughed by Lemass, but in a speech suggesting that he wasn't as opposed to the Just Society as was commonly believed he also pledged that 'the co-operation we will work for and hope to get is necessary because our concept of government is a democracy without limits', one that was 'neither narrow nor confined'.

He warned that 'merely ruling with a parliamentary majority does not necessarily achieve democratic aims.' What this Government desired instead was to 'build a society in which power is shared and in which decisions are arrived at after consultation with those who are most affected . . . where authority of course exists but where it is seen to be benign, because it is recognised as being just.'

This was heady stuff, but most new Taoisigh are informed by such sentiments as Cosgrave's pledge that 'we will not operate by Government decree, as we do not claim any monopoly of wisdom; but we will consult and seek advice before we act.' It rarely, however, lasts.

Cosgrave welcomed Lynch's offer on the North, feeling that 'we are obviously on the threshold of a new start'—one that could 'result in substantial improvements'. However, he rightly introduced a note of caution: these developments could equally 'result in a breakdown of law and order and in an even more serious situation than has existed there.'

Still, he declared, it time for the 'policy of realism', in all parts of Ireland, to 'press home its advantages over the policies of myth and catchcries.' For 'what is Ireland but the people of Ireland, all the people in all parts of Ireland?'

He noted that Ireland was still a young state; but, in a point often forgotten even today, we had 'seen much progress and a great growth in maturity'. He looked ahead 'with judgement, discretion and, I hope, moderation and responsibility, as well as enthusiasm,' and with the aspiration that this would be a Government 'indelibly marked with justice', one that would enact good laws 'governing the relations of the people with each other.'

After the unwonted idealism Cosgrave returned to more familiar territories as he flintily thanked Lynch for his promise of constructive opposition and was 'glad he has profited from my good example in the seat opposite.'

There was even a sample of dry wit to be found as the Taoiseach concluded by noting: 'This Government has been described as one of many talents, and commentators and informed writers . . . all agree that it is a talented team. I need hardly say that I am glad to have got a place on it.'

Others, such as Garret FitzGerald, were less pleased.

Chapter 19

HONEST JACK GOBBLES
THE LOT AS JOHN KELLY
PLAYS NOSTRADAMUS

5 July 1977

They should have been an odd, or at least a cantankerous, couple, but the marriage between Liam Cosgrave's Fine Gael (together with its Just Society wing) and a Labour Party that had been characterised by Micheál Ó Móráin of Fianna Fáil as consisting of 'left-wing political queers from Trinity College' was remarkably stable. They had also been remarkably short on luck, as the oil crisis of 1973 had led to a sudden reduction of 20 per cent in economic activity. The Government had compensated by increasing borrowing from 8 per cent of GNP in 1973 to 16 per cent by 1975. But the intractable nature of the crisis meant that in 1976 the Minister for Finance, Richie Ryan, was considering cutting the children's allowance, school transport and food subsidies.

Meanwhile, in the other staple Irish crisis, the spineless capitulation by Harold Wilson of the British Labour Party to the Ulster Workers' Council had destroyed the Sunningdale Agreement for a power-sharing Northern Executive.

With the Government's economic reputation already in tatters—by 1975 inflation was at 25 per cent and unemployment had exceeded 100,000 for the first time since 1942—its reforming liberal credentials were severely damaged by allegations of the rise of the Garda 'Heavy Gang'.

The stumblebum controversy in which the Minister for Defence, Paddy Donegan, had, probably correctly, called President Ó Dálaigh a 'thundering disgrace', which led to a brief political crisis and the resignation of the President, had also damaged the coalition's reputation. Others would contend that RTE's satirical programme 'Hall's Pictorial Weekly' (which disappeared from the knowing RTE airwaves very soon after Fianna Fáil returned to power), with its portraits of 'Richie Ruin' and the 'Minister for Hardship', did far more damage.

Even with a fair wind it was always going to be a struggle to defeat the man Liam Cosgrave openly admitted was the 'most popular Irish politician since Daniel O'Connell'. Such indeed was the love the voters had for Honest Jack that the historian Joe Lee observed that they 'to a great degree treated him as something of an injured household pet in need of constant solace and comforting.'

There was a steelier side to Lynch, but for this election the bright young strategist Séamus Brennan decided that it might be better if Lynch's campaign was dominated by 'balloons, Jack in an open-top car, T-shirts and battle buses'. And, just to be certain, there was also a giveaway manifesto, which would become infamous among the voters after they had snaffled all its contents. There was actually no need for the manifesto, for in a truly touching example of political innocence the coalition had commissioned a survey whose results they received only after the election was called. After the Government of all the talents was told, against the predictions of all the nation's political correspondents, that they were facing a rout, Michael O'Leary wryly summed up the mood, noting that the only sound in a silent room was of 'coffee cups tinkling against saucers'.

Lynch's own future woes, even in the moment of his 24-seat triumph, were captured by the corrupt spin-doctor Frank Dunlop, who recalled that after 'a particular hullabaloo, as a man in a white suit and polka-dot shirt was shouldered to the front door' of the Dáil, an incredulous Lynch asked, 'Who in the name of God is that?' It was, of course, the infamous Pádraig Flynn from Co. Mayo, who would play no small part in destabilising the august Taoiseach.

The Camorra too was back, in the sibilant form of Charlie Haughey, and while few commented, everyone noticed. For now, as Honest Jack eased back into power the way you might slip on a well-worn pair of carpet slippers, the mood of pastoral certainty brought Rupert Brooke and 'Stands the Church clock at ten to three? And is there honey still for tea?' to mind.

In a typical example of the ongoing supremacy of the Mercs and perks culture in Irish politics, the first big row was over who would secure the modest prize of the Leas-Cheann Comhairle's job rather than over any ideological divides. Traditionally this went to the opposition, but on this occasion a Taoiseach who had an excess of TDs and a deficit of places informed Fine Gael that when it came to such perks the previous coalition had 'gobbled the lot', and he was going to follow that precedent.

Other than the return of Haughey, the most interesting feature of the new Government was the appointment of Martin O'Donoghue to a new post of Minister for Economic Planning and Development. Lynch told the Dáil that 'the management and development of the economy will be the immediate concern of the Government' but that 'the direction and co-ordination of this function is a task of such magnitude that it imposes an almost impossible burden on a minister who is also charged with the administration of the public service.'

A new phrase went into political circulation as Lynch said one of its functions would be 'co-ordinating dialogue with the social partners'. There would be, he promised, 'a phased programme of public service reform, which I intend to have developed further.' Like many a Taoiseach before and after him, Lynch claimed that public service reform would 'be of fundamental importance to the effective discharge and implementation of the programme of national renewal and development upon which we are now embarking.' And he somewhat optimistically noted that 'the Public Service Advisory Council in their report have rightly, in my opinion, drawn attention to the fact that without conspicuous political will and commitment public service reform will not occur.' According to Lynch, 'the new Government will not be found wanting in this respect.'

Understandably, given the scale of his victory, Lynch claimed that 'the Irish electorate, as always, have proved themselves to be most discerning and discriminating. They have rejected the coalition Government.' But in a message to his own party as much as to anyone else he said 'the same Irish electorate will be equally discriminating in the next general election if the Government do not create the real economic progress . . . our people are entitled to expect.'

The shining new Fine Gael leader, Garret FitzGerald, admitted that the party could not defeat the new Government but had 'the duty by our negative vote here today to register this party's rejection of the basis on which this electoral victory was won.' He presciently observed that 'in a situation where our economy is expanding, and indeed where the expansion of the economy is accelerating . . . the measures proposed by the new Fianna Fáil Government involve a massive further increase in borrowing.' FitzGerald stated that, not for the first time, the pursuit of such 'irresponsible policies' has 'caused alarm in the international community.' Beginning as he unfortunately would go on, Garret indulged in a blizzard of statistics about how the economy was rising by 5 per cent, agriculture by 4 per cent and manufacturing by 10 per cent. Given that the coalition had halted the rise in unemployment and had reduced inflation to 14 per cent—for the time that was good!—he castigated a Fianna Fáil policy 'aimed at buying the support of different interest groups.'

It was certainly clear that the Just Society wing of Fine Gael was back in town as FitzGerald criticised policies 'aimed at those who own private cars, not towards those who use public transport.' In what would evolve into a continuing theme for FitzGerald, and for the next decade of Irish politics, he also attacked Fianna Fáil for having, 'for the sake of votes and office . . . reduced politics to an unprecedented auction for votes.' FitzGerald promised to 'try from these benches to give a moral lead to the nation, to combat materialism, the growth of which Fianna Fáil have so unfortunately encouraged in this election'.

Neil Blaney, of all people, echoed Garret in condemning this auction politics, in which 'the sky was the limit and it was a bit of the dog's own tail that was being fed to it by both parties'.

The hand-to-hand combat continued as the debate veered over to the promised abolition of road tax and a new scheme of house grants. Richie Ryan, who had been satirised mercilessly for the previous four years as the Minister for Hardship, said, 'This is a disgrace. Dáil Éireann is being asked to write a blank cheque for slush money'. Worse still, he claimed, we were borrowing money from the EEC to 'abolish motor taxation'.

Barry Desmond of the Labour Party slammed the £1,000 housing grant. 'This scheme is a farce. It was thought up on a superficial basis to impress the unfortunate and tragic young people who are trying desperately to get a new home of their own.' In yet another example of the politics of *plus ça change, plus c'est la même chose* Desmond claimed that 60 per cent of it is being 'siphoned off on a speculative basis into the hands of certain construction companies who could not care less about what they charge'.

Sadly, John Kelly was wasting his breath when he claimed that there was a need for the country to develop the concept of a responsibility in which the people, 'individually, and as families and communities, carry a responsibility for their welfare and future'. They cannot 'expect political parties to do the job for them in return for votes'. He warned that if it were not done the day would come when 'this country, burdened by impossible promises, its currency torn away from sterling,' would find itself 'unable to pay its bills' and 'dragged to its knees by a revolution'.

The Leas-Cheann Comhairle, however, had suffered enough of such predictions and told the Dáil they were actually 'dealing with local government', which, in fairness, was an entirely different thing.

In his reply, Lynch tartly dismissed Garret's claim that Fianna Fáil were guilty of 'irresponsibility in our election manifesto'. He noted of his predecessors' fourteen-point programme that 'never were there so many obvious areas of unfulfilled promises' and 'never was an outgoing Government so emphatically rejected by the electorate'. Under Honest Jack, of course, Fianna Fáil were 'not going to gloat over our victory, nor are we going to accept it in a complacent manner'. But, fatally, he also dismissed Fine Gael's admonishments about 'the modest scale of borrowing that we propose in order to create the kind of employment we believe is necessary and possible'.

Typically for the time, there was one moment of unanimity: the Dáil would indulge in a three-month adjournment, from Wednesday 6 July to Wednesday 12 October. Those were happy days.

Chapter 20 ∾

'TIS AN 'IRISH SOLUTION TO AN IRISH PROBLEM'

28 February 1979

There was something uniquely belonging to the 70s surrounding the Supreme Court's decision in the McGee case on the provision of contraceptives to the public. This refers not so much to the issue as to the activism of the Supreme Court, which regularly forced the political system to defend and protect the rights of citizens. Happily, for politicians at least, the modern judge is more concerned with pension rights than with inalienable rights.

The necessity of liberalising the provision of contraceptives had already provoked one political crisis. Liam Cosgrave, then Taoiseach, had voted against and facilitated the defeat of his own Government in 1974. Unsurprisingly, the contraceptive hare had since been lying safely in the political long grass until, as a special treat for Charlie Haughey, Honest Jack transferred the issue from Justice to Health and told Haughey to be getting on with it.

The subsequent debate, and Haughey's famous 'Irish solution to an Irish problem', certainly didn't accord with his rakish, musketeer image. But Haughey was capable of adopting many masks. Several years earlier, having summoned Haughey to the palace over Edna O'Brien's novel *The Country Girls*, Archbishop McQuaid had noted 'the rising politician's disgust at its contents'. Like so many 'decent Catholic men with growing families', Haughey was, according to McQuaid, 'just beaten by the outlook and descriptions.'

As it was, Haughey's response would have impressed even Talleyrand. Speaking on the curious bill he had finally cobbled together, Haughey had as his first priority (understandably) the dispelling of the 'unfounded criticism that the Government is unnecessarily introducing legislation legalising the sale of contraceptives.' It was instead responding to a situation in which there had not been 'any controls over the importation of contraceptives' and in which 'it is, at present, legal for any person, irrespective of his or her age or marital status, to import contraceptives, provided they are not being imported for subsequent sale.' Happily, the bill Haughey was introducing would now 'control the availability of contraceptives and restrict effectively their supply to certain authorised channels for family-planning purposes.'

The aspirant Taoiseach also made it clear that he was sympathetic to the view that 'the availability of contraceptives through a large variety of sources and, for example, from slot machines and similar dispensers, should not be tolerated' and that 'advertising of artificial contraceptives should not be permitted in journals or newspapers in general circulation.' Critically, Haughey would also be establishing 'a comprehensive natural family-planning service', because he was 'convinced of the value and importance of providing such a service.' The aspirant Taoiseach even managed, with a straight face, to cite the role of organisations such as the National Association for the Ovulation Method in Ireland and told the gaping TDs that later that year he was 'arranging to hold, with the assistance of the World Health Organisation, an international seminar on natural family planning . . . during the course of which the latest developments in natural family-planning methods will be reviewed and discussed.'

Haughey also promised 'instruction or advice in relation to methods of family planning which involve the use of contraceptives', but he warned that this 'can be done only under the general direction and supervision of a registered medical practitioner.' Section 4 of the bill also ensured that 'contraceptives shall be sold only by chemists in their shops and that they shall be sold only to persons named in a prescription or authorisation given by a registered medical practitioner.'

Haughey also noted that when it came to the actual provision of contraceptives 'it seemed to me most appropriate that the responsibility for providing guidance and assistance in relation to decisions on family planning . . . should reside with the family doctor.' He declared, 'No other single professional person is as well qualified as he', adding that such a decision placed family planning 'firmly in the context in which, I believe, it should be placed, that is, in the context of family medical care provided by the general practitioner.'

The careful Haughey also included controls on the 'importation of contraceptives into the state.' There would be 'a provision for the importation, in personal luggage, of limited quantities of contraceptives required by a traveller for his own use.' The Fianna Fáil tactic of solving every crisis with a grant was also in evidence as Haughey noted that it had been represented to him that research into 'methods of natural family planning, and studies of the outcome of trials of methods of natural family planning, were inhibited by an acute shortage of money.'

Conscientious objectors to condoms were looked after in section 11, which made it 'very clear that no person will be required under the provisions of the bill to take part in the provision of a family-planning service, to give a prescription or authorisation for the purposes of the act' or even to be involved in the 'advertising or display of contraceptives'. In a delightful legislative diversion, Haughey also had to amend 'the Censorship of Publications Acts to take count of the fact that this bill will authorise the provision under certain circumstances of artificial methods of contraception.' As he noted with a commendably straight face that 'it would be unrealistic and illogical to provide in the bill for the availability under certain circumstances of artificial methods of contraception and to continue to ban books which advocated or referred to such methods,' one could only wonder what Donogh O'Malley would have made of it all.

Donnycarney's Renaissance man sailed on, however, sternly warning that there would be 'substantial penalties for persons guilty of offences under the act, penalties which are considerably heavier for second offences and for continuing offences than they are for first offences.' In particular it would be an offence 'to forge a prescription or authorisation or to be unlawfully in possession of such a forged document.'

Haughey piously expressed the hope that 'deputies will accept that this bill is the result of careful and earnest consideration of a difficult situation and that it is a sincere attempt to meet that situation in a reasonable and acceptable manner.' Rather like Solomon, with whom he had a few similarities, our aspirant Medici prince admitted that 'this legislation will not satisfy everybody', but the 'time has now come when the parliamentary process should prevail.' In a phrase that would haunt him, he claimed that the bill 'seeks to provide an Irish solution to an Irish problem.'

The debacle was a catalyst for one of John Kelly's most unforgettable contributions. Kelly, who was actually a natural conservative, observed that we 'really are a strange people, that five or six ageing men are willing to sit in this parliament and solemnly discuss urine dipsticks in order to decide whether we are going to legislate along the fine tightrope of morality the people expect of us.'

Kelly acutely wondered when we had ever applied 'that exquisite care to deciding other moral issues, to the justification of violence in any part of this country . . . to deciding issues of morality such as dishonesty towards the state, such as failing to make correct income tax returns.' Instead we were engaged in discussions that could only be found 'in a country inhabited by leprechauns whom life had spared from most of the major decisions'.

In a touching display of faith in the *bona fides* of Honest Jack, Kelly slammed the 'pretence that the matter before us is primarily a health matter'. While it may be 'accidentally a health matter', this was yet again a moral test for the Republic. Kelly berated those who had fallen for the claims of

Haughey's apologists that the legislation was some class of sophisticated response, for we were actually witnessing yet another case of 'political cowardice'. Mindful of the previous Government's experience, Kelly admitted that there 'is a case for prudence with a wafer-thin majority', but he added that 'there is nothing to be said for it when you have eighty-four rearguard legionaries, members of a radical party compared with whom we are a crowd of musty old grannies on these benches, and the people on the Labour Party benches are living on the moon.'

A disappointed Kelly felt that Haughey 'would have done himself credit if he refused to be saddled with this dead and stinking albatross of a subject', which 'had to be tarted up as a health measure to be respectable.' In a stark analysis of where Fianna Fáil now stood Kelly noted that 'this is what the radical party are driven to fifty years after their foundation.' Like any former Government whip, Kelly was a realist who knew that 'this is a country where people are not encouraged by their political leaders to make straight decisions, and to think straight about simple issues a certain amount of whoofling, compromising, bargaining and window-dressing may be unavoidable.'

However, such was the abject state of Fianna Fáil now that sexual permissiveness, 'which for many people is an outcrop of love . . . maybe not always, but for many people it is . . . must be stamped down even by the party of radical reality.' As Kelly sharply observed, 'that could not be allowed. It could not be said that Deputy X or Y could be allowed go back to the peninsula he lives on and have people pointing the finger at him, that he was permissive about lovemaking, but he can hold his head high if he is permissive about murder.'

It was all a bit much for Niall Andrews of Fianna Fáil, who asked, 'On a point of order, is it in order for a speaker to impute permissiveness to murder, as Deputy Kelly has done? He is imputing to the Fianna Fáil party—'

A rather nervous Leas-Cheann Comhairle interrupted, 'If Deputy Kelly imputes permissiveness to murder to any member he is completely out of order.'

But Kelly noted that it was time to cease 'trying to legislate in this private, intimate, notoriously volatile and mercurial area of life in the way we have been doing since 1935'. He added ironically of the abuse of condoms that 'I know I am treading in a minefield—I am not sure what an abuse might be.'

John Horgan of the Labour Party also took the historical route, noting that such was the fear and terror that sexual matters inspired in the new state that the 1934 committee had met in private to discuss the matter, before deciding that 'the sale of contraception should be controlled by similar conditions as those which control the sale of dangerous drugs.' One suspects that Haughey wouldn't have been too unhappy had a similar position been taken on that particular issue.

Noël Browne, meanwhile, sharply rejected the unwise statement that the bill was an Irish solution to an Irish problem. It was instead 'concerned with protecting the political interests of Fianna Fáil', to such an extent that the 'minister is providing a family-planning bill the bias of which is towards the least reliable form of family planning.'

In a rare moment of kindliness Browne claimed that it was 'an oversimplification simply to concentrate on the Minister for Health, Deputy Haughey'. He was a 'sophisticated politician in a working-class Dublin constituency . . . and quite obviously if he had his way—this is not a defence for a politician—I suspect he would not have produced this document.'

Once Browne had concluded by claiming that this was a bill 'riddled' with the 'Catholic sectarianism of Irish republicanism', Haughey stated that he had 'never sought to suggest that this bill was ideal' but that 'it represents a sensible, mature, responsible solution to a complex problem in our society.' The embattled minister ruefully added that 'in devising this legislation I have sought to tread the middle ground. I am faced with the necessity to make artificial contraceptives available to married persons or for family-planning purposes.'

He was, however, neither the first nor the last Irish politician to discover that there was, alas, no such thing as a safe 'middle ground' when it came to Ireland's great moral wars.

Chapter 21 ~

MR HAUGHEY 'COMES WITH A FLAWED PEDIGREE'

11 December 1979

In retrospect the seventies were the greyest decade of the new state. It was the age of Formica, and it had neither the virile optimism of the sixties nor, with the exception of the North, the dramatic nihilism of the eighties.

All that, however, was about to change. When it came to that overwhelming majority (Fianna Fáil had won eighty-four seats in 1977), Jack Lynch had been correct to worry about the dangers of 'carrying a full jug'. In the first year the economy had grown by 7 per cent, inflation had been halved and twenty thousand jobs had been created. But the Taoiseach's economic guru, Martin O'Donoghue, had been more than previous in promising 'an everlasting boom and full employment by 1983.' Instead, as the world economy turned sour, the Government by 1979 was so unpopular that a march by PAYE taxpayers drew, uniquely for Ireland, a million participants.

Meanwhile, in a rare event for the normally astute Fianna Fáil, the threat and the even speedier withdrawal of a proposed levy on farmers managed for once to unite the farmers and the PAYE workers in anger while, more significantly still, it also alienated the Fianna Fáil parliamentary party, which suffered the ire of both.

All records for strikes and stoppages were being broken while at the same time the corrosive consequences of extreme republicanism were embodied by the assassination of the British ambassador and by threats to Southern ministers. Amidst all this uncertainty, as the collapse in support for Fianna Fáil and Lynch spread even to his own Cork back yard, anxious eyes were increasingly turned in the direction of the new Messiah.

Since his dramatic *Paradise Lost*-style fall Haughey had worked himself cautiously back into the top echelons of the party. He never overtly challenged the leadership, but he did go on what was memorably described as 'a half pilgrimage, half recruitment drive' among the party's semiliterate backbenchers. Haughey's inclinations were a lot closer to the delights of giving lectures at the Harvard Summer School on 'Art and the Majority', in which he could muse about the relationship between the Prince of Salzburg and Mozart. But when it came to securing the leadership of Fianna Fáil it was Pee Flynn, Lynch's man in the polka-dot shirt, rather than the Prince of Salzburg, who would see him home.

Though nothing was yet known of Haughey's tangled personal finances, the aura of corrupt ambition that surrounded him in the eyes of some meant that the debate on his nomination for Taoiseach took place in a hushed and expectant Dáil. The man who had increasingly dominated the political consciousness of the state, and who was both more hated and more loved than any Irish politician since Parnell, was at the edge of the Taoiseach's desk. Though expectations for drama were high, and despite the fact that the amount of sulphur in the air brought 1932 and de Valera to mind, few expected that this would be a day that would set the terms of political debate for a decade.

They shouldn't have been so surprised, for Haughey versus Garret wasn't just the clash of the coming men: it was a Shakespearean battle of civilisations and cultures, one between the politics of the tribe and the modernity of a Fine Gael leader who would have been a metrosexual, had the term then existed. And FitzGerald's speech would live up to its billing with its sustained elevated tone, which was not then, nor indeed is it now, the norm in that house, which elevated FitzGerald to the secular status of an anti-Pope to Mr Haughey's new dynasty.

The mood was set early when Garret eulogised Lynch's 'warmth, spontaneity and sincerity which attract our people naturally.' Poor Lynch, today honest, was a man brought down 'before his time by smaller, ambitious men who have little mercy for a man who has served them and his country well.'

FitzGerald then set the scene for the most dramatic speech on the nomination of any Taoiseach with the warning that 'the occasion of the election of a Taoiseach is not any ordinary debate.' He pleaded for recognition 'of the difficulty of responding adequately or sensitively to this unique situation', one in which he had to speak 'not only for the opposition but for many in Fianna Fáil who may not be free to say what they believe or to express their deep fears for the future of this country' and who 'oppose this man [Haughey] with a commitment far beyond the normal.'

In an era when the political consciousness of many had been formed by Richard Nixon, the melodrama of the affair could only have been enhanced by FitzGerald's hope that 'I may be equal to it, that I may say what needs to be said and can be said, recognising how much I cannot say, for reasons that all in this house understand.' The fact that few, including possibly Garret himself, actually knew what it was that he couldn't say only added to the drama.

In the best traditions of oratory FitzGerald claimed he took 'no pleasure' in what he was about to do, for he had 'known Deputy Haughey for more than thirty-five years' and had 'never suffered insult or injury from him nor exchanged with him bitter words at any time.' But though he 'would find my task today easier if we had not had this long relationship with each other, a relationship that was never intimate but never hostile,' this didn't stop the daggers from flying. He said of Haughey that, unlike his predecessors, 'none of them was ever alleged, even by his most unrelenting enemy—and some of them had unrelenting enemies on both sides—to have entered public life for any motive but the highest.' Then came the line that would set the FitzGerald-Haughey feud in stone. FitzGerald coldly observed that while 'a recollection of the virtues of past Taoisigh allowed us to draw sustained hope for the future of this state . . . Deputy Haughey presents himself here seeking to be invested in office as the seventh in this line, but he comes with a flawed pedigree.'

The intensity of the atmosphere was epitomised by the sight of Haughey's own aged mother watching from the gallery while FitzGerald darkly claimed that her son's motives

> can be judged ultimately only by God, but we cannot ignore the fact that he differs from his predecessors in that these motives have been and are widely impugned, most notably but by no means exclusively, by people within his own party . . . They and others . . . have attributed to him an overweening ambition which they do not see as a simple emanation of a desire to serve but rather as a wish to dominate, even to own, the state.

He would also be a Taoiseach without a genuine mandate, as FitzGerald alleged that

> the second aspect of the election of this man as Taoiseach which must disturb deeply every democrat is that, whatever may be the result of the vote—and I think that is a foregone conclusion—he knows, I know, and they all know that he does not command the genuine confidence of even one-third of this house, never mind one-half.

However, though 'no previous Taoiseach has been elected in similar circumstances', FitzGerald ruefully admitted that 'as democrats we must respect the forms of democracy even when the true spirit of the democratic system is not breathed into these forms'. But 'the feet that will go through that lobby to support his election will include many that will drag; the hearts of many who will climb those stairs before turning aside to vote will be heavy.' They would give their 'formal consent' but 'withhold their full consent', because they were 'repelled by other defects which they see as superseding all considerations of mere competence, political skill or adroitness.'

Haughey's supporters were not spared either, as FitzGerald noted of a Government quaking in its boots that

> it is not from such as these that Deputy Haughey won his majority. His majority comprises men judged inadequate in office in the past; men ambitious of office but disappointed of it hitherto; men fearful of losing office because they backed the wrong horse; and, above all, at least eighteen men who scraped home narrowly in 1977 and who, fearing for the seats that were so unexpectedly won for them by the gamble of the manifesto, have now switched their bet to another gamble, the gamble of Deputy Haughey.

The speech concluded with a clever apologia. 'It is distasteful to have to argue the merits of an individual rather than a policy, and to reflect so critically on the performance and character of a parliamentary colleague I have known for many years.' No-one could argue, though, that Garret hadn't managed to leave his distaste behind.

It was impossible for anyone to surpass FitzGerald's seizure of the spirit of the age. But the debate continued with a level of vitriol that seemed more appropriate for the post-Civil War era. The acerbic leader of the Labour Party, Frank Cluskey, was one of the gentler contributors, noting that Haughey was the epitome of the rise in the middle of the 1960s within the political and business world of

> a group of young, well educated, very clever, highly articulate young men, who also had one other quality: they were totally ruthless, and they had a clear indication of what their personal ambition was . . . They had another thing in common: a philosophy of life that was dominated by the principle that the end justifies the means. Those people, small in number, set out to acquire great personal wealth, influence and political power.

He added that Haughey,

> being of the same mould, or, as he might prefer it, out of the same stable . . . was only too willing to ensure that, as far as he could, by virtue of the political office he had, he would facilitate them in every way in the achievement of their ambition: the acquisition of great personal wealth, influence far out of proportion to their numbers.

Cluskey ended with the wise piece of supposition that soon reached the status of prophecy. He suggested that Haughey would be 'undoubtedly entitled to the same degree of support and loyalty which he gave to his predecessor.' Labour Party leaders of that time knew a great deal about the nature of loyalty in divided parties.

After Garret the sense of drama was most acutely captured by the normally urbane John Kelly, who claimed that Haughey's triumph would cause consternation and fear for 'hundreds of thousands of Irish people.' An *Irish Times* editorial suggesting that the nomination of Haughey should be discussed in a rational way sparked the response from Kelly that 'it would be well for the "Irish Times" to bear in mind that this is Dáil Éireann, not the Reichstag.' He concluded with the claim that there was something about Haughey's temperament that 'ought to make the rest of us take fright.'

Noël Browne, never a man to calm a troubled scene, said that his 'awful nightmare is that this man is a dreadful cross between Richard Milhous Nixon and Dr Salazar' and that Haughey's election was the triumph of 'sectarian nationalists' and 'crypto-Provos'. The bitterness was epitomised by his claim that when John Kelly had asked

> whether it was not time to bring an end to the Civil War, or some phrase of that kind, it was Deputy [Vivion] de Valera, to my horror, who said, 'Your invitation is refused.' That is the mentality of the kind of support this man has in the house.

The troubles continued into the next day. John Horgan of the Labour Party noted of the defeated George Colley that 'I felt some sympathy as I saw him sitting there yesterday as if the marrow had been sucked out of his bones, listening to himself being proposed as Minister for Tourism and Transport, Minister for CIE's Overdraft, and for giving grants for bed-and-breakfast places in hotels round the country.'

Even the normally sanguine Ruairí Quinn joined the mood with the claim that 'we are faced with a palace revolution which has all the subtlety and finesse of the Ayatollah Khomeini in Iran, with a little less bloodshed.'

Haughey, in contrast, was in the mood for playing down everything that had been said. In a terse response the new Taoiseach said it was not his 'intention to make anything in the nature of a major statement of policy.' He did, however, pointedly refer to 'a new beginning' and said he 'was very heartened by the countless messages of support I received from people from every part of Ireland.'

Typical of the continuing priorities of Irish Governments he said his 'first objective is the attainment of peace, with the economy being second.' He did admit, in his usual stilted style, that there were major problems on the economic front, where we 'will probably have a balance of payments deficit of the order of £650 million this year, which must be reduced.'

Haughey concluded by saying that 'Deputy FitzGerald will agree that this seems to be a time of incredible rumours of every sort' but that many had 'no foundation'. But the nature of the spectacle that had unfolded was best captured in Bruce Arnold's observation that what should have been 'a celebration of victory' had instead turned into 'a spontaneous and relentless impeachment'. There would be more to come.

THE HORRID EIGHTIES AND THE GREAT AGE OF GUBU

'I FOUND MY FOOT IN SOME STRANGE DOORS LAST WEEK'

30 June 1981

On coming to power Haughey had attempted, in between sorting out his personal finances, to put the state's affairs in order. In a speech that mirrored some of his own affairs, Haughey told the nation in the iconic televised address of January 1980 that we were 'living away beyond our means', at a rate 'which is simply not justified by the amounts of goods and services we are producing.' The dangers of deficit financing had struck to such an extent that 'to make up the difference we have been borrowing enormous amounts of money . . . at a rate we just cannot continue.'

The new Taoiseach may have expressed the hope that 1980 could be the year in which 'we find a better way of doing things', but instead, in one infamously profligate year, when the final figures came in Garda pay had been underestimated by 30 per cent and the army's by 28 per cent, and social welfare was over budget by an impressive 45 per cent. The ESRI, meanwhile, revealed— unsurprisingly in circumstances such as this—that inflation had reached 20 per cent and that Ireland's banks were facilitating wholesale tax evasion to retain their deposits. The Haughey experiment, in short, was effectively bust.

Normally politicians such as Garret FitzGerald, who believed that 'the whole purpose of representative democracy is to have a system which doesn't give people what they want if they want the wrong thing', do not thrive in the Irish political system. On this occasion, though, the electorate were—only barely—in the mood for political honesty. It was needed. As FitzGerald memorably noted, he had been delighted to be elected Taoiseach 'until I got my seal of office and was told the country was bankrupt. That wasn't a good moment.'

When it came to the Dáil debate, Haughey certainly had an odd pair of proposers in the selection of George Colley and Brian Lenihan. Mind you, Garret's two proposers—the youngest TD, Ivan Yates, and his former and future *bête noire,* Oliver J. Flanagan—were equally eclectic.

Colley's nomination of Haughey was a short affair consisting of the single sentence 'On behalf of the Fianna Fáil party I nominate Charles J. Haughey as Taoiseach.' One supposes that the brevity was understandable.

Unlike at the accession of Haughey, there was no high-flown rhetoric. Instead the debate was short and businesslike, but there was a discernible undercurrent of bitterness. Surprisingly the Labour Party didn't contribute at all. Other than the *dramatis personae,* the debate was, given the finely balanced state of the political arithmetic, inevitably dominated by independents.

Noël Browne, almost four decades on from his first Dáil appearance, was certainly clear in his views on Haughey. He noted that 'over the past four years I raised a number of . . . matters of private morality and private conscience, matters particularly affecting minorities, matters important in the context of the Northern Ireland question, matters like divorce, contraception, capital punishment and so on' with him but found his 'attitude to be completely rigid, unyielding, uncompromising and totally intransigent.'

This, allied to Haughey's performance in the Arms Trial debate, during which it seemed to Browne that 'he was either contemptuous of what we thought of his position or his integrity or he was afraid', meant that he couldn't vote for Haughey.

The scattered independent Seán 'Dublin Bay' Loftus made an ineffectual plea for a 'national government—the pooling of the brains of the best men and women in the country,' before the independent socialist Jim Kemmy, a stonemason, noted wryly, 'I found my foot in some strange doors last week.'

Kemmy was, to put it mildly, equivocal in his support for FitzGerald as he noted that 'the people voted, in their fashion, for change, although it may have been in a strange and inconclusive way,' but he promised to 'respect the decision of the people'. He slammed the new cult of 'government here by public relations and, at times, government by default, instead of government in the interest of the people.' Fine Gael, had they been listening properly, would surely have been more aware that Kemmy would be a turbulent priest: though he was voting for FitzGerald on the day, he said that if Fine Gael indulged in measures he opposed he would be the first person to 'pull the rug from under them. I can go back to my hammer and trowel in a few weeks or a few months'.

The independent Neil Blaney was even less impressed by the scene unfolding before him. Haughey's decision to cut and run had led to a 'rather foolish, unwanted chore' of an election that had provided the political elite with a deserved result of 'no clear verdict one way or the other.' Blaney, the last great republican irredentist, referring to the escalating violence in the North, was also anxious to note that

> we find ourselves here today also minus two members of the new, expanded Dáil of 166. Those two are in the H-blocks of Long Kesh. I would wish to have it go from here—from me if from nobody else—that we regret their absence, their inability to attend.

He might have hoped that 'collectively, we, as an elected new Dáil, whatever form the Government may take, will henceforth and forthwith clearly and in the open come out and be seen to be concerned about the tragedy that is unfolded by their absence here today', but the activities of Blaney's kissing cousins meant that no-one was queuing up to join him.

The endemically self-pitying Irish voters would have undoubtedly agreed, however, with Blaney's analysis that in 'an international economic situation that is anything but promising, and has indeed been difficult for several years,' the electorate had been given 'the sad, unenviable task of trying to choose between bad and worse.' And it would, alas, become increasingly hard to know which was which as the decade unfolded.

Few, with the exception of the increasingly delusional Haughey, would have disagreed with Blaney's other stark warning: in the wake of Britain's recent encounter with the IMF we were going to have to

> try to undo—in haste—some of the damage that has been done before we find ourselves in the position . . . of not having any real say in what we are to do about our economy in the future, but rather have it dictated to us, as indeed our sister island, England, had it so dictated not so very long ago—and she is a much bigger entity.

Haughey, who had done so much to bring us to that place, loftily informed the Dáil that Fianna Fáil would vote against 'the political haggling and bartering that have brought this Government into office.'

He would be a lot less fussy some months later. For now, though, Fianna Fáil would oppose 'the mixed bag of irreconcilables that the parties opposite purport to put forward as a Government programme of action.' It was a typical performance by Haughey, with poor Garret being told that Fianna Fáil had 'fought an honest campaign . . . We made no special promises or offered any election bribes or inducements'. In contrast, when it came to the new coalition, its 'programme is dishonest . . . It is not capable of being implemented.'

Fianna Fáil, in contrast, Haughey magisterially claimed, 'created thousands of jobs and have initiated major new programmes. We undertook the essential modernisation of our country's infrastructure.' Sadly, however, many 'of our plans will only come to fruition in the years ahead'.

FitzGerald, however, wasn't taking any of this stuff. He sharply declared that Fianna Fáil was 'rejected at the polls basically because of the perception by the people that that party failed to govern—a failure to govern that had no precedent in the annals of the country and which has led to the near collapse of our public finances.' A fuming FitzGerald added that 'in the couple of hours since I was appointed Taoiseach I have had many things to do' because of 'the nature of the changeover on this occasion'. But even in that time he had learnt something 'of the scale of the damage done. I have to say I am shocked to find the position is even worse than our most pessimistic—' At this moment his train of thought was disturbed by what in the record is politely termed 'interruptions', but an undaunted FitzGerald continued: 'I do not say that without careful consideration. It is not a propagandist remark: it is a factual remark.' Fianna Fáil had 'left behind them so much to be done that this Dáil will have to become the hardest-working Dáil, as was the Dáil when the national coalition Government were in power, in terms of the volume of legislation enacted and the amount of work done.'

Like many of his predecessors, FitzGerald, as Taoiseach, promised that this Government would 'govern by the process of listening and leading: we shall not cut ourselves off from the people.' In spite of his confidence that, like 'other administrations that did not have an overall majority, this Government will see through their term of office', Garret wouldn't get the chance to break that particular vow.

To a country most of whose citizens were at best broke, FitzGerald quixotically pledged to create 'something better than the materialistic society which has grown up so rapidly in recent years.' In truth, a country experiencing record levels of unemployment might have been entitled to hope that Garret would bring a little bit more materialism into the country.

At the adjournment Haughey had the last—and defining—word on the more prosaic realities that FitzGerald faced. Having established that 'it was not proposed to take any major financial measures next week', he asked, 'Will the Taoiseach be certain that he will have all his tortured independents here to support him?'

Mark Killilea (junior) of Fianna Fáil chuckled, 'I see some long faces at the back,' and they would get longer, for though Garret would have his eclectic little band for a slightly longer period, they were, essentially, like the rest of the economy, held on tick.

Chapter 23

EPHEMERAL CREATIONS BRING DOWN THE BEST GOVERNMENT WE NEVER HAD

27 January 1982

The horrors of the three elections of 1981–2 might of course have been avoided were it not for the only budget ever to be defeated by the Dáil. Ironically, given the capacity of Irish politicians—and in particular independents—for speechifying, it was in the end the man who didn't speak at all who brought down the budget of 1982. But it was the endemic incapacity of Fine Gael to listen to those politicians they believed to be their intellectual and social inferiors that really set the mine beneath the FitzGerald Government's foundations.

FitzGerald might have known his sums when it came to economics, but his mathematical capacities on the political front were rather more limited. In the 1981 election, in spite of the surge to Fine Gael, Haughey's drive for his own mandate as Taoiseach had been foiled by a razor-thin margin. This meant that, outside of Noël Browne, FitzGerald's Government was dependent on two other trembling pillars that needed careful nurturing.

One was the independent Seán 'Dublin Bay' Loftus, whose full name was as long as a list of EU accession countries, and the other, Jim Kemmy, was a philosophical Limerick stonemason. The duo, in common with Browne, had already endured a knee-trembler of a mini-budget as the new Government struggled to impose some degree of order on the state's deteriorating finances. Their willingness to vote for the first dose of reality that Irish politics had experienced in half a decade meant that a Government of academics and merchant princes was dangerously casual in securing the support of its accidental fellow-travellers.

In what was an immediate bad sign for the trembling deputies, the Minister for Finance, John Bruton, began his 1982 budget by expressing regret for 'the great length at which I must address the house on this occasion.' Happily, he was 'confident that, as a result of this budget, the budget speech I shall have to make this time next year will be somewhat shorter'. He was, one supposes, right about that.

The central thesis of Bruton's fiscal strategy was that 'budget deficits are demoralising: they encourage the myth that one can spend what one has not earned'. There would be no more of that, though. The new minister warned the deputies that 'as a community we face a new order in the world; an era of easy growth based on cheap energy, which lasted from 1945 . . . until approximately 1970, is now definitely over. We must now expand in a contracting market.'

In a forensic destruction of the chaotic running of the national finances under both Lynch and Haughey, Bruton noted that there had been overshoots in the planned deficit of 81 per cent in 1979, 58 per cent in 1980 and 62 per cent in 1981. His language echoed that of Haughey in 1979—'We cannot continue to pay ourselves more than our competitors'—but Bruton actually meant what he was saying.

The chilling critique continued. Bruton noted that 'the targets contained in the original January 1981 budget proved to be meaningless.' We had instead incurred 'the largest current deficit and overall borrowing ever . . . in the country.' More significantly still, in 1981 only a quarter of the total Exchequer Borrowing Requirement could be financed at home. This left us dangerously exposed to 'international fluctuations in the availability of funds.'

In language that carries a woebegone air of familiarity, Bruton told the Dáil that each minister would be 'reporting back to the Government by the 30th of April on the results of public expenditure reviews which are already being taken in conjunction with the Minister for the Public Service and myself.'

On the plus side, and there were few enough of those, Bruton had found an extra £250,000 for veterans of the War of Independence and their widows. A new Ombudsman's office—one that would cause plenty of difficulties for Haughey in its time—was also being established.

The trouble only really began when Bruton claimed that 'Government policy places a high priority on a more equitable system of taxation, and we intend that a greater burden of taxation will be borne by those who can best afford it.' In terms that are again all too familiar to modern ears, Bruton noted that 'the present tax base is too narrow.' The problem, as he would learn the hard way, is that expanding the tax base in Ireland is always a dangerous move.

There was a brief digression on the issue of tax evasion, with Bruton noting (as Haughey had some twenty years earlier) that it has 'moral implications'. Haughey had taken a somewhat different journey since, but all that would have to emerge.

Bruton, however, got back to swinging the axe as he warned that 'there is no reason in logic why short-term social welfare benefits should not be charged to taxation.' He then abolished a series of frankly incredible tax breaks on non-mortgage personal borrowing and business expenses, while Fianna Fáil greeted with some horror the news of a proposed windfall tax on development land.

As Bruton announced that the lower rate of VAT was being increased from 15 per cent to 18 per cent the fatal flaw finally reared its head. 'We have an exceptionally large zero-rated category in our vat system, covering some 27 per cent of all items.' This was 'far larger than in any of our EEC partners apart from the UK . . . The major zero ratings, particularly clothing and footwear, therefore have been removed.' The less than worldly Minister for Finance admitted that 'clothing and footwear are undoubtedly necessities of life.' But, he added, 'this category covers everything from the most simple garments to the most expensive and ephemeral creations of fashion.' The even worse news was that many of these 'ephemeral creations' were imported.

The grave was getting bigger, but Bruton ploughed on happily, for the great defence of statistics suggested that 'a tax on clothing and footwear will . . . bear less heavily on lower and lower-middle income households'. Statistics counted for little among the ranks of a Fianna Fáil party that, though it didn't realise it at the time, was about to be the beneficiary of one of the greatest political blunders in the history of the state.

In the disjointed aftermath of the budget, Fine Gael deputies would be even more horrified to hear that 'the possibility of omitting children's clothing and footwear from the increase' had been considered. While Bruton was 'aware that this is done in the UK . . . I am also aware of the major difficulties which it poses in practice and of the anomalies it has created.' He had considered 'it better therefore to compensate parents directly through the new child benefit scheme.'

The axe continued to come down hard on a variety of other delights. Typical of the taxation rates that were then applicable, the top rate of VAT was 30 per cent. There were new taxes on video players, televisions and late-night drinking, of all things, and Bruton also declared that 'an area of discretionary expenditure which I consider does not bear its fair share of tax at present is expenditure on foreign holidays . . . It is a measure of the unreality of our living styles that, notwithstanding the recession in the economy generally, more people than ever before were able to take their holidays abroad in 1981.'

The home front didn't look any prettier, thanks to an increased motor tax 'to encourage longer usage of cars, provided of course that we can satisfy safety requirements.' Bruton may have come from a different side of the Civil War tribe from de Valera, but he appeared equally determined to impose a regime of frugal comfort, if not actual discomfort, upon us.

All this, together with reduced food subsidies on items such as butter, meant that we would still have a distinctly high exchequer borrowing ratio of 13.8 per cent, as distinct from 16.9 per cent in 1981. Prudence, alas, had certainly been on a long holiday: from 1977 to 1981, £5 billion had been added to the national debt, and 25,000 extra public sector jobs had been created.

The reply of Martin O'Donoghue of Fianna Fáil gave no indication of the drama to come. He did note that 'even children's clothing is going to jump from a nil rate today to 18 per cent', but the effect was lost, as the professor made a priority of attacking the Labour Party for its failure to live up to its election slogan, 'We want jobs, not promises.' O'Donoghue's weary final observation—that the Dáil 'will have opportunities as the debate continues in later weeks to develop on all these things'—wasn't indicative of a man expecting a snap election.

Haughey laid it on with a trowel, claiming that this was 'a savage and antisocial budget'. The embattled Fianna Fáil leader continued to reside in a fantasy world where there was 'no problem or crisis in the public finances, nor is there any difficulty on the balance of payments front, which could justify the savage imposition on ordinary families that this budget represents.' It was almost as though he thought he could treat the economy in the same cavalier way he treated the misfortunate AIB bank manager in charge of his finances when he condemned the absence of 'one single optimistic aspect' in a budget dealing with these 'alleged' difficulties.

The somewhat exotic Fianna Fáil TD Niall Andrews was particularly exercised by leisure issues, feeling that the coalition 'must consider very carefully the question of introducing a tax on foreign holidays.' He admitted that 'the initial imposition of ten pounds for a holiday does not appear to be a great deal,' but he warned that 'it is important that Irish people should be encouraged to travel abroad to see what is happening in Europe and America.'

It was characteristic of the frankly appalling standard of parliamentary debate that some Fianna Fáil TDs genuinely expressed concerns about the effect the tax would have on invalids going to Lourdes. Gene Fitzgerald of Cork meanwhile claimed that an increased tax on beer was the 'last straw'.

But even as Haughey expressed the hopeful view that the Government was 'walking steadily towards a crisis'—many thought 'unsteadily' would have been more appropriate—John Kelly claimed that there was 'a glimmer of hope' in the budget. 'For the first time, in my memory at least, we have a Minister for Finance who knows what is meant by taxation equity . . . the cornerstone on which any kind of social understanding here must be built'.

The conclusion bore no inkling of what was to come, with Bobby Molloy and John Kelly crossing swords over an exemption for those travelling to Lourdes from the new tax on persons travelling out of the country on charter flights.

Then, suddenly, an astonishing tableau emerged in the Dáil as the first budget vote was called. Excited Fianna Fáil TDS began to cheer and jeer as Garret went down on one knee in front of Jim Kemmy, who simply told him, 'Sorry, Garret, the die is cast.'

Raymond Smith, a colourful chronicler of a colourful age, wrote afterwards:

> My memory from that night will always be of the moment when Ray Burke, the Fianna Fáil Chief Whip, unrestrained jubilation written on his countenance, came down the stairway waving the paper containing the winning vote. He couldn't hide the 'By God, we did it' air of triumph as he walked up to Charles Haughey and shook his hand before handing the paper to the Ceann Comhairle, John O'Connell.

Afterwards, Garret is believed to have famously asked, 'Is there any way we can un-dissolve the Dáil?' But, of course, there wasn't.

Chapter 24 ~

| A DUO OF DESPAIR

9 March 1982 and 14 December 1982

Moving away from abnormal depression, 9 March 1982

The period 1981–2, for all of the colour and drama that is inevitable when three elections closely follow each other, raised the despair of the electorate to new heights. Garret perhaps came closest to describing the trench warfare of the period when, on finally winning the war, he described what had gone on as a 'curious process of attrition'.

The wretched nature of Haughey's brief second Government was succinctly captured by Bruce Arnold, who described it as being something 'conceived by accident, born in confusion . . . doomed from the start to a short life . . . without being a merry one . . . [as] the sickly creature wailed its way from one affliction to the next.'

The confusion that had led to its conception was, of course, Bruton's tax on children's shoes. After that little accident a buoyant FitzGerald had expressed his delight at being able to go to the country with an honest policy platform. Fianna Fáil, in contrast, was a house divided, before and after its equivocal victory. In its aftermath the bitter division was epitomised by the calling of Séamus Brennan to the Taoiseach's office before the announcement of the Government. He should have started getting worried when Ray Burke sweetly whispered, 'Congratulations,' for Brennan had been specifically called to be told he was getting nothing.

As Haughey stitched together the necessary support the critical vote of Tony Gregory meant that fiscal rectitude also went out the window. Instead, at an encounter in which Haughey simply told Gregory, 'You know what I want; what do you want?' both swiftly got what they wanted.

In the Dáil on that fateful day, independents once more dominated the nominations process. Inevitably, Neil Blaney said:

> Putting it without any strings attached, we want it to be clearly known throughout the world that we want Britain out of this country. On that I got a good and receptive hearing from Deputy Haughey. I did not get quite

the same hearing—nor was I disappointed—from Deputy FitzGerald.

Jim Kemmy, meanwhile, noted of the tight result that we were going to have to 'all learn to live dangerously in politics'. That was certainly true, but Kemmy was being optimistic in his hope that 'this tight situation in the balance of power will bring about greater public accountability by future Governments'.

For Tony Gregory, the star of the hour, 'two major considerations dictated our approach to these negotiations . . . First, to try to get clear commitments . . . Secondly . . . to make a decision that would encourage the development of progressive and class politics.' With commendable understatement, Gregory noted that 'this was no easy task'. According to Gregory, Garret's response, 'though sincere and genuine, was most pessimistic and did not approximate remotely to the commitments given by Fianna Fáil.'

FitzGerald's speech was somewhat more tranquil than his first critique of Haughey. The deposed Taoiseach promised to constructively 'support all reasonable measures that may be necessary to maintain the real underlying level of borrowing'. Like all defeated party leaders, FitzGerald claimed that it was not 'an exaggeration to say we in government have transformed the economic climate of politics and that on all sides the politics of promises is the politics of yesterday's men.' The views of FitzGerald's former ministers about his observation that 'the achievement of this new realism was painful, but so is any worthwhile achievement' are not recorded.

Lest Haughey become too enthusiastic, FitzGerald anxiously hoped that 'the Taoiseach does not—as he did before—change his mind about the need to secure our financial solvency.' After Gregory, the omens were not good as FitzGerald warned:

> In 1977–8 net foreign borrowing by the Government totalled about £110 million; in the subsequent two years this rose roughly by a factor of ten, to £1,075 million . . . If the present build-up of foreign debt were to continue unabated, Ireland's credit rating overseas might be downgraded.

On this occasion even Garret was eclipsed by a stellar contribution from our old friend Oliver J. Flanagan, who lashed 'the campaign of disgraceful vilification' of Haughey by the media.

As this sparked the unprecedented sight of Fianna Fáil supporters cheering the response of a Fine Gael TD to the nomination of a Fianna Fáil Taoiseach, the Ceann Comhairle was moved to 'ask the members of the public in the gallery to cease: applause by them is not permitted.'

Oliver J, though, wouldn't be stopped so easily. 'I too was a victim of vilification by the media after the Locke's Tribunal of 1948,' he said, before warning the press gallery, 'It is only right when a new Government take office that it should be made very clear here that it is this parliament and the Government who run the country, not a group of journalists or pen-pushers.' Fine Gael's front benches were also less than happy when Flanagan essentially rejected his own party's policies. The Fine Gael populist instead believed that, in this life,

> balanced ledgers will not fill any hungry stomachs . . . There is no point in putting forward a well-balanced account . . . on a table to a husband and wife who have six or eight hungry children around that table. That is the kind of policy that has us where we are today. Get on with the spending.

It was an offer that Fianna Fáil would need no encouragement to fulfil.

In a speech laced with future ironies Haughey noted that the 'return of the Fianna Fáil Government to office today is an historic occasion, since it marks the fiftieth anniversary of the election of the first Fianna Fáil government in 1932.' Since that day, Haughey claimed, 'our people have always looked to Fianna Fáil for good, stable government as an essential precondition of the achievement of our national objectives.' On this occasion he too believed that 'the entry of this Government into office will bring the political uncertainty of recent times to an end.'

In spite of our economic woes Haughey maintained that his priority continued to be 'the quest for a solution to the tragic problem of Northern Ireland.' Other than this 'the immediate task of our Government will be to restore confidence on a basis of stability which we alone are capable of providing.' The new Taoiseach pledged that Fianna Fáil would 'mobilise the resources of our country to return to the path of progress and achievement. We will move away from the abnormal and depressing atmosphere that has recently prevailed.'

'A curious process of attrition', 14 December 1982

In one of the more perceptive books on the earlier Haughey era, *The Boss*, by Joe Joyce and Peter Murtagh, it is noted that Haughey's greatest weakness was that he thought 'he could make things happen by declaring them to be so.' The world, sadly, was somewhat less malleable.

Nothing typified the 'abnormal and depressing' nature of Haughey's short-lived minority Government more than the Malcolm MacArthur affair, in which a murderous fantasist, who had bludgeoned a nurse to death and blown the head off another stranger, had been found in the flat of Haughey's Attorney-General, Patrick Connolly, who then took the extraordinary step of leaving the country to go on his holidays.

MacArthur, though, was just one example of how the promised 'Camelot of Charlie' had been transformed into a foul palace of 'grotesque, unbelievable, bizarre and unprecedented' events. Together with the infamous Gregory Deal, Haughey's determination to seize and maintain power, along with the growing belief of his more uncouth supporters that dissenting from him was the equivalent of treason, had been the catalyst for real fears that even the Gardaí were being taken over and used as an instrument of Haughey and his ill-regarded Minister for Justice, Seán Doherty.

When Haughey inevitably fell, the third leg of this terrible troika of electoral despair was inevitably a squalid, ill-tempered affair epitomised by Fianna Fáil scaremongering about how Fine Gael was planning to let 'armed RUC men' patrol the streets of Dublin. It all mattered little, except perhaps in putting the slightest of dents in the majority of the Fine Gael-Labour Party coalition.

In the Dáil, as he faced inevitable defeat and the possible loss of his leadership of Fianna Fáil, Haughey astonishingly was far more concerned about 'the restoration of good order in this house'. The deposed Taoiseach grandiosely fretted about how 'over a period of years the situation in this regard has steadily deteriorated. We have had increasing disorder, procedural wrangling, arguing with the chair, and in many cases an abuse of the point of order.'

Garret, as the new Taoiseach, understandably felt he had more serious priorities. He noted that, 'having had the experience of being Taoiseach for eight months, I am aware what the burdens of office are, and I am aware also, as members are, of the gravity of the problems facing the country.' He somewhat lamely expressed the hope that he would

> mobilise to a greater extent than perhaps we have been able to do in the past the efforts of all in the Dáil in the interests of the nation, and that, by opening up procedures of the Dáil in new ways, the opposition can be given the fullest opportunity to contribute and to participate in the whole work of formulating policy and of working, where possible, towards a consensus.

Inevitably, over future fractious years, consensus would be an elusive friend. For now, though, Haughey, as was his wont on such occasions, promised to 'go into opposition with, I hope, dignity and honour.' It was a remark that must have occasioned the occasional wry smile in the wake of subsequent events such as Haughey's morally squalid opposition to the Anglo-Irish Agreement, which even achieved the rare feat of embarrassing Brian Lenihan.

For now, though, Garret issued his thanks to Haughey for his 'courtesy and co-operation', Haughey expressed his 'appreciation of the kind and courteous words just spoken by the Taoiseach', and we then settled down to business as usual, as the ceasefire didn't make it as far as the nomination of Garret's new ministers.

Instead, Haughey begrudgingly said it was 'not open to us to question the right of the people to vote in any way they wish, or even to deplore the outcome. Nor indeed do I see this as an occasion for petulance or party polemics.' The high-minded (on this occasion at least) opposition leader noted, therefore, that he would 'not indulge in personalities or comment in any way on the individual members of the Government, despite the fact that I and my colleagues have often in the past on such occasions been forced to endure much in that regard.' He did, however, note that Fianna Fáil saw it as 'being of deep significance that Deputy John Bruton has not been returned to the Department of Finance,' and he wondered if this had been informed by a Labour Party embargo on his appointment or by the desire for a 'flexible approach'. Haughey, with his usual cunning, had spotted the Achilles heel of the bright new Government.

After Haughey had warned that 'this is no time for hedging or ambivalence on the imperative need to bring down as quickly as possible the annual budget deficit,' the ascetic-looking Workers' Party leader, Tomás Mac Giolla, in an early critique of the politics of celebrity, claimed that the election had been debased by nasty personal squabbles. 'Would the leader of Fine Gael shake hands with the leader of Fianna Fáil? Would they smile at each other?' The public, Mac Giolla observed, had been far more 'entitled to know what they would do in Government.' But while Haughey 'told them pretty clearly what he would do, and it certainly was not very nice . . . the new Taoiseach did not tell us a thing.' After noting that this rare reticence had done the new Government's chances of being elected absolutely no harm at all, Mac Giolla was right to 'await with some trepidation the policies the new Government will pursue.'

FitzGerald, meanwhile, was absolutely clear in his view that in the phasing out of the budget deficit there would be no flexibility. There was, he warned, a real danger now that it might be 'steadily more expensive, and perhaps even impossible, for us to borrow to meet the needs of investment in the future' if this were not done.

Garret noted that Mac Giolla was right to suggest that the last eighteen months had been a 'traumatic period in Irish politics'. He added that it had been 'an unhappy period, no matter what side of politics one is on, but out of it has come through a curious process of attrition, with respect to public opinion, a growth of a sense of reality among the people that there are problems which must be faced painfully.'

Fine Gael's eternal optimist concluded by hoping that 'we . . . in this Dáil will be seen in retrospect as one of the most constructive Dáils in the history of the state.' Though he didn't know it, the curious politics of attrition had another five years in them.

Chapter 25

DESSIE O'MALLEY STANDS BY THE REPUBLIC

14 February 1985

By 1985 almost all the optimism that had accompanied FitzGerald's election victory had been squandered. The moving of Bruton from Finance, as Haughey had correctly divined, was fatal, as fiscal decisiveness was replaced with paralysis by analysis. In Northern policy the Government had been severely wounded by Margaret Thatcher's unintentionally brusque 'Out . . . out . . . out' response to the attempt by the New Ireland Forum to define a future path for the Northern conflict. And the much-prayed-for (in a secular way, of course!) constitutional crusade had been spectacularly derailed by the debacle of the abortion referendum.

As Haughey waited wolfishly for the apple of the Taoiseach's office to fall gently into his avaricious hands, the national mood was depressed further by the poignant tales of the victims of Ireland's continuing moral civil war. It is remembered now as the age when a tribunal that was supposed to be about how gardaí had secured a series of false confessions over the death of a baby turned into a trial of the sex life of the central character, Joanne Hayes, who would be asked about such things as 'the quality of the pain' she experienced in giving birth in a field. A nation that was still wrapped tightly in the swaddling clothes of devotional Catholicism would be further shocked by the story of the fifteen-year-old Ann Lovett, who had died giving birth to a secret child at a secluded grotto devoted to the worship of the Virgin Mary.

If that iconography had caused an outbreak of national self-questioning, the strength of the *ancien régime* was epitomised by the bitter court case that evolved after an unmarried schoolteacher, Eileen Flynn, having given birth to a child by a married man with whom she was openly living, was dismissed from the Catholic primary school where she worked. At one point during the case the judge had mused that it wasn't unknown in certain countries for women to be 'condemned to death for this sort of offence'. He hastily added, 'I do not agree with this, of course,' but it was too late to stop the inevitable, and somewhat understandable, furore.

Other 'eternal verities' also continued to survive. The state might have been experiencing an existential fiscal crisis alongside its social battles, but as the Labour Party hobbled along ineffectually the political scene continued to be dominated by the post-Civil War monoliths of Fianna Fáil and Fine Gael.

As the economy sank ever deeper into the mire, the last thing that an increasingly fissiparous Fine Gael needed was a further dispute over the provision of contraception. The matter, however, had been taken out of their hands following a Garda raid, on foot of a complaint, of a clinic in Dún Laoghaire that was being over-liberal in its dispensing of contraceptives.

The vicious mood within the Dáil in the wake of the decision by the Minister for Health, Barry Desmond, to normalise the sale of contraceptives was epitomised by the Fianna Fáil response when the embattled Desmond referred to secret meetings involving Haughey and the Irish Hierarchy. It had provoked the normally pleasant Brian Lenihan to say that 'the minister is a very objectionable little man', and the feral mood intensified amidst claims as the debate began that Fianna Fáil was censoring the list of speakers to ensure that Haughey wouldn't be embarrassed by any displays of independent thought.

Before Dessie O'Malley's speech the nature of the times was captured in some preceding contributions. Joe Doyle, who uniquely combined being a Church sacristan with being Garret FitzGerald's running-mate, referred to the 'possibility of some people being upset by the making available of contraceptives free of charge to medical-card holders'. Fretful TDs referred to contraceptives as 'the devices' in a manner that suggested that they had been designed by paramilitaries, and a Fianna Fáil TD, Pearse Wyse, who would subsequently join the PDs, asked if there would be 'an escape clause whereby a nurse may refuse to sell non-medical contraceptives'.

The slightly less sheltered Labour Party TD Michael Bell introduced a lighter note to proceedings when he told the arch-conservative Fianna Fáil TD Rory O'Hanlon that

> thirty years ago, aged eighteen, I went to London to work. I went into a barber's shop to have my hair cut, and the barber offered me a handful of contraceptives. I bought them. The reason I bought them was that I thought they were shampoos.

The tension of the occasion and the tightness of the Government majority meant that Desmond, not normally a politician who undersold his case, stressed that Ireland's legal prohibitions were repressive 'and do not exist in any other country in the world except . . . Iran and Pakistan.' Few could deny that some logic informed Desmond's plea for a more tolerant, open society. Shockingly, Desmond noted that he was 'the first Minister for Health to provide moneys for . . . a sexual assault treatment unit with a professional staff' and 'to authorise research into . . . the incidence of incest, which affects sixteen-year-olds, twelve-year-olds, ten-year-olds and many young people'— incidents which 'we have kept . . . under the carpet.'

The disconsolate minister might have wished to God 'we could settle down, get this bill through the house at 5 p.m. today and resume our normal, happy social relationship one with the other', but the reality was summed up by Alan Shatter's claim that 'we are witnessing Civil War sexual politics.'

Poor John Kelly dolefully observed that it was as though 'one had been put into a time machine and we were still in 1935, that if one looked around a little more closely and rubbed my eyes one could find Seán MacEntee and Seán T. O'Kelly'.

Even as Kelly wondered of one opposition speaker 'how is it seriously possible for an adult man, no longer in his first youth, to talk like that,' and as Brendan Griffin of Fine Gael suggested that we might 'introduce identity cards to assist the chemists,' the sense of having gone through some strange time-warp was intensified by our old friend Oliver J. Flanagan, who thundered about how 'this is the first time in the history of this house that a bill has been passed with the waving of the red flag and the clenched fist outside . . . with abusive remarks from the crowd outside about members of the Hierarchy and others—which were despicable to listen to'.

Then, suddenly, in a rare case of 'cometh the hour, cometh the man,' Dessie O'Malley raised the debate out of the querulous mire in which it had become lodged. He was an unlikely hero of the liberal left, for, during a previous moral furore he too had opposed the legalisation of contraception lest it give comfort to the advocates of 'fornication'.

On this occasion a completely reinvented politician cut to the core of the issue. In O'Malley's view, whatever about the rights or wrongs of contraception, 'issues much greater have raised their heads in relation to far deeper matters . . . which far transcend the details of the bill and which are of grave importance to democracy on this island.'

As was so often the case in the Haughey era, when it came to moral issues O'Malley claimed that 'in the past ten days or so the most extraordinary and unprecedented extra-parliamentary pressure has been brought to bear on many members of the house. This is not mere ordinary lobbying: it is far more significant. I regret to have to say that it borders at times almost on the sinister.'

O'Malley noted that article 6 of the Constitution stated that decisions about the state for the common good are 'exercisable only by and on the authority of the organs of state'. It was a proposition that was often taken for granted, but 'today we must declare whether the people', as represented in parliament rather than in shadowy vested interests, were 'sovereign'.

Today's debate, he said, 'can be regarded as a sort of watershed in Irish politics' for a second reason: if the house were to fail, the two most delighted groups would be 'the unionists in Northern Ireland and the extremist Roman Catholics in the Republic,' who are 'bound together by the vested interest each of them has in the perpetuation of partition.'

He added that it would also define the nature of Irish republicanism, for

'republican' is perhaps the most abused word in Ireland today . . . It consists principally of anglophobia . . . Often it is displayed by letting off steam in the fifteen minutes before closing time with some rousing ballad that makes one vaguely feel good.

In a position that represented a genuine personal revolution against his previous allegiance to the old confessional ethos, O'Malley said, 'In a democratic republic people should not think in terms of having laws other than those that allow citizens to make their own free choice in so far as private matters are concerned.' He dismissed the state's obsession with sex with the query: 'Do we not need to remind ourselves that God gave Moses nine other commandments?'

Like many an embattled Catholic politician before him, O'Malley cited the speech of the American politician Mario Cuomo about the duties of a Catholic legislator 'to assure our freedom' by allowing 'others the same freedom, even if occasionally it produces conduct by them which for us would be sinful.' In Ireland, however, O'Malley belatedly admitted that pluralism is 'a bad word here. You are supposed to be ashamed of wanting a pluralist society in this country.'

After a brief query as to how we could persuade unionists that the recent Forum report wasn't a 'bag of wind, a lot of words' if the Dáil voted this bill down, O'Malley recalled the Mother and Child Scheme debate. 'It is incredible that members of this house and of the Government of the day could be as craven and supine as they were.' But, he wondered, in this different country 'has the atmosphere changed? Because when the chips are down is it going to be any different?'

O'Malley admitted that it would be easy to take the smart politics of being 'one of the lads, the safest way in Ireland', but he did not

believe that the interests of this state, or our Constitution and of this Republic, would be served by putting politics before conscience in regards to this. There is a choice of a kind that can only be answered by saying that I stand by the Republic and accordingly I will not oppose the bill.

It was a speech that signed the death warrant for O'Malley's career in Fianna Fáil, from which he would be, with marvellous irony, expelled for conduct unbecoming. In a house where debate between opposition and Government had become increasingly embittered, the instinctively generous Desmond, though, was moved to 'thank Deputy O'Malley for a contribution which, in retrospect, will be reminiscent of the Treaty debates of this house. The debate has been a watershed in many respects.'

As the bill passed by an alarmingly thin margin, little did Desmond, or indeed anyone else, know just how dramatic the consequences of O'Malley's qualified act of rebellion—the defender of the new Republic abstained, rather than voting for the bill—would be.

For now, though, an excited Gemma Hussey simply recorded: 'Today we defeated the bishops and Fianna Fáil and Oliver J. Flanagan!'

Ironically, even as Garret FitzGerald evolved into a political ghost, and as liberal Ireland hunted despairingly for a new icon, Fine Gael, despite Hussey's temporary delight, would ultimately be the biggest losers from the formation of the PDS.

Chapter 26

FRANKENSTEIN'S MONSTER AND PEE FLYNN STALK THE LAND

14 May 1986

G arret FitzGerald might have promised a constitutional crusade during the halcyon days of opposition, but in the wake of the horror story that the Government's well-intentioned attempt to sort out abortion had evolved into, John Kelly of Fine Gael spoke for many when he noted that, for a Government that could still achieve things, even thinking of 'indulging in a year-long catfight about divorce' was enough to 'make its friends despair'.

In truth, Kelly was being optimistic, for the coalition Government had, when it came to economic matters, essentially lost the confidence of the country. Once again, as in the 1950s, the language of elegiac despair had settled over public discourse like a shroud as a Government frozen by good intentions floundered so ineffectually that the national debt would double during its term in office.

The erosion of faith in the FitzGerald Government was all the more depressing because of the faith he had inspired before the election. First Haughey and now a second icon had been proved to have feet of clay.

In such a situation as this, more people than Kelly realised that starting a war on a third front wasn't the wisest of tactical decisions. And even though the initial opinion polls on divorce were encouraging, the issue faced an uphill struggle in a state whose sectarian character meant that it had taken until 1981 for the law on 'criminal conversation'—according to which a husband could sue a wife's lover effectually for damages to property—to be abolished.

The bad news for the Government was that, despite Haughey's fine words when Fianna Fáil had lost power, Garret's nemesis was in no mood for co-operation. The coalition attempted to appeal to the better instincts of the electorate. Fianna Fáil, in contrast, had taken the somewhat cannier stance that property rights would exercise more of a bearing on the result.

In the chamber the tetchiness before the debate was epitomised by the attempt by Terry Leyden of Fianna Fáil to raise a point of order on videos. Poor Terry was immediately slapped down by Alan Dukes's cold remark that 'the deputy is a bit of a video nasty himself.' In truth, when it came to the divorce referendum there were nastier and more powerful forces at work than Terry.

Rather like Noël Browne in the Mother and Child Scheme, Dukes admitted at the beginning of the debate that he had attempted to fireproof himself against the Catholic right by holding with the Taoiseach 'full discussions with all the main churches on a range of topics arising from the joint committee's report dealing with marriage'. The ill-starred future Fine Gael leader claimed that one of the critical factors behind the introduction of divorce was that failing to recognise change in Ireland ran the risk of the law losing touch 'with the lives of a growing number of people, and that could only result in the law coming into disrepute.'

Dukes, however, went to some pains to assure the house that divorce would apply only if a court was satisfied that marriage had failed for at least five years, that there was 'no reasonable possibility of reconciliation between the spouses, that any other condition that might be prescribed in law had been complied with, and that adequate and proper provision having regard to the circumstances is made for any dependent spouse and children.'

Unfortunately, even as Dukes claimed that 'the concept of "failure of marriage" has been used in the proposal rather than . . . "breakdown of marriage", since in the Government's view it indicates more clearly the idea that the marriage has ceased to be a marriage in anything but name,' he was creating the impression of a man backing out from, rather than kicking down, the door.

In contrast, Michael Woods provided us with one of the finest examples of nuanced fence-sitting Irish politics had ever seen. The language of nod and wink was in vogue from the start, with Woods wailing about how the Government see 'the provision of divorce as the greatest social need of our time, and consequently they have committed all their energies and political resources to a national campaign for divorce.' Though he wasn't saying anything, Woods quickly made it clear he was with the 'great and always silent majority of Irish men and women', who had other priorities.

While in his view the Government seemed to want to 'put into the Constitution the most liberal divorce scheme so far devised in any modern society', Woods slyly claimed that he still believed they were well intentioned. The problem under this scheme, though, was that first families would 'become constitutional orphans' no longer able to rely on the protection of the state against any unjust discrimination or oppression 'in areas such as taxation, social welfare and education.'

'Yes' votes were already slipping away as Michael warned that within the farming community a first wife could lose her home as a consequence of the Government's unwitting creation of a 'constitutional Frankenstein which may sleep for a time but then rise and stalk the land.'

As the peasants started reaching for their pitchforks, Michael was so anxious not to be seen to be openly for or against the proposal that an exasperated Mary Flaherty of Fine Gael was moved to ask, 'Where does the deputy stand? We are no wiser at the end of an hour.'

The formidable Fine Gael backbencher Alice Glenn certainly didn't creep around the issue. In a classic example of how, in liberal eyes, the devil always gets the best lines, she said, 'It occurs to me that any woman voting for divorce is like a turkey voting for Christmas.'

One of the proposal's few Fianna Fáil supporters, Charlie McCreevy, implicitly admitted that the referendum was lost before it began. He castigated the way, when there are moral and social issues to be taken on, 'politicians appear to act on the principle "There goes the mob, I must follow".'

After McCreevy had said, 'One cannot prevent people dying merely by banning funerals', it all inevitably took a turn for the surreal, with the turbulent Fine Gael TD Liam Skelly warning against divorce on the grounds that 'separated women are subject to attention from unscrupulous men, in the main, who take advantage of their weakness . . . to indulge in temporary affairs, which cause even more problems'. In particular, 'these parasites live off the women and take a portion of the small amount of money they get to buy themselves drink.'

The escalating spectacle explained the dispirited performance of Dick Spring, who like any Labour Party leader could see a lost cause a thousand miles ahead. After he claimed that 'the essential reason for the debate . . . is that people should be allowed to choose', even the former musketeer Brian Lenihan sent remarkably clear signals with his concern that 'a very real issue of conflict will arise in relation to the rights of the first family as against those of the second and third families.'

There was no shortage of ambushes from former allies. The independent TD Seán Treacy, who, much to the delight of the rest of the Labour TDs, had left the Labour Party, condemned this 'distressing tactic' of diverting people's attention away from the economy. He thundered, 'So far as the people are concerned, it is the old saying "If you cannot give them bread or work, give them a damn good circus" . . . So we have this new coalition circus of divorce to contend with.' But Treacy warned the poor liberals that 'we are the proud inheritors of a great tradition, a rich culture, a religion to which we have held fast down through the ages and will never relinquish.'

The liberals might have sneered at Treacy's warning to be 'careful that we of this generation do not win for ourselves the name of the new soupers, who sold their souls for soup, for twopenny rolls and for hairy bacon,' or at Oliver J. Flanagan's claim that the real motive behind all this was that 'our people are being asked to give the seal of respectability on adultery.' But Oliver J, in asking, 'Who will pay for this?' was saying what the voters were thinking.

As Oliver railed against the 'dreadful, awful, disastrous situation we are facing'—one in which 'western society is becoming more like society before the Middle Ages . . . rudderless as regards values'—and as he tore into the evils of 'nightly visits' to a new phenomenon known as the 'singing pubs', an increasingly desperate Government began to focus on Fianna Fáil's 'absentee warlord', Mr Haughey.

The liberal Fine Gael TD David Molony slammed the absence from the country of Deputy Haughey, 'the leader of the main opposition party', while Barry Desmond chuckled that 'he is in the cathedrals in Strasbourg . . . locked in contemplation.'

It was in fact a bad move, as a furious Pádraig Flynn snapped, 'That is miserable, and the deputy knows it,' before launching into what the then Fine Gael minister Gemma Hussey would describe with some horror as an hour and a half of 'extraordinary Dáil roaring and ranting'.

Flynn admitted that 'marriage and the family are under great pressure at present,' but he believed this was being 'brought about by the very difficult unemployment position, the level of poverty, the great hardship that renewed emigration is causing so many families.'

Though he expressed the pious desire to 'avoid acrimony', Flynn soon warned that marriage when there is the possibility of divorce becomes 'a temporary contractual arrangement', which would put children 'at risk under certain circumstances.' Haughey's most loyal spear-carrier of all—well, until he became Albert's loyal spear-carrier—claimed that Haughey 'dearly wished' to be in the Dáil, but the Fianna Fáil leader was busy in Europe helping out a singularly ungrateful Government.

After Pee blustered about how 'arrangements had been made to meet many important personages in very high office in certain places in Europe', there was more than a slight air of tongue in cheek to be found in his surprise at the idea that there 'might be some grand alliance between what we do here and what the Catholic Church, in their right, are going to do in so far as this campaign is concerned.' Gemma's *bête noire*, however, also carefully observed that 'the Christian ethic cannot be lightly set aside'—well, except perhaps on matters of taxation—and 'introducing divorce would give respectability to actions totally at variance with Christian ethics.' In what was undoubtedly a clever speech, Flynn admitted that 'we cannot legally enforce morality or impose virtue by law'. But certain laws 'can make virtue more difficult', and why should the Dáil 'pressurise others to cater for the difficulties of the few'?

Mary Harney didn't fare too well as Flynn told Ireland's permanent victim, 'I do not accept that politicians or political parties are trying to frighten or terrorise the women of this country. Personally I do not think the females of this country are that easily terrorised.' He would, in time, discover that the hard way. For now, though, Flynn happily recalled a series of earlier clashes with Mary Robinson in which he had put her in her place, before dismissing Alan Dukes's claim that the Government was fully committed to the protection of marriage with the clever point that this aspiration wasn't compatible with 'seeking to introduce divorce, resulting in the dissolution or dismantling of existing legal marriage contracts.'

Flynn was in full flow now as he warned that the claim by the minister that divorce legislation would be 'child-centred' was 'an abuse of the English language and the established thinking as far as divorce is concerned', for divorce 'is individual-centred, and in no country is it granted in the interests of children.' In a prescient analysis he said the referendum would not be 'that close', believing that 'when all the arguments are set down in a clear, balanced and responsible way the vast majority of people will not see divorce as a solution to marital breakdown.'

After an oration like that, poor Gemma Hussey's view—that 'divorce or separation of any form are not a perfect solution to problems; but unfortunately the problems exist, and they do not lend themselves to perfect solutions'—provided the 'Yes' side with thin enough gruel.

John Kelly, at least, was entertaining as he claimed that the performance of the opposition was epitomised by a vignette in the Members' Bar: the 'happy shouts of laughter' convinced him that 'there was an old Marx Brothers movie on television.' In fact, he admitted, 'I was not far wrong: it was Deputy Brian Lenihan explaining to the people of Ireland his party's position and explaining why his leader was not here'. Kelly understood 'Deputy Haughey's position all too well: he has to keep in with everyone. I recognise the ethos of his party.' He noted that this had recently been 'trenchantly put by the man who was then Fianna Fáil chief whip, Deputy Ahern', who may not have 'realised he was being reported at a meeting for Fianna Fáil women' that had resulted in the *Irish Times* headline: 'Bertie Tells FF Women Sell Your Soul'.

Kelly quoted two paragraphs, the first of which said:

> The Flurry Knox of Irish politics laid it on the line. Keep your balance. Keep well in with everybody. Say hello to your local TDs and councillors even if you hate them and you might get nominated at your local convention.

Further on, Kelly noted that Ahern was quoted as saying:

You have to walk the line. Take the middle ground. You may hate your TDS but you must do what is required. We all have to swallow humble pie and I have been doing it for years. But if you keep at it—this unremitting diet of humble pie—you can break through.

Kelly noted of Bertie's opinion that he 'did not take it from the wind', and he was right: when it came to Mr Haughey, who was 'caught between his hillbillies and "Hot Press",' he too was doing 'the cute thing' and lying low 'like Br'er Fox'. Kelly mused that 'we suffered for a long time from absentee landlords, but we are now suffering from an absentee warlord.'

Haughey would subsequently declare his 'unshakeable belief in the importance of having the family as a basic unit of our society. My experience of life tells me that this is the best way in which to organise society.'

Like so many others, it was, in the context of his life and times, a statement that was beyond satire.

Chapter 27 ∿

MAC THE KNIFE CONFRONTS IRELAND'S ECONOMIC CRISIS

31 March 1987

The definitive victory of the right in our ethical wars, and the continuing status of the economy as the sick man of Europe, meant that a strange lack of fervour was the dominant characteristic of the 1987 election and the subsequent manoeuvres for the Taoiseach's office. The inevitability of Haughey's return had sucked the air out of the political fires. But, unlike the First Coming, the return of the fabulous wanderer was accompanied neither by excitement nor by hope, nor even by fear. Haughey had been a miserable Taoiseach and a wretched leader of the opposition, to such an extent that he had in the aftermath of his defeat in 1982 barely hung on to the leadership of his party. Ironically, one of the central themes of his defence had been the warning that when it came to Fianna Fáil its future and its leader should not be 'decided for it by the media or alien influences, by political opponents or, worst of all, by business interests pursuing their own ends.'

His opponents in Fine Gael and the Labour Party, though, had been hollowed out to the point of despair, and to some mutual detestation, by the travails they had experienced in government, where theory met practice and lost out by a substantial margin. These factors, along with the continuing gentle decline of the economy, meant that the real point of drama for the incoming Government consisted of its first budget. It was a defining moment for Haughey and his Government, for as the shades of Dr Blythe gathered around the Department of Finance, Ireland really was in the Last Chance Saloon.

Three weeks after taking office, as Ray MacSharry delivered a full budget, it was some comeback for the Minister for Finance too. As with the Taoiseach, there was no shortage of uncertainty about the nature of the new man. In the infamous fallout from 1982 it had been discovered that MacSharry had taped a conversation with his Fianna Fáil colleague Martin O'Donoghue in an attempt to discover if money was being paid to opponents of Haughey. It had led to MacSharry being pigeonholed with Seán Doherty.

But in spite of MacSharry's Dublin 4 status as one of Haughey's litter, all politics is about character, and it was known that he wasn't short of that particular trait. He was a rough-hewn, self-made individual who had fought the banks off in his time and was respected, grudgingly, for being one of the few Fianna Fáil politicians who didn't live in a state of fear and terror of Mr Haughey.

These characteristics meant that from the onset on budget day there was no ornate rhetoric about corners being turned. Instead, MacSharry briskly observed, 'It is time to give a new sense of direction to the economy and to harness more effectively the resources that are available to us.' Had other politicians warned, as he did, that 'it is evident that conditions are extremely difficult and that there is no room at all for soft options,' it would generally have been taken with several pinches of salt. But MacSharry's clipped Lemass-style tone contained that invisible thing called authority.

This meant that when he said there could be 'no concessions to interest groups, and all sections of the community will have to bear some of the burden,' all sectors listened. As MacSharry warned that 'clear signals' are needed 'if interest rates are to be reduced and confidence restored,' and that the objective, 'therefore, has been to reduce the budget deficit and the borrowing requirement below the targets proposed earlier,' a caesura had been placed in front of the well-meaning drift of the FitzGerald Government.

The indictment of the previous Government was tart as MacSharry noted that 'the economy has shown no growth at a time when other economies have been experiencing steady if unspectacular growth.' However, there were at least 'good prospects that the international economic environment will remain favourable over the next few years. Growth in world trade could be reasonably buoyant'.

In a classic example of how old and new problems rarely change, MacSharry noted that 'some of our difficulties, especially those related to the high level of interest rates, follow from the unidentified outflow of funds in recent years.' In short, Ireland's banks were starved of capital, owing to the decision of our tax-dodging elite of builders, businessmen, barristers and professionals to transfer their assets abroad with the connivance of the self-same banks.

MacSharry also warned that 'pay increases in excess of what employers can really afford and of the economy's capacity to bear have contributed greatly to our economic difficulties.' The minister conveniently forgot that Fianna Fáil had regularly opposed such pay increases because they were too small and told the Dáil that, now that Fianna Fáil was in power, future pay increases, 'if warranted at all, must be below the rate of inflation'.

There was no other option, as the self-indulgent way we had been governed now meant that 'the annual cost of servicing the national debt is a severe burden on the economy as a whole and on the individual taxpayer.' This was so to such an extent that 'the stage has now been reached where virtually all the receipts from PAYE are absorbed in servicing debt.'

A decade after Haughey's famous 'living away beyond our means' speech, Ireland had finally reached the point where we 'simply cannot afford our present level of public services'. Indeed, the situation, then as now, was so dire that 'for as long as public expenditure and, in consequence, taxation and borrowings remain at present levels, productive activity in the economy will be stifled'.

There was, astonishingly, no attempt to gild a single lily. MacSharry emphasised again that 'the message I have to deliver is unpalatable'. But while it might have sounded entirely logical to claim that 'we cannot be content to announce our intention to curtail spending while at the same time deferring action,' after a decade of duplicity and dithering, faith had all but collapsed in the capacity of Irish politicians to actually do what they said they intended to do.

Ironically, much of the speech was as much a vote of no confidence in MacSharry's leader as it was a critique of the inactivity of the previous Government, as 'the national interest must take precedence over sectoral concerns.'

Then, as now, unemployment was also eroding the fiscal and social capacities of the state. Some indication of the sense of urgency MacSharry was trying to inject into a country hollowed out to the point of moral dereliction by despair was given in the declaration that 'the Government has decided to initiate a national job-search programme, commencing tomorrow.'

In what really wasn't a good budget for vested interests MacSharry also bluntly told our teachers, who had been so assiduously courted in opposition, that 'the exchequer cash that will be available to educational institutions will be reduced.' He informed the public sector that when it came to the size of their pay bill 'there are two major factors accounting for the size of this bill: the rates of pay and the number of public servants. Action must now be taken on both fronts.'

There was none of the sort of 'Come on, the lads, we're all in it together' rhetoric that normally reveals that the Government's core is soft. MacSharry instead continued to confine himself to tight factual statements about how the Government 'has already set a headline as regards pay restraint by the announcement on the 13th of March of the decision to postpone indefinitely any action in relation to the interim report of the Review Body on Higher

Remuneration in the Public Sector.'

The era of Gene Fitzgerald, who, when he was appointed to be Haughey's catspaw in Finance, pleaded with the financial correspondents, 'Ah, lads, go easy on me,' was definitively over. Power was also moving subtly from the Taoiseach's office to the Department of Finance, and MacSharry told the Dáil that, from this point, 'in the civil service no vacancy may be filled without the consent of the Minister for Finance,' who will have the authority 'to redeploy staff within the civil service as required.'

Amidst all this gloom there was one source of delight as the grim minister informed the house: 'The National Lottery was launched last week, and I am pleased to note that it is enjoying considerable popularity.'

We quickly returned, though, to business as usual. MacSharry noted that the Government 'has decided to abolish three of the four housing grant schemes.' This wasn't Fianna Fáil as we knew it, but when MacSharry noted that 'in terms of GNP today's figures translate into . . . an Exchequer Borrowing Requirement of 10.7 per cent of GNP,' there were no alternatives to rationality.

The man who would become known as Mac the Knife did at least attempt to end on a hopeful note. His clipped but optimistic pragmatism was again redolent of a Lemass as he noted, 'There is an air of despondency that is unwarranted.' Optimism, he claimed, 'does matter', and, 'as things come right, success will be self-sustaining. Jobs will become available again.'

Michael Noonan, hard though it may be to believe, as opposition spokesperson on finance a mere twenty-five years ago, summed up the budget in the claim that 'this is grand larceny of our policy as put before the electorate.' The problem, though, was that Fine Gael had not implemented those policies in government. The even worse news was that Fianna Fáil, having definitively robbed the clothes of Fine Gael, would retain office because it at least was implementing rather than talking about the necessary reforms.

Noonan could jib at how 'prayer without good works does not achieve salvation' and at how, if the minister imposes his cuts rigorously on schools and hospitals, 'it will make our education cuts look like the teddybears' picnic,' but after Ruairí Quinn noted that the builders who backed Fianna Fáil 'will be looking for their cheques back' there was more than a slight element of whistling past the graveyard in Noonan's assertion that 'it is a good time to be in Fine Gael, because there is a certain sense of satisfaction in looking around the house at all the people who have been stealing our clothes for so long.'

Sadly, relations were no better between Fine Gael and the PDs. Noonan had one swipe of the cutlass in the observation that, when it came to the PDs, while 'one revered deputy in this house' referred to them as the 'military wing of the Fine Gael party . . . I prefer to think of them as the provisional wing of Fianna Fáil.'

That most unlikely Provo, Michael McDowell, however, slated 'the derision and scorn . . . cast upon the Fianna Fáil benches for doing what his party [Fine Gael] were too gutless and too afraid to do themselves.'

The unhappiness continued into the next day. John Bruton chastised the duplicity of Haughey, who, as Bruton recollected it, frequently castigated in his magisterial fashion the monetarism of the Government.

Unfortunately, but typically, Bruton met his match in Albert Reynolds, who warned, 'I suppose it is only human that there should be a certain element of sour grapes in a contribution by a man who has produced two budgets for this house, neither of which has been passed.'

It might perhaps have been better for Fine Gael and the country if they had been.

Chapter 28 ∾

'A FURTHER SIGNIFICANT DEVELOPMENT IN THE POLITICAL DEGENERATION OF FIANNA FÁIL'

12 July 1989

The 1987 minority Fianna Fáil Government was the best of Governments—when set against an admittedly low benchmark—that fell for the worst of reasons. Its collapse would also have more serious long-term political consequences than was the norm in Irish political life. After the deal was sealed Haughey may have proudly stated that 'nobody but I could have done it,' but the problem for him was that a growing number of his TDS, in particular his powerful Minister for Finance, Albert Reynolds, believed that only Haughey would have been foolish enough to end up in the sort of scrape in which Fianna Fáil had been forced to abandon its last core value and go into coalition with the PDS.

When it came to the Fianna Fáil-PD coalition that emerged in 1989 it is easy, looking at it with modern eyes, to underestimate the scale of the task facing Fianna Fáil's devious old pilot. Within the mythology Fianna Fáil created so assiduously, single-party government was the sole element of the 'unique genius' of a pragmatic, non-ideological party that couldn't be 'polluted'. It wasn't without reason that it was considered a Holy Grail, for such a devaluation of the Fianna Fáil coinage, once done, would mean that voters would 'never fear a hung Dáil again'.

Haughey's position within Fianna Fáil was further weakened by the fact that it was he who had essentially forced the election, thanks to an opportunistic huff after the Government had been defeated after refusing to increase the amount it was to pay into a fund for haemophiliacs who had received infected blood transfusions. As was so often the case, though, after the election an initially feeble position was strengthened by Haughey's enemies, with Alan Dukes demanding seven ministries and a rotating Taoiseach's position as the price for his support.

However, the maths of 77 Fianna Fáil and 6 PD seats meant that some form of arrangement with the PDS was a rather more attractive solution. Haughey initially attempted to secure support for a minority Government on the grounds that he couldn't sell it to the party. Haughey, however, was dealing with an equally wily old fox. Dessie O'Malley, leader of the PDS, simply smiled and told Haughey he should 'not make the mistake of underestimating his capacity' as a salesman.

It took some time for the sale to be contemplated, let alone completed. On 29 June the Dáil met and for the first time in its history failed to elect a Taoiseach. It soon acquired the habit, though, as two further meetings also failed to do so. The outlook appeared to be bleak for Haughey, with observers noting that no-one was in control of a Fianna Fáil party that was 'like a cork bobbing in the ocean'. But even as Pee Flynn and Albert Reynolds expressed their vociferous opposition to coalition, Haughey made use of his patented political strategy of sitting tight and waiting for the ball to come to him.

Fractious negotiations were opened, and Fianna Fáil was slowly reeled in. Nothing captured Haughey's duplicitous nature better than the moment when, even as Pee Flynn was declaring on RTE that rejection of coalition was a Fianna Fáil core value, Haughey told O'Malley at a private meeting that he had crossed his political Rubicon. Inevitably the aftermath wasn't warm: in sealing the deal with the PDS, above the heads of Bertie and Albert, the politically frail Haughey had used up capital he could ill afford to lose.

On the floor of the Dáil the dénouement was very civilised. Haughey noted that the result of the general election placed 'the responsibility on my party, Fianna Fáil, of forming a Government.' He claimed he had been 'convinced, after several discussions with the other party leaders, that it was not possible to form a minority Government.' While it was

> our preferred solution, the formation of such a Government depends on the tacit support of one or more of the opposition parties, and this was not forthcoming . . . As the days passed into weeks following the reassembly of the Dáil, the reality became clear, the conclusion inescapable, that the only possible alliance that could give this country four years' stable government, at this crucial period in our history, was one between Fianna Fáil and the Progressive Democrats.

The new, reinvented Haughey said stability was necessary.

> The process of national recovery, already successfully under way, must be sustained. Our difficulties are not over, and any departure from a

disciplined approach to public expenditure, to Government finances, to incomes and to other costs would be disastrous.

And on the plus side there was also the glittering prize of 'our presidency of the European Community', which would 'give us the opportunity to exercise an influence on developments' in Europe and the world. Charlie wasn't going to miss his chance to hob-nob with François, Helmut and the rest of his fellow-leaders.

On the domestic front there was also the intention to continue the

extraordinarily successful approach to the management of our affairs when the present [social partnership] programme has run its course. The contribution that all of the social partners have made to national recovery has been immense . . . I would like to assure them that the same spirit of co-operation and consultation will continue.

The measure of how the country was turning was captured when Haughey observed that all

the measures in our programme are subject to the overall financial constraints of an improvement in the Exchequer Borrowing Requirement to no more than 3 per cent of GNP by 1993. If it proves possible to improve on that target, and to virtually eliminate borrowing altogether, this will be done.

It was as though the horrors of that earlier decade had never occurred, as Haughey even dared to promise that there would be tax reform 'subject to economic and budgetary circumstances.'

Haughey was definitely correct in his view that 'the formation of this administration is a new departure in our political life.' Whatever about himself, though, he was being optimistic in believing that 'my Fianna Fáil colleagues . . . are making a wholehearted, sincere commitment to this new administration.' He would also, in time, be revising his thanks to Deputy O'Malley 'for his role in the formation of this Government' and his looking forward to the 'contribution that I know he will be able to make to its success from his personal talents'.

The Taoiseach concluded by noting that his Government would be informed by the words of Addison: ''Tis not in mortals to command success, but we'll do more, Sempronius; we'll deserve it.'

In contrast to Haughey, Alan Dukes began in utterly bedraggled style. The nominal leader of the opposition decided that, as distinct from attacking the Government, he would focus on 'the parties which describe themselves as the "left", who had 'washed their hands' of the nation's problems. The ailing Fine Gael leader quickly received the sharp response from Michael Bell that 'we have washed our hands of you.' Dukes then tore into a Labour Party that was 'offering to the electorate, and particularly to their own supporters . . . a combination of political impotence and analytical sterility.' In a typically lofty performance Dukes claimed that 'the real lives of ordinary people are neither improved nor affected in any way by poseurs who espouse divisive class politics and then abdicate their duty to the people they claim to represent.'

Oddly enough, the Fine Gael leader's claim that, seeing as the left had abandoned the political battlefield, Fine Gael would 'fight for the people who are represented by the Labour Party and the Workers' Party' didn't go down at all well with those he planned to replace. Brendan Howlin tartly observed, 'As you did during the last two-and-a-half years.'

While Ruairí Quinn forgave Dukes on the basis that he was, 'after all, a disappointed Taoiseach,' things took an even more hostile turn after Emmet Stagg commented of Dukes's observation that 'a coalition Government can now be set in place' that 'you must be disappointed that you are not in it.'

As Dukes snarled, 'I will be back to you in a moment,' and as Stagg snapped at his constituency colleague, 'Any time you like,' the opposition were fighting among themselves rather than with the Government.

Dukes did cut to the core of Fianna Fáil's fatal flaw when he chided their view that government was a 'possession', claiming that it was instead 'an art, a science, a duty, an obligation; it is anything but a possession.'

However, it was the ascendant Labour Party leader, Dick Spring, who took the plaudits. He sympathetically noted that he 'certainly can understand that the leader of the Fine Gael party may be somewhat confused, since some weeks ago he had a pact with a party [the PDS] who have now crossed the floor.' Spring suspected that Dukes's problem was that he was 'experiencing some difficulty finding his way into opposition. He certainly has not been in opposition since he announced his Tallaght strategy some two years ago.' Ultimately Spring's most prescient observation was that what had happened between Fianna Fáil and the PDS wasn't so much 'an agreement as a truce, not so much a prescription for the future as a burying of the hatchet.'

The ever-sharp Proinsias de Rossa received a less than enthusiastic reception after stating that the Workers' Party had forced Fianna Fáil and the PDS to recognise their right-wing souls. He enthusiastically claimed that more and more people were embracing 'socialism based on the principles of the French Revolution—the principles of liberty, equality and fraternity' and that the new coalition 'marks a further significant development in the political degeneration of Fianna Fáil.' Though it was once 'radical and reforming', it had now come 'more and more under the influence of the speculators and the asset-strippers.'

O'Malley got off to a less than impressive start. His sanguine claim that the PDS had always 'made it clear that we are prepared to participate in government with like-minded parties' was undercut by the cutting observation of an alas anonymous TD: 'Why did you ever leave it [Fianna Fáil], then?' O'Malley ignored this minor technicality and carolled about how 'courage and generosity' had been needed to 'put past differences to one side' and to create a 'stable, sustainable Government.'

A few Mercs had also helped, but in language few would have thought possible half a decade ago O'Malley acknowledged 'in particular the courage and skill exhibited by Deputy Haughey in recent weeks—courage and skill which I know he possesses in abundance and which have been utilised in the national interest during this time.'

Tony Gregory understandably noted with some irony that his deal with Haughey in 1982, which secured 'houses for the homeless of the inner city, jobs for the unemployed and medical cards for pensioners' was labelled 'stroke politics' by the media. In contrast, Gregory wryly observed, when 'deputies here . . . haggled and bartered for Mercedes cars and high-paying positions in cabinet' the same media 'applaud this as the dawn of a new era of Continental-style politics'.

Intriguingly, the most impressive piece of prophecy came from John Bruton, who noted that there had been 'an abandonment of the spirit of collective responsibility . . . in the selection of the Fianna Fáil members of this coalition Government.' Bruton, who knew a great deal about unpopularity, noted that Brendan Daly and Michael Noonan, 'who earned considerable unpopularity because they were pursuing collectively agreed Government policies in regard to army pay and the issue of rod licences, have been sacked simply because they became unpopular'.

Bruton warned that this 'indicates that any minister in this Government who finds himself . . . unpopular is liable to be dropped in order to court some superficial and temporary popularity for those who remain behind after he has left.' Even Bruton, however, couldn't have guessed how often that would occur, or where it would end. Little also did he realise how topical his curiosity would one day become about how 'the portfolio of Communications seems to have become the personal property of Deputy Raphael Burke', who has 'been moved twice from one department to another, and on each occasion he has brought Communications with him as if it somehow or other belonged to him.' After Bruton wondered what 'the secret agenda' that 'Deputy Burke, and he alone, is capable of fulfilling in that area' really was, a happy Burke merely observed, 'Stick around.'

Mr Bruton, however, would have to 'stick around' another decade for the answer.

AN EVIL SPIRIT LEAVES AND A WARD BOSS COMES

Chapter 29 ~

AN EVIL SPIRIT GOVERNS
THE REPUBLIC

31 October 1990

When a somewhat eccentric student with an interest in some of the more obscure aspects of the Presidency almost brings you down you know you're in trouble. Yet that was precisely what happened to Mr Haughey in the debate that ended the ministerial career of his 1960s fellow-musketeer Brian Lenihan (senior). The *casus belli* was a set of tapes made by the student, and subsequent Fine Gael employee, James Duffy with the then Fianna Fáil presidential candidate.

The taped interview, about alleged phone calls made to the President in 1982 in an attempt to avoid an election after Garret FitzGerald's Government had fallen, didn't tally with a claim by Lenihan on 'Questions and Answers' (a minor but somewhat self-important RTE current-affairs programme) that no such calls had been made.

In what many viewed as a reprehensible act, the interviews (in which could be heard a heavily medicated Lenihan) had been released. After Lenihan, in his usual charming but utterly accident-prone way, had famously claimed that 'on mature recollection' no such calls had been made, the affair quickly developed into yet another ethical crisis—one so great that the increasingly frail Fianna Fáil-PD Government was facing a motion of no confidence.

At the debate Lenihan, like Hamlet without the prince, was a ghostly bystander at his own execution. Fianna Fáil's embattled Tánaiste might have been the headline act, but this debate was all about Haughey. Then again, for the last two decades it had always been about Haughey.

It was also another occasion when Dick Spring, leader of the Labour Party, again seized the opportunity to cement his role as *de facto* leader of the opposition with an attack on Haughey that was almost as coruscating as Garret's 'flawed pedigree' speech a decade earlier. By now, though, Haughey was a lion approaching winter, for, while the façade and the imperious gestures still existed, Fianna Fáil's fabulous leader increasingly resembled a hollow man.

The economy was still thriving, but Haughey's eclectic history was quickly catching up with him. The Goodman scandal and a growing number of others meant that the truth about the past was beginning to seep up through the floorboards like some cadaver in one of Edgar Allan Poe's short stories.

Though this was a difficulty for the PDS, Haughey's real danger came from his own, according to whom defiling the sacred tabernacle of single-party government was an act of sacrilege too far. The mood within the party hadn't been helped by concerns that, like one of those Chinese leaders, Mr Haughey was planning to go 'on and on'. Such a prospect was particularly unattractive to his ambitious Minister for Finance, Albert Reynolds, who was preparing to do to Haughey what Haughey had done to Lynch.

The storm clouds were gathering, and the survival of the Government was in question, but Haughey combatively dismissed the motion of no confidence as inappropriate and as a 'crude piece of electioneering, an attempt to use Dáil procedures for presidential election purposes.' The Taoiseach loftily compared his record, whereby 'for nearly four years now the country has had the benefit of good, effective government,' with an opposition who had 'no alternative policies of any note or any achievements they can look back to.'

In contrast, despite the somewhat tattered state of Haughey's mane, this self-confessed economic basket case was being praised by a 'heartened' IMF, which had noted our 'resolve to stay the course', and a 'pearl of great price' called social partnership had just been secured. This was now a country in which the International Financial Services Centre, Tallaght Shopping Centre and Intel were all thriving, and yet, Haughey contended, we were supposed to believe that 'all this tremendous achievement is irrelevant and fades into insignificance compared with the Tánaiste's inaccurate description, in a private interview with a research student, of events that happened eight years ago'.

Happily, Mr Haughey could never maintain a dignified tone for too long, and he soon unleashed his inner gurrier. The kindliness of his gentle, guileless Tánaiste had facilitated 'someone he took to be a bona fide research student', without his being aware of 'the student's close association with the Fine Gael party.' Ranks were being closed when Haughey warned that he would 'rather any day have a Brian Lenihan who would, for whatever reason, give an impulsive, inaccurate version of what happened eight years ago than a group of Fine Gael conspirators who, with a cold and ruthless determination, planned to trap and destroy a decent man.'

Though he was now only a humble backbencher, Garret, the Taoiseach's great nemesis, was soon drawn into the frame. Haughey claimed that FitzGerald had 'bequeathed Alan Dukes to Fine Gael, and as the enormity of that mistake becomes increasingly evident he once again seeks to avert attention by renewing his campaign of vilifying his opponents.'

There was even what appeared to be a genuine moment of emotion when Haughey countered claims that he had threatened to end the career of an army officer on the night of the infamous phone calls. He reminisced about how his father was

> a distinguished army officer . . . I was brought up to believe in the integrity of our Defence Forces and the army, and I have the highest regard for them. I would never, and never have, insulted an army officer or our Defence Forces in any way, and I never will.

He was, of course, lying, but we would only find that out later.

We soon returned to the more ornate style of public discussion, Haughey concluding with the high-minded observation that 'it is a matter of deep regret to me that a campaign which we intended should be conducted at a high, dignified level, and in a tone and manner fitting for an election of a President, should be . . . deliberately dragged down'.

Though Alan Dukes was the leader of the opposition, his flat speech was totally overshadowed by the *tour de force* of Dick Spring. In a well-crafted introduction Spring said, while Lenihan is 'liked and admired on all sides of the house on a personal basis . . . he cannot be regarded as being immune from the vital need for high political standards simply because he is a nice man.' Anyway, Spring contended,

> this debate is not about Brian Lenihan, when it is all boiled down. This debate essentially is about the evil spirit that controls one political party in this Republic, and it is about the way in which that spirit has begun to corrupt the entire political system in our country.

Haughey's 'greed for office' and 'disregard for truth' meant that this was actually

> a debate about the way in which a once-great party has been brought to its knees by the grasping acquisitiveness of its leader. It is ultimately a debate about the cancer that is eating away at our body politic and the virus that has caused that cancer: An Taoiseach, Charles J. Haughey.

Spring warned of 'the viciousness within Fianna Fáil' that it must not

> be allowed to develop, for the sake of all of us. We had plenty of it in the twenties and thirties, but it must stop . . . It must be stopped by the authority of this house.

Like Garret a decade earlier, he claimed that

> there is an ethos underlying Fianna Fáil politics now. It is that ethos that
> forced Des O'Malley and others out of Fianna Fáil. It is not the ethos of
> Seán Lemass, Jack Lynch or George Colley. It is instead the ethos so clearly
> illustrated on the Brian Lenihan 'Late Late Show', when the audience was
> invited to chuckle at stories about how Brian dealt with a 'sharp little bitch'
> who happened to be a nun, or of how gardaí were threatened with
> disciplinary action for trying to carry out their jobs.

In a cutting aside, Spring noted:

> No doubt the same ethos informed the Taoiseach when, as it has been
> alleged, he . . . threatened to end the career of a member of the army if the
> officer concerned did not put him through to the President. If it was
> proved that a member of Provisional Sinn Féin made that telephone call
> he could be sentenced to seven years' penal servitude; but when the leader
> of Fianna Fáil does it we are supposed to accept it as part of the way we
> run our politics.

The cut-throat nature of the debate continued as an emotional John
O'Connell, who knew far more of Mr Haughey's secrets than was good for Mr
Haughey, compared the opposition to 'snarling dogs who have scented blood'.
They, and in particular Fine Gael, had been 'hijacked by adventurous
mercenaries who will only bring about the party's destruction.'

Liam Lawlor, who found himself in the unusual position of defending his
constituency adversary, adopted his 'plain man of the people' persona and told
John Bruton to 'get out of the old university-campus environment of lecturing
everyone and fighting for his motions whether they are fact or fiction.'

Even Brian Cowen had a hand in the debate, with an interesting
contribution. The new Fianna Fáil deputy, who would defend many a lost
cause, said he was 'not interested in old battles between Deputy FitzGerald and
anybody else. Deputy FitzGerald has had his day.' Lenihan, in contrast,

> is the same honourable man who was in my house thirty years ago
> beginning a Seanad campaign. I will make my opinion very lucid for the
> house: if I am given a choice between pegging out thirty-three years of
> public service and a misleading, overemphasised role on tape to a political
> student—about whom I know nothing and have no intention of saying
> anything—that will be a sad day for Ireland.

Michael D. Higgins was in combative form, dismissing Haughey's opening salvo with the observation that 'it has been said that the economy is doing so well it would be a pity to draw our breath for ethics'.

Ray Burke, unsurprisingly, was in no mood for any ethical discussions. In typically understated style he claimed that the 'the accomplishments of this Government and of its predecessors since 1987 have been nothing short of phenomenal,' given that Fianna Fáil had inherited a nation in a 'most pitiful' state—one whose young people were practically leaving the country 'in the darkness of the night'.

Michael Woods loyally pitched in with wails about how, 'already, instability is creeping back in, the stock market is getting shaky and interest rates will rise if the Government collapses'.

Disappointingly—well, for Fianna Fáil at least—the party's *bête noire*, Garret, wasn't feeling at all guilty. If he had 'contributed to precipitating, even if accidentally, a general election on the issue of integrity in public life,' Garret instead would be 'proud that this issue may have proved to have been my swan song.'

Outside of Lenihan, the other absent ghost at this spectral feast of vitriol was the PDS, but Pat Rabbitte made sure to drag the latter onto the floor of the Dáil. Sadly, he was less than sympathetic to the dilemma being faced by the PDS, who were once again being cast as Government saviours, or executioners. He chuckled, 'Now, as Deputy O'Malley makes the lonely trek in leading his parliamentary party across to Molesworth Street, he is reminiscent of the duck that hatches out on Leinster Lawn and crosses to St Stephen's Green with her ducklings every summer.'

Alan Shatter raised other hares over the nature of governance in Ireland with the biting observation that 'there were great headlines some months ago about the Dublin planning scandal . . . Yet in a year and a half we found it impossible to get a comprehensive statement from the Minister for Justice or the Minister for the Environment as to what is happening in that area.' Seeing as the two gents were Pee Flynn and Ray Burke, Shatter shouldn't have been too surprised by that lacuna.

Inevitably the same Pee Flynn provided us with one moment of light relief with a parable about how he had 'learnt a lot of lessons in politics. But paranoia, self-protection and mistrust of colleagues—I like to think I am a little too young for those lessons.' But even as Flynn slammed the opposition's 'Halloween-type approach to opposition', in which you 'dress it up in old clothes, paint a little piece of imitation gore on it, knock on the Government's door and say, "Boo!"', the trapdoors were opening.

The dénouement was stark and unexpected. Haughey swept into the house and curtly announced:

I regret to have to inform the house this evening I requested the Tánaiste

... to resign as a member of the Government ... Deputy Brian Lenihan has been a friend, a loyal and trusted colleague, with whom I have served in the Dáil and Government for well over a quarter of a century.

Haughey coldly noted that he wanted

to make it clear that, as I said this morning, there is a clear dividing line— and I think the people understand that—between the Government and the presidential election. I would hope that this reluctant action of mine will serve to emphasise the difference between the two, and I assure the public that I am totally supporting Deputy Brian Lenihan for election as President.

But as he sat alone after the vote it was already clear that, whatever about Lenihan, the sands of Haughey's fabulous career were falling much faster through the political hourglass.

Afterwards the scenes were elemental. At one stage, in the Dáil bar, Conor Lenihan ambushed O'Malley, grasped his hand and hissed, 'Are you happy with your pound of flesh!'

Meanwhile, as Fianna Fáil began to talk openly about the post-Haughey era, Dick Spring was the hero of the hour.

That too would inevitably pass. Instead, little more than a year later, in the wake of Spring's coalition with Fianna Fáil, Eamon Dunphy would colourfully capture the mood of the country in the *Sunday Independent*. 'The Minister for Foreign Affairs ... is a disgrace to his county and his country, and, to borrow a phrase from Brendan Behan, "a bollocks of the highest order".'

Chapter 30 ~

'I HAVE DONE THE STATE SOME SERVICE'

11 February 1992

The magisterial study of Charles Haughey, *The Boss*, claims that in power he behaved like

> an actor savouring the role that had been given to him . . . The main point about power was that it thrust Haughey into the limelight all day for every day that he kept it. He loved the trappings of power . . . the ability to have his whims gratified. He played the role for all it was worth, occasionally hamming it up by replacing comment with imperious waves of the hand. He never wore a watch, waiting on some aide to have him where he should be on time.

It is a portrait that explains much about Haughey's status as a political chameleon, as it was simply having the role of Taoiseach (and the finance it brought with it), and not what he could do with the office, that dominated his motives. But all plays, and all actors, face a final curtain, and Haughey's time had come to a close. Though a mousetrap had brought his long run to an end, the fire had been getting hotter under Haughey's feet since that Faustian deal with the PDS was signed.

Near the end Haughey had comprehensively seen off a final leadership challenge, but he knew all too well that his support was inspired more by pity and opportunism—crossed with fear—than by any genuine desire that he might be staying. With the arrival of the PDS he was, critically, no longer master in his own gilded mansion anyway. So, slowly, like some vast latter-day statue of Saddam Hussein, he tottered around the stage until the breath of a political ghost such as Seán Doherty was enough to finish the job.

Even at the close the Taoiseach persisted in that patented ornate, courtly style of speaking that disguised so much more than it revealed. In spite of the rodomontade, though, more than a few would have blinked at Haughey's opening claim that 'over thirty-five years in Dáil Éireann I have developed a deep affection for this house and its traditions.' Still, it wasn't a day for carping, as the man who would subsequently occupy the full attention of two tribunals of inquiry claimed that Dáil Éireann is 'the democratic forum of the nation to establish which our forefathers made many sacrifices and of which they would be proud' and paid tribute to 'the great figures who have passed through its portals in my time'.

So the old rouge of sentiment covered all blemishes as Haughey, who had brought secrecy in government to new levels, urged 'all deputies to continue to stand up for and enhance the standing of the Dáil and the status of its members and to foster a sense of pride in all our democratic institutions.' The departing Taoiseach, who had for so long been painted as a closet fascist, also claimed that 'when we look around this troubled world I think we can consider ourselves fortunate we have these democratic institutions.' Of the many reforms he said had been introduced to the Dáil he had 'no doubt this process will continue.' The irony was surely unintended as he added, 'For my part, I have done a fair amount to improve the conditions of deputies.'

There was even a magisterial wave of the hand to the plain people of the country as the last real chief thanked above all 'the people of Ireland for the support they have given me over such a long period of years and indeed for the great affection they have shown me from time to time.' In his entertainingly aristocratic fashion the Taoiseach bade them 'a fond farewell' and warned his successors that 'the work of Government and of the Dáil must always be directed to the progress of the nation.'

Haughey expressed the hope that 'I have been able to provide some leadership to that end in my time', and in a speech laced with ironies he also claimed that 'I have always sought to act solely and exclusively in the best interests of the Irish people'.

Even before our tribunals, public attention afterwards focused mostly on the inevitable quotation from *Othello*. '"I have done the state some service; they know't. No more of that".'

The issue of service would come up again, but for now Haughey sailed serenely on, carried along by a breeze of fine sentiments about how 'we should always keep in our minds, too, that government has much wider dimensions than merely managing an economy.' In fairness, Haughey's career, more than that of most politicians, had lived up to his view that in political life 'there must be concern and commitment that all shall participate in the fruits of progress, a caring attitude towards the least advantaged, a love of our heritage and culture, a desire to protect our environment, a deep attachment to the values that are precious to us.'

Haughey, who knew hope was budding in this regard, called on the political process to respond constructively to the 'great universal yearning for peace' in Northern Ireland. We could look forward to 'a great future in a united Europe, exceeding anything in our past, if we take the right decisions and stay on course.'

He humbly noted that it wasn't the time to list achievements. 'Let the record speak for itself. If I were to seek any accolade as I leave office it would simply be: he served the people—all the people—to the best of his ability.'

John Bruton appeared to be overwhelmed by the historic significance of the departure of this figure, whose promise—and the threat he posed—had dominated the Irish political imagination for more than four decades.

However, amidst the banalities about Haughey's capacity as 'an effective and imaginative manager of public business', Bruton provided the house with one colourful moment with his chortling that he doubted very much that Haughey 'will confine himself to the cultivation of chrysanthemums.' It was a prophecy that came to pass, though not in the manner Haughey, or certainly Bruton, might have anticipated.

Dick Spring, who had harried the old rogue possibly more effectively than any of the rest of Haughey's myriad of political foes, observed that 'the outgoing Taoiseach, Deputy Haughey, quoted last week from Shakespeare's "Julius Caesar" to telling effect in this house when he referred to the heavens blazing forth the death of princes.' But Spring's mind was drawn

> not to Shakespeare but, closer to home, to Flann O'Brien, whose tribute to another folk hero, Fionn mac Cumhaill, ran like this: 'I am an Ulsterman, a Connacht man and a Greek, I am my own father and my son, I am every hero from the crack of time,' which I think is appropriate.

Spring noted that this was the day that would bring an end to 'a long and turbulent era in Irish politics' for a man elected leader of Fianna Fáil, and Taoiseach, 'in an atmosphere of high expectation', one who brought 'to the job a prestigious range of talents and skills perhaps unparalleled in the modern era.' In Spring's view the tragedy was that, although the controversies by which Haughey was surrounded 'can only be answered in the cooler light of history', his defining persona would for ever be that of a man consumed with 'hunger for high office'. Spring's warning that 'it would not be appropriate to list now all the questions and controversies which helped to make the last thirteen years so turbulent' was at a minimum pragmatic: it took two tribunals a decade to do this.

But the Labour leader managed a fair summary. Those years had been ones of 'achievement and failure, promise and betrayal, hope and despair, idealism and cynicism, style and mediocrity, triumph and disaster.' Though Spring was content, when it came to such complexities, to leave it up to historians, he did admit that he will 'always wonder what might have been, particularly if he had the confidence to give free rein to his skills'.

However, Spring was never a man to wallow for too long in sentiment. His hope was that, after the thirteen years of Haughey, politics could 'be restored to a more honourable and consistent ground,' for which 'our country will be the richer'. Though this hope was somewhat tartly expressed, it was, to put it mildly, fair comment.

But there was kindness too in the desire that 'in future, now that he is free from the never-ending ambition for office, I hope his talents will find true expression, perhaps in the further development of the cultural life of our country, to which he has made a genuine and long-standing commitment.'

Even Dessie O'Malley, Haughey's other great nemesis, added to the festschrift, noting that Haughey had been

> a man of very considerable distinction and ability. He deserves what we hope he will now have: many long and happy years of retirement. I wish him and Mrs Haughey well in that time.

Ironically, such would be the scale of the great unravelling that followed that even Haughey's wife would not be granted any tranquillity.

It would begin a week after Haughey's resignation as Taoiseach and leader of Fianna Fáil, when a certain Ben Dunne would disappear unnoticed on a golfing holiday to Florida and end up being carried, hog-tied, out of his hotel, leaving behind him a trail of cocaine, escort girls and soon-to-be-discovered bank drafts. Mr Dunne's misadventures would mean that, far from having reached the beginning of the end, in a very real way we were only at the end of the beginning of the great Haughey soap opera.

As for Haughey, a year earlier he had exclaimed, 'What else would I be doing if I wasn't leading Fianna Fáil? It's my life.' Now he was about to find out.

Chapter 31 ~

HOLLOW, NERVOUS LAUGHTER AS THEY PASS THE GRAVEYARD

11 February 1992

This date was a busy one by the standards of the Dáil. One Taoiseach, Charles Haughey, had been carried out and another, Albert Reynolds, was about to be cheered in. As is always the case in such affairs, despite Reynolds's relatively high profile as the creator of, challenger to and eventual executioner of Haughey, no-one quite knew what to expect of him. It was hoped, however, that after the political stagnation of Haughey's last years Reynolds might restore some vitality to the Irish political scene. The mood was perhaps best encapsulated by the canny Seán Duignan, who had left his 'grand, safe job' in RTE to work with Albert because he had been attracted by 'his breezy blend of small-town mateyness and up-she-flew optimism'.

It certainly started with a bang. Years later Albert noted of the first act of his dramatic—and all too short—reign that 'it was over in fifteen minutes. I called them in one by one, and I said, "You won't be appointed, thank you." And they all went out, most of them too shocked to even question me. It was all so fast I could have done with a revolving door.' Duignan, though he was typically colourful, wasn't exaggerating when he described it as the 'great chainsaw massacre'. Mary O'Rourke memorably recalled that Reynolds had been eating a ham sandwich, bits of which had been splattering in her direction, as he sacked her.

At least she wasn't alone: Albert had engaged in the greatest political massacre seen in Irish politics. In one short hour he axed eight members of Haughey's old Government, including such heavyweights as Ray Burke and Gerry Collins. The number was even further augmented by the despatching of a vast number of sleeping ministers of state who had never troubled the pens of the nation's journalists—or, for that matter, troubled themselves—with an original thought. Somewhat typically, the only senior member of the ancient Haughey regime who survived the charge of the Country and Western wing of the party was Bertie Ahern.

None of this had been anticipated at the somewhat less than dramatic debate about the nomination of Reynolds as Taoiseach. Unsurprisingly, since Albert had essentially assassinated him, there was an absence of a long adulatory speech from Haughey.

Peter Barry, given the less than enviable task of nominating John Bruton, who was almost as unpopular in opposition as Haughey was in government, was almost as unenthusiastic. But when the Fine Gael blue-blood Barry found himself being laughed at when he attempted to suggest that there should be a general election he stilled the mockery with the cold observation that this was 'the hollow, nervous laughter' of Fianna Fáil as they 'pass the graveyard'.

Meanwhile the best Jim Mitchell could come up with for Bruton was that he was 'a thoroughly modern man'. In truth, if there was one quality Fine Gael's affable big farmer, who often resembled a James Dillon-style refugee from the old Irish Parliamentary Party, didn't possess it was modernity.

Dessie O'Malley's decision to re-pledge his troth with Fianna Fáil meant that the irascible PD leader was subjected to many interruptions. There was, however, more than a slight element of whistling past Barry's graveyard in O'Malley's hope that there would be 'fruitful, constructive and positive interaction between our respective parties'.

Roger Garland, a poorly regarded Green Party TD, made the most prescient point of all. He fretted about the possibility that Reynolds might be 'embarrassed by any further revelations at the beef tribunal inquiry, because the last thing we want is another series of crises which resulted in the situation we are facing today.'

After the vote, Albert continued to be the invisible man of the affair. He thanked everyone for 'the great honour being conferred on me' and essentially left it at that. The announcement of the new Government, however, certainly grabbed everyone's attention.

In its aftermath Bruton loftily dismissed the Reynolds shuffle as a mere 'exercise in snakes and ladders, where so many have gone up and so many have gone down.' He slammed a political process that facilitated 'the triumph of the superficial over the real', of 'personality over policy', and asked why Ireland, 'unlike other island nations which have become world leaders, or at least regional leaders—like Japan and Taiwan, which are no better blessed geographically than we are—remains in Europe's second division.' Sadly, the less than compelling nature of Fine Gael's 'modern man's' speech was epitomised by the plea of the Ceann Comhairle that 'conversation in the chamber and in the lobbies must cease.'

Dick Spring, in contrast, continued to own the opposition benches. Like

Bruton, he criticised Reynolds's failure to 'set out, however briefly, his intentions, aims, ideas and vision for his leadership of Fianna Fáil.' Spring wryly noted that 'obviously he has been very preoccupied over the last number of days' and that perhaps 'the title of this show should be "Gone with the Wind"—or perhaps it was even a hurricane that brought in this Government.'

Spring did admit that Reynolds had 'taken not only the Dáil but the whole country by surprise by the nature and the scale of the appointments made here today,' for it was probably 'the first time in the history of the state that eight members of a Government were sacked in a cabinet reshuffle—nine if one includes the former Taoiseach, Deputy Haughey.' He astutely observed that

> none of the Fianna Fáil ministers, with the single exception of the Minister for Finance, Deputy Ahern, held onto his or her portfolio—strange times . . . The new Government put before the Dáil today is undoubtedly Taoiseach Reynolds's own choice. For that reason I say he is playing for very high stakes.

For Spring this 'political courage' was indicative of the fact that, 'at least in terms of style, he has made an encouraging start.' He expressed the hope that the independent streak of Charlie McCreevy and David Andrews would not 'cause the Taoiseach any trouble, although I could not guarantee that, of course.' But he also wisely noted that the new Government's mandate was 'a fragile and tenuous one, depending as it does on the mood of the Progressive Democrats.' He warned Albert that for the PDs, having effectually 'presided over the removal of a Taoiseach and a Tánaiste, obviously the only thing left is to destroy the Government'.

Pat McCartan, a Workers' Party frontbencher, was relatively restrained in noting that 'many commentators forecast we would see major changes in the Government, but . . . what we have seen here is not just the formation of a new Government but the day of the long knives.' He conjured up images of a Corleone-style bloodletting as he noted that 'old scores have indeed been settled, and favours have been repaid.' McCartan admitted that 'an injection of new blood was certainly necessary, but some of these appointments are extraordinary in the extreme.' He noted in particular of the appointment of John O'Connell as Minister for Health that 'people who depend on the public health services can draw little comfort from his appointment if he still holds the views about patients being left overnight on trolleys in corridors; he uttered the immortal words that "a trolley is just a bed on wheels".' McCartan also called for a new openness and observed that 'extracting the simplest of information from Government ministers was an extraordinarily tedious and often painful process.'

O'Malley, meanwhile, eschewed the difficult politics of beef and focused on the North, where a series of atrocities that were horrific even by the standards of that place had occurred. It is fashionable in the new age of retired Provo chic to forget the role of Albert in bringing peace to the North, but there were real traces of despair in O'Malley's observation about the sort of evil 'in the hearts of certain people' who can 'coldly and ruthlessly blow up a busload of workers or indiscriminately shoot up a bookie's shop full of people.'

Alan Dukes, recently deposed as leader of Fine Gael, was typically dismissive about a new Government where all that happened was that 'the pantomime horse had changed around and what used to be the tail is now the head, and what used to be the head is now the rump.' He was particularly unimpressed by the promotion of Brian Cowen, who had up to now 'been remarkable to me only for being what I might call the chief vulgarian of the Fianna Fáil backbenchers'. Dukes warned that if Cowen was 'to make an impact' as a minister 'he will have to show a great deal more delicacy and finesse.'

BIFFO didn't . . . and he did.

The chilly nature of the debate was evident in Pat Rabbitte's response to the sacking of Noel Davern after a brief couple of months as Minister for Education that 'the decision to despatch Deputy Davern back to snagging turnips is not likely to be to the detriment of our children's education.' It was symptomatic of a mood in Leinster House that was as bitter as any of the excesses of the Arms Trial or the Civil War. The working out of the Haughey era had been, and would continue to be, a vicious process.

Little did Rabbitte know how much his observation about politics being 'a funny old business when you see the circuitous route by which Deputy O'Connell finally realised his ambition' to be Minister for Health would mirror his own future.

O'Connell was a celebrated Labour Party poll-topper who split with his party, went independent and joined Fianna Fáil. He was initially an intimate associate of Haughey and played a central but subtle role in his resignation before finally being appointed to the Government by Albert.

We are a strange country.

Meanwhile, after all the other dramas, Albert continued to be a ghost at his own inauguration. He simply noted, 'I would like to take this opportunity to say a very sincere word of thanks and appreciation to all who participated in and contributed to a debate that was conducted without rancour, without acrimony, and reflected the mood that is throughout the country today.'

In the rapidly emptying Dáil chamber the glossy-eyed Fianna Fáil ministerial victims of the greatest Government purge in the history of the state might have begged to differ.

Chapter 32 ∿

A BIT OF A SHOCK AS BRUTON 'RISES AS A PHOENIX'

15 December 1994

He might then have been only a minister, but Albert irrevocably lost the liberal intelligentsia the moment when, on RTE's 'Live Mike' programme, in a stetson and a white cowboy suit, he sang about putting 'your sweet lips a little closer to the phone'.

What he should really have sung was 'The Gambler' by Kenny Rogers ('You gotta know when to hold 'em, know when to fold 'em, know when to walk away and know when to run'). The problem, you see, with Albert was that he never knew when to fold 'em, and that's why the PDS first and then the Labour Party ran away from the Fianna Fáil leader's embrace.

Nothing exemplified his accident-prone nature more than the collapse of the Fianna Fáil-Labour Party coalition. In retrospect it is astonishing that an economically successful Government that had just brokered a Northern ceasefire would fall because of the appointment of a little-known barrister to an utterly unknown post. But at the time of the Harry Whelehan debacle, over the theoretically prosaic matter of a lost extradition warrant for Brendan Smyth, with Albert laid low by 'mad monks' and Pat Rabbitte speculating about conspiracies involving the Church and sexual abuse that would 'rock the foundations of the state', it felt quite different.

As it turned out, the truth about the Church's hidden affair with paedophilia was far worse than the suppositions. But at the time such was the level of anxiety that on one famous occasion the normally unflappable Dick Spring, on hearing some new information from the Attorney-General, Eoghan Fitzsimons, about the Smyth affair, exclaimed, 'Oh, Lord, Eoghan, we'll both be back in the Law Library.' Even this, though, was surpassed by Ruairí Quinn's sanguinary remark about the Labour Party's last visit to Reynolds's office.

'We've come for a head—Harry's or yours—and it doesn't look as if we're getting Harry's.'

The final fall of the Labour Party-Fianna Fáil coalition might have been the worst of weeks for Fianna Fáil, but the accidental beneficiary, John Bruton, had suffered from no shortage of the slings and arrows that come with being the leader of Fine Gael in opposition. In the wake of Fine Gael's failure to get into government in 1992, the subsequent wretched state of the party was epitomised by a confused *coup d'état* led by such political giants as Alan Shatter and Jim O'Keeffe. On the announcement of the heave O'Keeffe offered his resignation to Bruton, who chortled, 'There's no need, Jim, you're all fired anyway.' Subsequently Michael Lowry noted with some justification that were Fine Gael 'a private company we would be put into liquidation.'

Then, suddenly, a gap in the market appeared. The subterranean tensions within the less than cordial Fianna Fáil-Labour Party *entente* were best captured by Fergus Finlay's horrified recollection that after the deal in 1993 he had first been embraced by a well-known pro-life Fianna Fáil senator, before turning the corner and immediately becoming the recipient of another bear hug, this time from Seán Doherty.

Despite occasional furores over the 'vindicated' leaking of the report of the Beef Tribunal, in which Finlay himself was memorably described as entering Government Buildings like an 'Old Testament whirlwind of wrath, biblical beard quivering like Moses about to smite the idolaters of the golden calf,' it had been a progressive Government with real economic and foreign-policy achievements.

In fairness to the Labour Party, when Dick Spring had controversially signed up for the Fianna Fáil option in 1993 there were no guarantees that the offer of a threesome involving Fine Gael and the PDs would have ended up any better. Spring had, of course, famously noted before the deal that he believed 'one political party in this house [Fianna Fáil] have gone so far down the road of blindness to standards . . . that it is impossible to see how anyone could support them in the future without seeing them first undergo the most radical transformation.' But politicians, particularly ones from Co. Kerry, have long memories, and it is unlikely that Spring ever forgot one particular Government vignette from the FitzGerald coalition when the loudest guffaws had come from John Bruton after Alan Dukes, in his normal lordly fashion, said, 'Labour, once bought, should stay bought.'

However, the excess of legacy issues from the long Haughey era couldn't be smoothed over—not even by a Bertie. The subsequent negotiations over the bright new Rainbow Coalition that would follow were understandably at times confused. At one point a sharp early-morning exchange, in which Ruairí Quinn exploded when Richard Bruton claimed that a particular issue hadn't been resolved, and Quinn snapped, 'For Heaven's sake, we hammered it all out,' was ended only when Brendan Howlin said, 'No, that's what we agreed with Fianna Fáil, remember? Not with this lot.'

If it all came as a 'bit of a shock' to Bruton, you can only imagine how distraught Fianna Fáil was. The party huddled together in a fugue of grumbling horror, and when it came to Taoiseach's nominations—in spite of all the talk about Bertie's 'immense political experience' and 'outstanding record of public service'—it was clear that Reynolds's heart, traumatised as it was, wasn't in it. And when you start reaching for such achievements as the candidate for the Taoiseach's office having been 'a very distinguished Lord Mayor of Dublin', you're reaching bottom-of-the-barrel country.

What must have hurt Albert most was the spectacle of an 'outgoing Government and minister handing over an economy in excellent shape, with glowing prospects.' It didn't happen with Fianna Fáil that often, but in a situation in which a record number of jobs were being created, and in which tax hikes were being replaced by cuts, if the new Rainbow played their cards right Fianna Fáil feared that even Bruton couldn't mess this up.

The speech by Nora Owen nominating Bruton was cut from the finest of blue serge. She noted that 'at the very centre of his political character there has always resided the principle of accountability.' As with Bertie, we struggled on the great achievements front, with Owen enthusing about Bruton's role in the reform of the Oireachtas. But she managed one brief lyrical moment. 'John rises as a phoenix from the distressing ashes of a Government which treated truth . . . and accountability as of small importance and betrayed the trust of the people and of this house'.

Bruton made for an an odd phoenix, and an accident-prone one at that. Paddy Harte, who seconded the new Taoiseach, recalled of the 1969 election that Bruton 'was too young to vote for himself and indisposed on election day because he was in hospital.'

Dick Spring was understandably brief, but Proinsias de Rossa did try a little harder. But while the former member of Sinn Féin the Workers' Party noted that, in spite of their 'very different backgrounds, political and otherwise', he believed Bruton to be a 'fair and honest man', nobody, except Bruton, was falling over themselves with joy.

Albert provided the wisest, most patriotic observation of all. 'I have been privileged to have led one of the most successful Governments in the history of the state . . . It matters not how long one occupies any position in political life, but what one achieves'.

In some respects it is now clear that the psychic shock of Fianna Fáil losing office because of the 'wrong crime' played a central role in turning a party that had not been particularly idealistic since the 1960s into an utterly cynical operation.

Mary Harney, now leader of the PDS, was of course already there. The puzzled Harney said, 'If somebody told me a few months ago that a County Meath farmer would bring Democratic Left into his first Government I would have said, "Bring the men in the white coats to see me".' In a very long speech, in which she appeared to forget that it was actually Bruton who was becoming the Taoiseach, Harney left plenty of hostages to future misfortunes. She embarked on a prating lecture about how public spending 'should approximate to inflation. The country must begin to live within its means if we are not to throw away all the benefits from economic growth.' The sourness continued with a warning about how

> we all know the high cost to the economy of the mad spending of the past
> . . . People at a conference last night spoke about the bright new rainbow
> of renewal. It seems it is more like the red rainbow of ruin.

Sadly, Harney's discomfiture had scant effect on a Fine Gael party that was already in 'never mind the ideology, feel the Mercs' mode.

Ruairí Quinn, meanwhile, referring to the 'red rainbow of ruin' line, simply sniggered, 'Is that yours, Michael [McDowell]? Well done—the scriptwriter of the year award.'

Harney then claimed that 'the Government that is about to be elected today does not have the moral authority that derives from a mandate from the people.' Years later she wouldn't be at all so fussy about such ethical issues.

Such was the length of Harney's speech that when it finally ended the Ceann Comhairle was moved to note, 'I wish to dissuade members from making rather long speeches.'

In contrast, an excited John Bruton, as is generally the case with new Taoisigh, was full of humility. He admitted that the position of Taoiseach was a 'high office', but it was also, in his view, a 'humbling one'. It was 'a high office because the holder is rightly held responsible for the good governance of this Republic,' but it was a humbling one 'because, in our democracy, the Taoiseach does not discharge his duties by virtue of his own merits—or, dare I say it, by looking into his heart—but derives all authority from . . . the Dáil, the duly elected parliament of our people.'

Bruton somewhat unexpectedly promised that his rule would be informed by the precedent set by 'Gaelic Ireland', when the Taoiseach was 'one who led by example rather than by exhortation, by character rather than coercion, and who exercised such authority as he had as a service to the people.' Then, in a rhetorical flourish that would haunt our brave new leader, he pledged to 'seek simplicity in Government and national policy' from a Government that would 'go about its work without excess or extravagance and as transparently as though it were working behind a pane of glass.'

The perceptive Seán Duignan, who had been Albert's press secretary, noted that 'John gives a hostage to fortune right away, saying the Government must always be seen to be operating behind a pane of glass. That will be the day.' He was right, too, for within months Bruton's performances in the Dáil strangely conformed to Ray Burke's old theory that 'if the other side don't ask the right questions . . . they don't get the right answers.'

Though Bruton had in the past acquired nicknames such as Brutal Bruton, the centre-left status of the new Rainbow meant that the Taoiseach made a brave attempt, from the start, to contact his inner Just Society man. He managed to achieve a synthesis of the competing ideological impulses of his Government in the observation that

> in recent times we have had two views discarded . . . First, that the state should substitute for private effort; and, later, that there is no such thing as society. Both are wrong. The state must support; it must not substitute. Otherwise it will end up enslaving, and there is such a thing as society. We are our brothers' and sisters' keeper.

In the circumstances, Bertie Ahern's response was generous. He ruefully noted that Bruton was 'the first Meath man to become Taoiseach, and Meath men have caused not a little trouble for Dublin for many a year.' Ironically, Ahern was to leave his own hostage to fortune as he piously stated:

> Like his predecessor on this side of the house, Deputy Bruton should reflect that it is the quality of what he achieves as Taoiseach that is important, not how long he manages to stay there. That will be the true mark of his success and of his contribution to the welfare of the nation.

A wistful Ahern added, 'There is no war in Ireland this Christmas. Who could have believed that was possible this time last year?' He promised of the new Rainbow that 'although our first experience of multicoloured administrations was not entirely encouraging some time ago . . . in the festive spirit we will give it until after Christmas.'

Bertie, though, was also anxious to remind the Dáil of Wordsworth's warning—'The Rainbow comes and goes'—before promising that 'we in Fianna Fáil will try to ensure that it goes as quickly as possible.'

The Labour Party's mood was enhanced even further when Michael McDowell complained that 'if there were ever an indication that the levers of power are in the hands of the Labour Party it is indicated symbolically by the fact that Deputy Quinn has been granted the Finance portfolio.'

Meanwhile, Ahern, the new and most unhappy leader of the opposition, warned that under the previous coalition 'things went from bad to worse . . . The national debt doubled.' And in a statement echoing that of Lemass he warned that he did not want 'on return to office in a few years to have to start from scratch' in repairing the country again.

After David Andrews patronisingly observed that 'it is tremendous for a young politician like Deputy Kenny to finally make it,' the real feelings of anger and horror that had been churning away within the newly disempowered Fianna Fáil ranks only really surfaced when an incandescent Brian Cowen snarled that 'the political philosophy of Fianna Fáil goes much deeper than the length of a dipstick in the petrol tank of a state car.'

How little he knew about his own party.

Chapter 33 ～

WE ARE IN SURPLUS: LABOUR'S LAST BUDGET

22 January 1997

The 1997 budget was awaited somewhat more eagerly than others. Of course, all budgets are important, but this was the fiscal prologue to what was shaping up to be no ordinary election. As the economy boomed, and as cranes began to flock across the Dublin skyline, the sense was growing that whoever won what would be one of the most finely balanced contests in the history of the state would be set for a long period of power.

Mary Harney might have predicted an age of red ruin, but the tenure of Ruairí Quinn, the Labour Party's first Minister for Finance, had been marked by levels of growth and prosperity surpassing the achievements of Lemass. And in another example of how money solves all difficulties, Bruton, contrary to all predictions that he would go mad in government, had gone native and forged a cohesive, united Government.

Fianna Fáil was in a particular state of terror. An uneasy truce had been achieved between its various factions, but Bertie Ahern knew that it wouldn't last beyond an election defeat that would possibly return Ireland's permanent party of power to the tundra of the opposition benches for another decade. The only hope Fianna Fáil really had was that an over-confident Rainbow would in some way blow what appeared to be a winning advantage.

In the Dáil, Quinn claimed that 'this is a budget about the concerns of today, the priorities for tomorrow and our plans for the future; it is a budget about change, compassion and confidence.'

The ever-practical Ray Burke was slightly more realistic. Quinn had barely drawn breath before Burke snapped, 'It's for the election.'

It certainly looked that way. Ethical Labour Party Ministers for Finance are always reluctant to use vulgar such phrases such as 'tax cuts'. But there sure was a giveaway look about things as Quinn contentedly told the Dáil, 'The full annual value of the additional amount which I am investing today in our society is, at over £650 million, the biggest in the history of this country.'

In the past the minister's proud declaration that social welfare was being increased at twice the rate of inflation might have unleashed the PD bloodhounds. But when unemployment had fallen by 31,000, and when 100,000 jobs had been created in two years, Quinn could do this and also provide for a 'significant current budget surplus for the first time in our history.' Better still, he was 'projecting a surplus not just for one year—1997— but for 1998 and 1999 as well.'

Glum indeed were the Fianna Fáil faces as Quinn noted, 'We have confounded those commentators who said that you cannot achieve social progress and fiscal responsibility at the same time.' Instead, the Rainbow changeling had secured 'the most dramatic economic and social development of our society since this state was established just seventy-five years ago.'

Just as miserable were the faces on the PD benches when Quinn, not a politician prone to rhetorical exaggeration, stated, 'Ireland is now a national and international success story.'

Even Bertie could only look on like the political equivalent of the plaintive doggy in the window as Quinn even robbed Ahern's social partnership baby from the cradle via the crow about how 'social partnership works', having 'produced real results at home' and 'caught the admiration of commentators abroad'.

There was one source of hope for the quietly distraught opposition when Quinn, ever the cautious mandarin, noted that the characteristic features of this new deal were 'moderate wage increases in the context of low inflation' and 'agreement on the management of the public finances, including a slowdown in the rate of increase in current public spending.' This wasn't precisely the sentiment a nation getting ready to party wanted to hear.

The normally perfectly mannered Quinn did allow himself one moment of grandstanding. After announcing the 'biggest tax reduction package in the history of the state' he expressed sympathy over the fact that all these reductions were 'making deputies sick'. In spite of any maladies, Quinn urged Fianna Fáil and the PDs to 'please listen' as he announced the reduction of the standard rate of tax from 27 to 26 per cent and an increase of £3 a week in all personal social welfare payments.

But as closet PDs such as Séamus Brennan were murmuring about 'an expensive election', and with Quinn listing the already-eaten bread of the ending of third-level fees and the abolition of residential property tax, a problem was emerging. Somehow the minister was making a bonanza budget sound like the annual report of a firm of chartered accountants. And claims like 'this year the IDA found that Ireland was the number 1 location for US investment seeking to locate in Europe' or philosophical dissertations about how 'the celebration of success should not be confused with the contentment of complacency' were not resolving the problem.

Charlie McCreevy, opposition spokesperson on finance, was certainly not impressed by the peculiar delights of this particular work of fiscal architecture. He adopted his most avuncular persona as he recalled that 'not far from here the slogan "God loved the world so much that he did not send a committee to save it" adorned the office of the senior partner of a very successful professional practice in this city.' In contrast, when it came to this budget, by 'the time the Tánaiste and Minister for Social Welfare, other fellow-socialist ministers, programme managers, advisers and assorted hangers-on were finished' it was inevitable that Quinn's budget 'would resemble the political equivalent of a camel, which we all know is a horse designed by a committee.'

As McCreevy sighed about how this budget had been a 'a glorious opportunity to leave a real footprint on Irish economic development, but instead we get barely a toemark,' Fianna Fáil's back-room strategists were already purring contentedly. The high-mindedness might have been continuing in public, with McCreevy asking, 'Has political comment become so vacuous that economic and budgetary decisions in an election year are measured solely on their perceived electoral pluses or minuses?' but the good news for Fianna Fáil was that the Rainbow had missed the boom-time bus.

McCreevy could bleat all he wanted about how the excessive stimulation of the economy during a period of record growth was a bad thing. But even as he donned the sheep's wool of conservatism, noting that we were in danger of spending our way out of a boom, more wolfish voices on the Fianna Fáil benches were observing that if we really were having this great boom, three pounds for the plucky pensioners didn't appear to be an awful lot.

Fianna Fáil continued to hide in full view as McCreevy entertainingly claimed that 'short-term popularity bought at the expense of future bankruptcy is not a worthy aim.'

It was a theory McCreevy would subsequently test to the full, but in opposition the man who subsequently said, 'When I have it, I spend it,' claimed, with a straight face:

> The Government has engaged in short-termism to an extreme degree. It has thrown caution to the wind. It has not provided for the rainy day . . . The budget is pro-cyclical.

The subterranean truth, though, was that even as McCreevy issued pious ejaculations about fiscal caution Bertie and Fianna Fáil were giving us the wink and the nod about the party that would be going down if it got into power.

Michael McDowell, in fairness, did his best to raise a stir with the apparently optimistic claim that this was the 'longest redundancy application form ever composed and signed by a Minister for Finance and an administration in the history of the state.' It was, he contended, 'a Bloomsday Gloomsday budget which is being put forward as something magnificent but turns out to be something very disappointing.' Sadly, ripples of laughter soon began to spread through a rapidly emptying house at the despairing claim that Ireland had 'a pre-Berlin Wall Labour Party in office'. McDowell's next fusillade—that this budget was 'the Rainbow Coalition's 1997 manifesto, in which it tries to appropriate the credit for all the good things it inherited'— was somewhat more accurate, as was his observation that the electorate was going to get back 'less than half the excess revenue collected in 1996'.

After McDowell noted the warnings by the Central Bank (apparently he paid attention to those, in opposition) that the 'current context of strong economic growth' meant that 'any tax reductions would have to be made only in conjunction with more stringent control of expenditure,' his prim caution was openly ditched by Harney, a PD leader who was experiencing growing cravings for power. Instead, she piously grumbled about how

> all the Labour Party could do for workers was take a penny off the tax rate. If anything was needed to prove there is no crock of gold at the end of this rainbow it is the pittance for the workers who try so hard.

In a chilling prophecy of the fiscal madness that Fianna Fáil and the PDs would indulge in to secure a quasi-permanent tenure in power, Harney nostalgically recalled that 'between 1989 and 1992 Fianna Fáil and the Progressive Democrats reduced the standard rate of tax by five percentage points and the higher rate of tax by eight percentage points. That was at a time when we did not have the boom we have now.' The implied message was clear: like Fianna Fáil, Harney was in the mood to party.

It was in retrospect a critical budget precisely because of the year that was in it. The greatest power any political party has is that of shaping an election campaign by means of the budget. Fianna Fáil, as we were to learn to our cost, were masters of the art.

In contrast, even as the Rainbow deputies rose to give the Minister for Finance a rare standing ovation, the all too circumspect Ruairí Quinn, while he hadn't blown the nation's finances, had frittered the election away.

Chapter 34 ~

A RAT IN AN ANORAK OR A
HUMBLE NORT'SIDE DUB?

26 June 1997

W e didn't grasp the significance of the event at the time. But there again the political essence of Bertie was that you never saw danger coming. It had been manifest from the moment he had moved for the leadership of Fianna Fáil. Indeed at the time it didn't look as though he had even been so proactive as to move. Instead, in the wake of the collapse of the Reynolds-Spring Government, Ahern simply allowed the devastated Reynolds to sleepwalk from his position as Fianna Fáil leader and be replaced 'almost before he realised it'.

In spite of Ahern's cautious personal style, and the somewhat supercilious attitude of the Sancerre-sipping socialists of Sandymount, some observers realised that his selection had brought a new dynamic to Fianna Fáil. It wasn't just that for the first time since 1959 it had a leader who was the unanimous choice of the party. Worried sources, particularly in the Labour Party, also observed that Fianna Fáil now had 'a leader who could fight for the Dublin PAYE workers' vote'.

Ahern had a number of other crucial qualities. In a youthful country he was a young leader who was seen to be more in tune with the mores of the evolving Celtic Tiger. Three years earlier his status as a separated husband had been viewed as a liability by his timorous political colleagues, who had little better to do than fret about where the Taoiseach sleeps at night. Since then Ahern had played a crucial role in the razor-thin passing of the divorce referendum. He had acute political antennae and sliced up the soft underbelly of the Rainbow in such areas as crime, where John O'Donoghue had become the Savonarola of 'zero tolerance', and education, where Micheál Martin filleted Niamh Bhreathnach of the Labour Party.

The only dark side to it all was that Ahern's victory had been accompanied by more than a sense of the boys being back in town: old Haugheyites such as

Ray Burke and Liam Lawlor didn't so much slink as barrel triumphantly back into the fold. But Ahern's capacity for gliding like a ballet dancer away from trouble, allied to the extraordinary implosion of the career Michael Lowry, minimised the consequences of their less than edifying return. The embrace by the Fianna Fáil leaders of celebrity, to the extent of being photographed handing a puzzled Sylvester Stallone a hurley at the opening of Planet Hollywood, together with Ahern's capacity to out-campaign the relatively ponderous Fine Gael leader, John Bruton, had played an important part in securing the close-run and, for many, surprising victory.

The result meant that, while it was a day few ever expected to see, it must have been scant consolation to Bruton when Dick Spring expressed his sense of honour in nominating him for the Taoiseach's job. We had moved a long way from 1992, when a haughty Spring had ushered a submissive Bruton to the edge of the dustbin of history.

In a conscious echo of Lemass, Bruton's other colleague, Proinsias de Rossa, noted that 'the country is being passed, temporarily, to the care of Fianna Fáil and the Progressive Democrats in far better condition than when Fianna Fáil last left office.' As we shall see, he was being rather optimistic about that temporary status, but there was no doubt that Fianna Fáil (and its little PD tail) was enchanted at the state of the country.

Bertie cleverly hauled out a relic of old decency, rather than Ray 'Rambo' Burke, to nominate him, for it really was better to let the high-minded David Andrews drawl about how the people had 'voted for change' and for a new leader who would lead 'from the front' and be 'fair, honest and decisive'. After Andrews concluded with the claim that he knew that Bertie had 'the iron in his soul to be a great leader and to make this country proud,' Mary O'Rourke was almost as ebullient about the 'calibre and character of Bertie Ahern'.

Mary Harney noted in her typically egotistical manner that she remembered 'saying here on 15 May, when I set out on the election campaign, that politics would be on trial. By the time the election was over I think I was on trial.' The aspirant Tánaiste said she intended 'to prove over the next few years that nurses, teachers and gardaí have nothing to fear. I want to see a dynamic public service serving our country.' In truth, with four seats, she would have very little say.

Ironically, the individual who came closest to unveiling the ethos of the new Government was the little-known independent TD Mildred Fox. As she listed off the deals—the construction of a secondary school, a district veterinary office, a sub-office of Wicklow County Council and a raft of other knick-knacks she had secured for her vote—the new Government had the grace to look a little shamefaced. But, despite all the opposition catcalls, poor Mildred was only experiencing at the local level what every vested interest would enjoy under Harney, the PDs and Fianna Fáil.

Ultimately nothing exemplified the 'party on' mood of the Government benches more than Jackie Healy-Rae, who told the house he was 'here on a mission to work for the people of south Kerry'. After Healy-Rae demanded a replacement for the closed Pretty Polly factory in Killarney and the extension of the tourist season the mocking response of the newly deposed Rainbow was epitomised by Spring's query: 'Does the deputy want one or two months?' Ironically, even as Healy-Rae warned, 'Don't write me off, I'm warning ye,' and despite all the supercilious commentary, Jackie would keep his seat longer than Spring and quite a few other Rainbow 'stars'.

In the aftermath of the vote a chastened Bruton congratulated Ahern as incoming Taoiseach. But he warned that 'there are many challenges facing this country in the years ahead', such as the 'growth in consumerist attitudes in our society, which damages care for others, which is the essence of politics just as it is the essence of good personal living.' Harney and Ahern would deal with such attitudes in their own unique manner by encouraging them. And as the new, reformed Bruton praised the success of social partnership, Bertie had his own plans for how that too would evolve.

For now, the new Taoiseach began on a modest footing, expressing his 'deep gratitude and appreciation to the Dáil for the great honour it has conferred on me by electing me Taoiseach.' One of the defining themes of Ahern's period as Taoiseach would be his determination to stay as far away from the same Dáil for as long as possible; but on that day he savoured the achievement of that for which he had schemed to secure for so many years.

Certain central themes soon emerged. Mindful of the debacles of the Haughey-Reynolds era, Bertie spoke of the 'partnership Government of Fianna Fáil and the Progressive Democrats'. In the new dispensation Ahern promised that 'the leader of the Progressive Democrats, Deputy Harney, our Government team and I will work long and hard and to the best of our ability to provide sound, stable and productive government,' and he somewhat edgily noted that 'many of the best Governments have been minority ones.'

Ahern's concerns were understandable, for the new political child was also unique in the sense that it was 'the first to be both a minority Government and a coalition.' Ahern, who had experienced quite enough collapsed Governments, made it quite clear, just in case it wasn't already, that 'there is a duty on us all to ensure the Dáil functions effectively in the interests of the people for the full length of its natural term or as near to that as possible.'

He noted that 'the last Dáil was unique, because for the first time there was a change of Government without a general election.' He then expressed the very genuine hope that it is 'not repeated in the near future'. It was

healthy for our democracy that all the larger parties and many of the small ones have had experience of government and of working together in different combinations in the past ten years. That has been good for this house. I came here in another period, when the choice was black and white, but that has since changed.

It would change even further under Bertie, who was determined to keep things as grey as possible.

The new leader may have been attempting to be kind when he noted, 'It can be reasonably said that the Rainbow Coalition did not lose the election: it was more a case of the opposition winning it.' Those who had just lost were unlikely to be consoled or to believe Bertie's claim that such a dénouement showed 'solid and constructive work in bringing forward well-considered and relevant policy positions, and private members' bills can provide a good preparation for Government and make this Dáil an interesting place in which to work.'

Those who knew the real Bertie would have been even less convinced by the claim that both he and Bruton, having known what it is like to have 'the cup dashed from one's lips at short notice', knew how 'to survive, not to take it too seriously and to live and learn from the experience with a reasonably constructive frame of mind. I have had to do that, and I agree with the Taoiseach [Bruton] that I am a better person for it.'

Ahern also made sure to offer his 'sincere thanks to my partners in the new Government, the Progressive Democrats.' In particular he wanted to thank Harney 'for all her work over the past number of weeks, many of which were difficult for her.' The PDs' difficulty had, of course, become Fianna Fáil's opportunity, but Ahern wisely refrained from commenting too much on that phenomenon.

Such was his capacity for dissimulation that few noticed the brief emergence of the Bertie ego when he talked about securing 'an honour which has been bestowed on only a handful of people.' Ahern, 'having spent twenty years here and having had an interest in politics from a very young age,' found it 'hard to put into words the honour of this position.'

The speech was infused with other ironies. He noted of the new TDs who had 'worked extremely hard to get elected to this house' that some 'will go on perhaps to hold the position to which I have been elected. Others will be appointed ministers or ministers of state in the future, leaders of opposition parties and to other positions.' Under cautious Bertie they would be waiting.

The cruellest irony, though, was provided by Ahern's benediction to those new TDs who were about to 'assume the great dignity that is part of being a member of this house.' Dignity, alas, would be the last word to be associated with Irish politicians by the conclusion of the reign of the great ward boss.

Chapter 35 ～

RAY BURKE DRAWS A LINE
IN THE SAND

10 September 1997

P. J. Mara once claimed that Ray Burke's defining political characteristic was his preternatural ability to 'see danger before it appears on the horizon'. It was an ability, though, that was to fail him spectacularly when a well-known local builder, Michael Bailey, and a cantankerous pensioner, James Gogarty, arrived in his home during the 1989 election and unburdened themselves of a cash donation of £30,000. Afterwards Gogarty would allegedly ask Bailey if they would get a receipt, only to receive the immortal reply, 'Will we fuck.'

In 1995 such concerns were a long way from Burke's mind. Instead, in the wake of Albert's resignation speech, the delighted Rambo brutally summed up the nature of the Leinster House merry-go-round, chirpily noting that 'the Praetorian Guard is changing.'

By 1997, though, as old ghosts rattled their chains, the swirl of rumour and counter-rumour surrounding the effective but somewhat less than fragrant political bruiser meant that his path to the coveted position of Minister for Foreign Affairs wasn't entirely smooth. The allegations about Gogarty, the minister and the £30,000 bung first began to surface in 1995, though Burke himself wouldn't be named at that time.

When it came to the formation of the Government, Mary Harney had somewhat typically quarantined the troublesome issue within the Fianna Fáil ranks. Bertie Ahern afterwards famously claimed that he had been 'up every tree in north Dublin' checking the issue. He, of course, had also sent the self-important Dermot Ahern on a couple of wild-goose chases, but the quality of Bertie's investigation was captured in the delicate query, 'Is there anything worrying you, Ray?' At the time, Burke, who had survived a number of Garda investigations, nonchalantly shrugged off the whiff of sulphur that was following him.

By July 1997, with the new Government barely bedded in, a lot of things were worrying Burke and, more importantly still, Harney. In the wake of Burke's outing as the recipient of the large cash sum, by September, as yet another ethical storm swirled around a Dáil that was back preternaturally early, Burke, the hardest of them all, and other than Bertie the last great survivor from the Haughey era, was fighting for his political and legal survival.

In typical style Rambo had decided that his best plan of campaign when it came to these allegations would be to get his retaliation in first. The recall of the Dáil to deal with the issue was, even by the standards of the time, a unique occasion: before we even got to Burke, the former Fine Gael minister Michael Lowry issued a personal statement about his own adventures with Ben Dunne.

In Leinster House there was a real sense that the credibility of politics had reached a tipping-point. The Haughey era had ended only six years ago, and the shadow he cast was still vast. Fine Gael too was floundering in an ethical tar-pit.

Inevitably John Bruton, back struggling again in opposition, had his eye on the big issues, pompously raising the necessity of banning mobile phones in the chamber.

Attention, however, was soon diverted to the travails of Bruton's former 'best friend, friends for ever', Lowry, who thanked 'the house for the opportunity to make this personal explanation' about his own special relationship with Dunne. In a fast-moving political world, however, Lowry was to a certain extent already history's litter.

In the confines of the Dáil all eyes were instead on Burke, a minister whose hands shook as he informed the house, 'I have come here today to defend my personal integrity, the integrity of my party, of the Government and the honour of this house.' As the chamber turned into a crucible the enormity of the implications were Burke to fall meant that the house appeared to be as shaken as the struggling minister. Burke, however, began strongly, noting that he was 'making this statement out of respect for the house and for those members of the house who have sought this statement in good faith'. He followed this with a rather more accurate explanation. 'I have been the target of a vicious campaign of rumour and innuendo. Since my appointment as Minister for Foreign Affairs this campaign has intensified . . . The story still keeps resurfacing in different shapes and forms'.

Burke resented 'having to dignify these allegations by responding to them at all,' but he believed that 'I must now do so.' He opened his explanation in casual style with the observation that 'the facts of the matter are that during the 1989 general election campaign I was visited in my home by Mr Michael Bailey of Bovale Developments Ltd and a Mr James Gogarty.' Then, in language that would dominate the next decade, Burke admitted, 'I received from him [Gogarty] in good faith a sum of £30,000 as a totally unsolicited political contribution. At no time during our meeting were any favours sought or given.'

He also admitted that 'with the benefit of hindsight it is clear that in accepting this contribution, even in good faith, I exposed myself to the risk of being the subject of malicious allegations of the type now being made.' But, the minister warned,

> any member who contests elections and depends on contributions to finance his or her campaign—unless he or she belongs to the fortunate few who inherit wealth—could find himself or herself where I am now had his or her path crossed that of a person who was prepared to make false charges against him or her, even if that person refused to honour those charges with a signature.

Burke did admit that the sum of money he had received was impressive. However, it had been small beer indeed when set against the ocean of resources that had been poured into Fianna Fáil's attempt in 1989 to secure that elusive second seat in Dublin North. During the campaign, Burke had 'organised and paid all the expenses of operating several canvass teams'. Literature had been printed and he had 'financed leaflets and carried out a vigorous personal campaign.' He sadly noted that 'members are aware a candidate's progress in a campaign is marked by ongoing levels of expenditure.' Even after the campaign he had 'functions to thank workers and supporters and paid the costs involved. All in all, the 1989 campaign was long and expensive.'

As a deputy sorrowfully observed that this had been the case 'for everybody', the house was almost agreeing by now with the minister's claim that 'any fair-minded assessment will demonstrate how quickly and easily considerable amounts of money are spent during a campaign. We are all here and know exactly what is involved.'

That in itself was surreal enough, but in corruption's version of the marriage feast at Cana the best wine was yet to come as Burke actually attempted to reinvent himself as an active warrior against rezoning. He produced—and it must have taken much searching—a letter from some years earlier to the former Fianna Fáil chairperson of Dublin County Council, Betty Coffey. This hitherto unknown soul experienced a brief moment of national fame as Burke read his letter to 'Dear Betty' into the record, though, sadly, certain members of the house struggled to keep a straight face at the pious concern expressed in it about 'considerable annoyance in the north county area concerning the recent rezoning decisions'.

By now Burke was a man in control. He informed the TDs that 'in February I will be a member of the house for twenty-five years,' and he had 'no intention of subjecting myself to a show trial to satisfy anyone's political agenda'. He may have been making a leap of faith as he claimed he did not believe that the 'decent, fair-minded people of the country want or expect me to do so.'

But the wily old campaigner quickly used the 'We're all in it together' defence and plucked out a Fine Gael press statement that noted: 'Solicited and unsolicited contributions to the election expenses of parties and of individual candidates are a normal, healthy, unexceptional part of the Irish democratic process.' Burke didn't confine his solicitude to Fine Gael either, noting that when it came to donations and personal affairs Dick Spring had also been subjected to 'what I call an impertinent question' from the *Kerryman*.

The embattled minister even went to some pains to prove that there was no 'massive surplus of funds following the 1989 general election.' The saintly Ray was 'reluctant' to make his personal financial affairs public, not because he didn't wish to provide 'information to the house' but because he believed he was 'setting appalling precedents for those who make personal statements to the house in the future.' He found it 'offensive to do this from the point of view of my family,' but in the interests of clarity he was placing on the record of the Dáil a letter from his bank dated 1989 renewing his £35,000 overdraft.

Though the house was silenced by Burke's rhetorical query, 'Does that sound like someone who, as has been suggested, was awash with cash?' the minister didn't escape unscathed from the subsequent questioning. Dick Spring began to wonder

> if the minister and I live in different worlds completely. Did the minister have any sense of something remotely odd about two gentlemen arriving with £30,000 in cash? . . . Did he for one moment think of the implications?

Pat Rabbitte echoed the puzzlement, asking if alarm bells had not rung, given that Burke was 'no stranger to controversy in the planning area'.

Burke, however, deflected all the criticisms with the observation that 'I have been accused of everything in recent weeks other than starting the Chicago Fire and being involved in the shooting of Michael Collins.'

Strangely enough, or so it seemed at the time, the one individual to rattle Burke was Jim O'Keeffe, a relatively harmless Co. Cork solicitor who tended to get frontbench positions in opposition and backbench positions in government. But his shot in the dark—'Since the receipt of the money in cash in 1989, did the minister lodge moneys in overseas bank accounts?'—appeared to shake Burke to the core.

Its impact was somewhat lost in the flux, but an angry Burke imperiously attempted to silence O'Keeffe by saying he had 'bared my soul to the house today, and I find the deputy's question offensive in the extreme'. It was, as we were to subsequently discover, also accurate in the extreme.

For now, though, we still knew nothing of the great old concept of 'walking around money', a company called Caviar or the rest of the filth that would fall out on the killing floors of the Mahon Tribunal. Instead, in the still safe territories of the Dáil, Burke used every trick in the book. Even the skeleton of his father, Paddy 'the Bishop' Burke, was dug up: a tearful minister noted that his father had 'served the house loyally for twenty-nine years . . . with many current members or their fathers.'

In spite of this record there had even been allegations that the land on which Burke's house had been built 'was originally purchased . . . from an inmate of the mental hospital in Portrane, Co. Dublin.' An emotional Burke said his father 'worked as a nurse in the hospital in Portrane until the mid-1950s. He had come from a humble background in the west of Ireland . . . The assertion in that article was a complete and utter lie.' Burke added that 'Land Registry documentation relating to my home' clearly shows that it and the site were 'bought in a normal commercial transaction' and that the house was 'built in the normal commercial manner'.

To put it mildly, the Flood Tribunal would discover a radically different tale. But for now a bristling Rambo told reporters outside that he had drawn a line in the sand. It was, however—as both he and we were to discover— drawn in quicksand.

Chapter 36 ∾

BERTIE SEES THE GHOST
OF TRIBUNALS FUTURE

7 October 1997

The problem with Ray Burke and donations was that the stories of the crooked house, and of every other crooked thing the crooked minister had done, wouldn't go away. Bertie could ramble on as much as he wanted about being up every tree in north Dublin, but the ball of wool that had been unravelling since as far back as 1993—when the Fianna Fáil Minister for the Environment, Michael Smith, had warned that 'the stage has now been reached where planning in Dublin' was a 'debased currency'—couldn't be tidied up, even by Bertie.

Since drawing his line in the sand Burke found that his position had been significantly deteriorating, thanks to a letter secured by John Ryan, then editor of *Magill,* at a wedding, of all places. In it Burke's friends the Bailey brothers, Tom and Michael, had somewhat embarrassingly warned that procurement of planning permission for the Murphy Group would be 'notoriously difficult, time-consuming and expensive'. Ahern's antennae were just as askew as those of Burke in 1989, as the Government claimed that the letter was just 'a normal business document using standard commercial language'.

Amidst further allegations about Saudi passports, a Government that hadn't even produced a budget began to wobble. Burke had become a pebble in the Taoiseach's shoe that ultimately had to go. Fianna Fáil fought like cornered rats to save him, but the growing apprehension that the sloppiness of the past might lead to the collapse of a third coalition Government led by Fianna Fáil meant that the jig was up.

The final circumstances were dramatic and poignant, as Burke resigned both from his ministry and from political life in the wake of the death of his brother. As the house dealt with the resignation, and as it finalised the establishment of the most costly and fruitless tribunal in the history of the state, the mood was dangerously bitter.

In the Dáil an unusually honest Bertie said it was 'with profound regret that

I have today accepted' Burke's resignation. The rest of the country might have thought Burke was a corrupt blight, but to Ahern he was still 'Ray'. That close relationship wouldn't last, but on this particular occasion a tight-lipped Taoiseach went to some pains to make it clear that he felt it 'a double tragedy for Ray and his family that he should feel compelled to tender his resignation at a time of bereavement and great personal stress.'

Though Ahern didn't look like a man signing his own death warrant, the suppressed anger that infused his speech was curious. In retrospect, though the road leading to Bertie's own chamber of secrets was a long and winding one, we should have realised that those who have things to hide often act in a spooked fashion. But for now Ahern was content to stress Burke's 'outstanding record of service', which in truth was so outstanding that it was invisible to the naked eye. The Taoiseach, however, claimed that in the peace process he had shown 'all the superb professional skills of organisation, communication and vigour for which he was so rightly renowned.'

The tribute continued. Ahern thanked 'Ray' for the 'consummate professionalism with which he also fulfilled his ministerial duties.' Burke, said Bertie, 'always distinguished himself in the ministries to which he was appointed by his great ministerial capabilities.' In particular, an unusually eloquent Bertie cited Burke's success in opening up 'a whole new era of local broadcasting'.

As Mary Harney's trembling-bottom-lip act went into overdrive, such was the chilliness of the mood that it was clear that one could quickly get oneself a smack in the face if one said the wrong thing. Ahern certainly believed that 'this country owes him a debt of gratitude for his work on behalf of the nation'. Such was the emotional state of the Taoiseach that his normally well-suppressed strain of self-pity was unleashed. He told a sympathetic house that 'those who choose politics as a profession know from the outset that they are putting their lives on the line in their determination to serve the public.' They had to face criticism in their 'every act', and 'their families, too, learn to take the brunt of stinging remarks which often overstep the boundaries of civility and courtesy.'

That by itself was bad enough, but it was risible for Ahern to claim that 'in the case of Ray Burke I see a more sinister development: the persistent hounding of an honourable man to resign his important position on the basis of innuendo and unproven allegations.'

A friend whom we would see a great deal more of in future made its debut as Bertie snarled about how 'some who would class themselves as protectors of basic civil rights have harried and hounded this man without according him the basic right of due process'.

As the man who had once put Liam Lawlor in charge of a Dáil committee on ethics slammed the 'sustained campaign' of 'incremental intensity' that had brought this good man down, it was clear that the honeymoon, insofar as there ever was one, between Bertie and the media was over and that the Taoiseach was the one issuing the divorce papers.

The conclusion was so thick with bathos that the only thing missing was a reference to the death of Boxer in *Animal Farm*. Bertie sighed about how 'there comes a time when even the strongest shoulder bows, the stoutest heart falters and the very best can resist no longer.' This, alas, had now happened to a 'proud, honourable man—loyal, true, persevering, principled, caring and committed—but tough, and a person who lost friends easily.'

The last phrase at least was true.

Such was the mood that when John Bruton dared to express his 'regret' at the 'circumstances which have led to Mr Burke's resignation at a difficult time for him personally and on a sad day for his family,' David Andrews of Fianna Fáil, who would succeed Burke, immediately rose to his feet. Andrews was normally a harmless old-school southside Law Library-style blusterer, but on this occasion he informed a half-amused house that it shouldn't have to 'put up with this humbug and hypocrisy'. It was farcical stuff, Andrews protesting that Bruton should 'have the decency not to make a speech. I intend to leave the house in protest. It is an outrage.' He added of poor Bruton that the 'deputy did not have the decency to keep his mouth shut when he knew Mr Burke's brother was dead.'

As Dermot Ahern snarled at the 'crocodile tears' of the opposition, even the normally acerbic Ruairí Quinn appeared to be taken aback by the intensity of the emotions on display. Quinn admitted he hadn't been surprised by Burke's fate, for 'clearly the pressure on him and his family had become intolerable.' However, though he noted that a Government already tight for numbers had seen its majority 'further eroded', the normally tough Quinn seemed to pull his punches.

When it came to Harney's contribution the crocodile tears were out in force. A Tánaiste who had been eroding Burke's position for months, to protect her own, bleated about the lost statesman's 'sharp mind' and about 'how determined and tough he was'. As ever, Harney traded on emotion, noting that she had seen Burke that morning, 'and he was a shaken man. Over the next few weeks I hope he will have an opportunity to take stock, have a rest and, perhaps, to reflect on what happened.' It turned out that Burke would have quite a substantial period of reflection.

Proinsias de Rossa cut to the core of the Tánaiste's hypocrisy, referring to her previous 'frantic efforts' to 'distance herself' from Burke. This was followed by a typically surreal *tour de force* from John Gormley, who recalled that when he told Burke not to take his criticisms personally he had received the noble response 'Never apologise for doing your parliamentary duty.'

When Dermot Ahern rounded on another of Gormley's remarks—'On occasion, it is hard to avoid feeling like a member of a firing squad, but we are in an adversarial system'—with the cold suggestion that 'it will turn on the deputy some day,' he was being more prescient than he knew. Not even Dermot, though, could have guessed he would be sailing in the same ship.

It had already been a fetid day, but there were more astonishing moments to come. A feral Noel Dempsey introduced the bill establishing the Flood Tribunal. We would find out subsequently that there were plenty of other issues to be concerned about, but Dempsey had one overriding objective: to raise 'as a longer-term issue with all members of the house the balance between whistle-blowing and public confidence in the workings of democratic institutions.'

The previous weeks, Dempsey claimed, had been 'deeply threatening to ourselves, the system we serve and the civil rights of the people we serve.' It was astonishing stuff, and there was better still to come, with Dempsey stating that we had seen 'an infinitely clever erosion of a reputation based not on upfront accusations and production of evidence but on instalments of venom.' The fall of Ray Burke had been 'a soap opera' with an 'unseen scriptwriter', and the timing of 'this planned poisoning' had been, according to the hyperventilating minister, 'chillingly exquisite'. We were now entering the world of Frederick Forsyth as Dempsey claimed that the whole Ray Burke affair had turned into an 'excited bloodsport' in which 'the phrase "bringing him down" has been used continually.'

Ray Burke as the new Dreyfus was a hard sell, but Dempsey was of the view that it was 'time to put an end to this corrosive cruelty dressed up as principled investigation.' He believed it was time we 'forced people who corrode public confidence to put their evidence on the table and support the accusations they make.' And he even appeared to be sincere in his opinion that we should be seeking to investigate those making allegations, rather than the allegations themselves, warning that 'it is time we cut away the undergrowth of rumours and nudge-nudgery and rebuilt public confidence.'

Alan Dukes was rather more suspicious, observing that it had 'taken a week of argument and twelve drafts of these terms of reference to get a debate on this motion.' He expressed his concern that the Government's enthusiasm for 'very broad terms of reference' was 'an obvious ploy to cast the net wide in the hope of finding other unspecified matters which would divert attention from the main issue' and allow Burke to slip the net.

And indeed it did, though not perhaps in the way Fianna Fáil was planning.

Dempsey took a momentary break from the hysteria, however, to claim that 'the terms of reference before the house reflect the urgency I am talking about: the belief, shared by us all, that this sorry situation should be cleared up in the shortest possible time.'

The tribunal subsequently sat for fourteen years at an estimated cost of more than €100 million and created more than a dozen tribunal millionaire barristers. To date, three people have served some months in jail as a result of its investigations.

Chapter 37 ∽

DRINKING CHAMPAGNE AS CHARLIE MCCREEVY BECOMES MIDWIFE TO THE CELTIC TIGER

3 December 1997

Oddly enough, once it was over, everyone forgot about Ray Burke very quickly. It did help that there were far bigger political fish to fry than the one they had to throw back into the sewer. One such fish was Charlie McCreevy's first budget, which provided a classic example of the fact that in politics sometimes it is what is felt in a debate, not what is said, that is its most critical aspect. In this case some of the more astute members of the self-declared Rainbow Government of all the talents must have felt a level of despair not dissimilar to that of Sisyphus as they silently watched their careers drown gently beneath the froth of McCreevy's ebullience.

If McCreevy was defined by anything it was that Cheshire Cat grin of cheeky satisfaction. Few could blame him either, for it was clear that the parsimonious age of the Rainbow, which was far less fiscally cautious than the political myth-makers on both sides attempted to claim, was over. Ireland was instead now going to party, and if McCreevy had his way with his 'ten books' (or budgets) our wine, dine and 69 them host would be in charge of the festivities for a decade. He didn't quite get there, but it was a damn close-run thing, and Fianna Fáil would live to regret the cutting short of the reign of their boisterous Minister for Finance.

All ministers love their briefs, but few could match the intensity of McCreevy. Olivia O'Leary, a canny observer of political affairs, famously stated that McCreevy in Finance 'was like a man with his arms wrapped around a plate of spuds, guarding it against any greedy raiders.' For a Minister for Finance he was certainly a uniquely powerful figure who treated incursions into his manor, even by Ahern, not to mention by mere ministers, the way a dog treats a stray cat.

From the very first budget, confidence was his lodestar, with McCreevy chirpily telling the dubious TDs of a coalition that had barely seen the autumn out of his delight and of the privilege associated with 'presenting my first budget to Dáil Éireann'. He promised he would be doing five more of them.

Though McCreevy claimed that 'those living through radical change rarely appreciate it at the time,' there was no chance of that happening here. This was a minister who had money, was intent on spending it his way and intended to be as loud as possible in the process. The last residues of the cautious accountant in McCreevy meant that he did carefully claim that 'a budget should not seek higher TAM ratings than it deserves' and that, 'instead of creative gimmickry and lucky-bag spending to win votes, today's budget is characterised by three things: spending, correction of tax inequities and overdue acknowledgement of the elderly.'

McCreevy warned that 'Ireland has in this decade undergone an economic transformation' and that we must 'prepare for the problems we face in the decades ahead.' But that was only hiding the great turning on of the fiscal taps behind a bit of decent drapery, as he projected 'a significant current budget surplus each year to 2000' and promised that by that year 'exchequer borrowing will be eliminated.' This was a world Irish politicians had never known before. The national kitty was so flush that, even under the great spender, Ireland would finally live within its means.

McCreevy, meanwhile, continued insouciantly to tell the opposition what it was missing, for 1997 had been the fourth successive year of strong economic growth, with fifty thousand more people at work, an inflation rate of 1.5 per cent and an exchequer borrowing ratio of 0.7 per cent of GNP. The concerned minister did point out that 'as a country we are still deeply in debt. By the end of the year alone it is likely to exceed £30 billion.' McCreevy warned that 'we must free up these reserves', as Ireland 'did not thank earlier administrations for spending their way into our pockets.' He added that 'we will not and must not lose control of our finances because of strong economic growth' and that the public service pay and pensions bill of £5.6 billion was 'expected to increase by 6 per cent over 1997, on top of an increase of 10½ per cent in 1997 itself.' Had we but known, these were actually cautious days.

What followed was a classic example of McCreevy's and Fianna Fáil's unrivalled ability to hold entirely contradictory positions with an entirely straight face. After that small outbreak of morality the gravy soon began to flow, with the promise of 'an unashamed and deliberate targeting of resources for old-age pensioners.'

With Noel Davern of Fianna Fáil chortling, 'Where are the socialists?' and with Ruairí Quinn asking, 'Where did you get the money?' McCreevy promised that spending on health and children would be 11 per cent higher than in 1997.

But the best was yet to come. McCreevy said, 'I now turn to my income tax proposals,' and piously observed that 'the Action Programme for the Millennium makes clear the Government's commitment to reduce the burden of personal taxation in order to reward effort and improve incentives to work.' The happy minister noted that 'for that reason I am allocating £517 million in full-year costs to the main personal tax reductions.' Unlike the outgoing Rainbow's abstruse calculations, this was a grand, round figure anyone could understand—the Fianna Fáil backbenchers certainly did.

This party, though, was only getting started. 'I am happy to announce that the standard rate of income tax and the higher rate will be reduced by two percentage points in both cases.' Better still, he said 'it is the Government's aim to reduce those rates further, as resources allow, and to achieve a 20 per cent standard rate of income tax over the next four budgets.'

From that moment on no-one, from the blind person's allowance to the elderly, was left out. In contrast, the opposition benches were reduced to individual shots from Brendan McGahon of Fine Gael, who asked, 'What about the punters?'

McCreevy didn't get around to incorporating a tax break for bookies, but the list managed to go on and on. The treasured corporation tax rate of 12½ per cent was set in stone, and capital gains tax was halved, from 40 to 20 per cent.

Jim O'Keeffe of Fine Gael flustered on about how 'the golden circle will be delighted,' but, as was the case with Fianna Fáil back then, the plain people of Ireland—together with the Fianna Fáil bar lobby—were not left behind either, by courtesy of McCreevy's decision not to increase excise duties on drink.

The conclusion belongs to another age. McCreevy noted that he had 'delivered a budget which has a significant current budget surplus each year to the year 2000, eliminates exchequer borrowing over the next three years, proposes a general Government surplus for the years ahead and reduces the debt burden.'

Unsurprisingly, he wasn't at all deterred by the claim by Donal Carey of Fine Gael that it was all a 'damp squib. Where is the PD tax revolution now?'

Instead, we got into the dangerous territory of philosophy, McCreevy musing that

one view of the Irish economy is that a river runs through it. In the 1930s the water level in that river was low, and the flow was sluggish. In the 1990s the river is in flood: the flow could not be faster, and the rising tide is lifting all boats.

Not even a shout by Brian Hayes of 'Save it for the ard-fheis' could stop the stream of consciousness about how a responsible Government sees the economy as having more in common with a canal than a river . . . and the Minister for Finance's function is close to that of a lock-keeper bringing the water level up in one area of the waterway, down in another, so that all boats can safely journey.

As Louis J. Belton of Fine Gael bellowed about the 'river of no return'—and Louis was more prescient than we (or, for that matter, he) knew—nothing could silence the phenomenon of the Fianna Fáil budgetary standing ovation. Hayes was right: the budget had turned into a Fianna Fáil ard-fheis.

Michael Noonan did his best as he warned that

the applause from the Government benches reminds me of a scene from a Victorian novel where distant and impoverished relatives are informed they are the beneficiaries of a huge inheritance and applaud the solicitor who reads the will.

There was scant attention, though, paid to the suggestion that we should

remember that the novel usually continues with the dissolute and spendthrift relatives scattering their inheritance to the four winds in as short a time as possible through foolhardy and improvident action.

Nobody on this day of days—and least of all the voters—was interested in the warning that the public were fearful that

somewhere in the backs of their minds they see a Minister for Finance returning from the races, calling into his department and finding the tiger thrown on the mat outside his office, his eyes rolling in his head, foam coming from his mouth, and the secretary of the department feeding him with worm powder.

Noonan might have correctly argued that the spectacle before him was 'more like bonfire night than budget night, as the minister, like an unsupervised youngster, places more fuel on the fire to see how high the flames will shoot,' but there was some prescience in his warning that the budget 'reminds me of the expansionary budgets of the late 1970s and the grief of the 1980s when payback time arrived.' Nobody, though, was listening to Noonan's claim that injecting the economy with £517 million of tax relief at the point where we're entering economic and monetary union was a dangerous game, or to his concern that soon 'a nurse, garda, schoolteacher, middle-grade civil servant and people in industry on almost twice the industrial wage will not be in a position to aspire to owning their own homes.'

Derek McDowell, the Labour Party's spokesperson, echoed Noonan's views. 'In 1988 George Bush made a famous and dangerous election pledge when he said, "Read my lips: no new taxes". Like Noonan, McDowell claimed that McCreevy 'proposes to borrow money to pay for tax cuts the primary purpose of which is to keep the Progressive Democrats alive.' And as with Noonan, no-one, except maybe Garret, could hear him.

There were further serious observations from McDowell that as European monetary union approached, McCreevy was 'gambling with the future of our economy' and that he had also 'played with the figures in a way which has not been done since the interfering hand of the former Taoiseach Mr Haughey dictated to the Department of Finance in the 1980s.'

By the end of the day, both Noonan and McDowell were twisting in the wind. The genie was out of the bottle, for McCreevy and, more importantly still, Fianna Fáil had been given the keys to a treasure chest of growth and cheap credit that would fund a new economic mantra called 'When I have it, I spend it.' And they did.

Chapter 38

HOPE AND HISTORY WALK HAND IN HAND

21 April 1998

S ince independence, no issue, other than Ireland's endemically fragile economy, dominated public life more than our uncertain relationship with our Northern neighbours. Even when the Irish cold war began to thaw in the 1960s, Seán Lemass admitted that he had 'no illusions about the strength of the barriers of prejudice and suspicion which now divide the people.' For a time after the meetings in Belfast in 1965 of Lemass and Terence O'Neill it was possible to agree with Lemass's belief that, 'given good will, nothing is impossible.' But by 1969 the North was again a Gethsemane for Irish politicians, with Jack Lynch admitting that 'the spirit of reform and international co-operation has given way to the forces of sectarianism and prejudice.' And perhaps because of, rather than in spite of, the North's status as 'John Bull's political slum', Britain bluntly told a series of Ministers for External Affairs that it was simply 'none of their business'.

That position softened in the eighties, though it had more to do with patient diplomacy by Garret than with Haughey's gift of a silver Georgian teapot to Margaret Thatcher. Ireland itself was well capable of contributing to the vast atmosphere of mutual incomprehension. In a display of somewhat less than welcoming Southern attitudes, a writer in the *Irish Press*, for example, helpfully suggested in 1970 that it might be a good idea to 'repatriate' Ulster unionists to such locations as that green and pleasant land of Algeria.

The pace of change accelerated in the nineties owing to the utterly unexpected emergence of Albert Reynolds as a peacemaker. The myth and codswallop of Charlie Haughey was replaced with Reynolds's entirely pragmatic view that 'here we were trying to develop an economy where tourism and inward investment were important,' but all 'the outside world was seeing of Northern Ireland was bombs and bullets.' In spite of the burgeoning relationship between Reynolds and John Major, the relationship was still tense between Ireland and Britain, so much so that during one famous exchange Major snapped a pencil in anger.

Even the end game that led to the Belfast Agreement was an uncertain affair. In the final week Tony Blair's most senior adviser, Jonathan Powell, said Blair had 'helicoptered into Hillsborough without a plan,' except that of eschewing excessive hype. Blair then promptly told the media, 'I feel the hand of history upon our shoulders.'

The final document was an imperfect one. Sinn Féin, somewhat typically, turned up for the photographs but didn't sign the agreement, and amidst all the hype and hope the historian Roy Foster somewhat warily, but accurately, defined its guiding principles as a 'combination of willed hopefulness and desperate weariness' that incorporated 'an intricate Balkanisation of Ulster'.

In spite of these flaws, within Leinster House it was still no ordinary day when Bertie Ahern, a Taoiseach whose reputation today is sustained only by his achievements in this arena, could say, 'I am laying before the house a settlement for peace in Northern Ireland.' This had none of the Blair-style hype about 'hope and history'. But the import of its promise, to secure that which four decades of Irish political leaders had dreamt of, meant there was no need for a garnish of metaphors. As Ahern noted, 'the agreement is historic in the true sense of the word.'

In a rare case of cross-party unity the Taoiseach wanted to 'thank in particular the party leaders, who on many occasions were helpful in that they did not ask questions. I appreciate that fact.' The next task was no less historic, for if the forthcoming referendums on Good Friday on both sides of the border were passed, Ahern said it would 'represent a concurrent act of self-determination by the people of Ireland as a whole for the first time since 1918.'

A lot of murky water had flowed under the sundered bridge of nationalism and unionism since then. Ahern's claim that the basis of the settlement was its 'recognition that we have to live together on this island, and for that we need peace, stability and reconciliation,' was informed by one cruel irony. The view that 'neither tradition has the means to impose its will on the other' made use of the same language as that of Cosgrave, FitzGerald and Lynch in the seventies. It had taken a long time and thousands of deaths, but finally some at least among the Unionist and Sinn Féin slow-learners of Sunningdale had evolved to reach the point in the political landscape that the SDLP had reached in 1973.

The Taoiseach attempted to sweeten the pill for the slower ones by noting that the removal of articles 2 and 3 reinforced the principle that 'it is the people who are sovereign and who have shared ownership of the territory of Ireland.' That, in conjunction with the removal of 'any British territorial claim of sovereignty, made without reference to consent, going back to the Government of Ireland Act (1920), the Act of Union or, for that matter, to 1170,' meant that neither side could any longer say, 'or appear to say, that the territory is ours, not theirs . . . Rather . . . it is shared by all of us.'

Of course, it being Bertie and Fianna Fáil, the agreement had to be wrapped in the swaddling clothes of de Valera. Ahern claimed that it

> reflects the political reality that we have long accepted for all practical purposes. As far back as August 1921 de Valera declared that 'we do not contemplate the use of force,' and in 1957 he told the Fianna Fáil ard-fheis that a forced unity would ruin national life for generations.

A lot of history had been buried in that particular statement, but Ahern deserved, perhaps, some leeway.

More ironies were to follow when Ahern looked forward

> with deep satisfaction and with high hopes and expectations to seeing the remarkable vision and abilities of John Hume, Seamus Mallon and their SDLP colleagues, who have honourably and very effectively upheld the standard of democratic politics for thirty years now, at last applied to the betterment of the lives of all who live in Northern Ireland.

In a measure of how much political objectives can change, Ahern also stressed the importance of the new North-South Ministerial Council. (He would soon be even more satisfied when the entourage of the most popular Taoiseach in the history of the state swept across the border in a fleet of ministerial Mercs, with a helicopter for Bertie. Awed onlookers said the scene resembled a mafia funeral, and it was certainly unlikely to have eased the troubled soul of David Trimble.)

Though Ahern urged 'everyone to have the courage to embrace a new and peaceful future,' John Bruton (understandably, given his experiences with Sinn Féin) was rather more wary. The Fine Gael leader warned that 'history is what we make for ourselves. There is no inevitable march of history in any direction.' He told the warring factions that for the Belfast Agreement to work 'we must replace the politics of aspiration with the politics of accommodation.'

Bruton was less than enthused about the curious D'Hondt system of representation, which requires parties 'to designate themselves as adherents of one of two opposite aspirations.' His was a position that intriguingly would later be echoed by Joe Higgins.

> As long as the two communities define their very existence in irreconcilable terms, arguments on almost any topic that appeal to one community will tend to create fear in the other community. This is a difficulty in selling the agreement.

Still, Bruton conceded that 'the genius of the originators of the peace process was that they made peace the issue, and peace was something with which no-one could really disagree, as Deputy Albert Reynolds pointed out here many times.' He also suggested that the evolution of the peace process would benefit from 'the power of the European ideal, for example of building a structure of co-dependence that would make war in Europe impossible,' something that 'sustained the world's greatest co-operative political achievement of the second half of this century.'

For this to happen, though, the very nature of Irish nationalism, which had 'long been a separatist one', would have to change. And indeed, seeing as the 'unionist ideology' had, since partition, 'stressed separation from the South as the touchstone of belief . . . the very nature of unionism and nationalism will have to change'.

As part of this process Bruton said 'the agreement itself and the institutions it creates must become the focus of a new loyalty.' In a rare synthesis of Fine Gael and Labour Party ideologies he said 'the definition of the "nation" in this draft is much more modern than the one that was put into the Constitution in 1937: the nation is now defined in terms of its people rather than its territory.' Bruton said this new definition was in line with James Connolly's maxim: 'Ireland without its people means nothing to me.'

Intriguingly, in the light of future developments, Bruton was then of the view that decommissioning should be 'a practical objective, not a totem pole.'

Ruairí Quinn said that 'as an architect' he was 'reminded of the task of constructing the great gothic cathedrals of Europe, which projects spanned generations and whose design evolved in detail over time.' What was of real significance was that 'the world is a very different place now than it was in 1974. The Irish people, North and South, were more insular then and, perhaps, less war-weary than today.' In relation to Sinn Féin he said that what was important wasn't so much that they had moved from the 'physical force tradition' to 'democratic politics' but that 'it appears they have arrived with their political base intact.'

David Andrews, Minister for Foreign Affairs, treated us to a contribution that was laced with too much self-importance for many tastes. He paid tribute 'to the memory of the great Éamon de Valera and his great Constitution, which has stood the test of time,' and he claimed that he deeply understood, 'as a consequence both of my own family history and of my long involvement in political life as a member of the Fianna Fáil party, the difficulty many people have in contemplating changes to articles 2 and 3 of the Constitution.'

Happily, Alan Dukes added a bit of realism to the saccharine sentiments.

As a member of a democratically elected parliamentary assembly, a democrat, a rationalist and a citizen of the state, I add my voice to the tributes paid to those involved in bringing about this historic agreement. It is the triumph of reason over prejudice, of politics over violence . . . and, most importantly, of honesty over rhetoric.

For Dukes, everyone was 'walking on eggshells because we do not want to offend people; but I may be thin enough to walk on eggshells without being worried about how many of them break.' He wondered:

> Why did Sinn Féin not see the world in the same way as John Hume saw it ten years ago? Why did Fianna Fáil not see the world in the same way as others saw it thirteen years ago?

They were good questions that received no answer.

Caoimhghín Ó Caoláin of Sinn Féin gave the agreement an equivocal response at best. He thanked those who secured the 'best result possible at this time.' He noted that what had been secured was not a 'settlement' but a 'basis for advancement'. In an even more lukewarm observation he expressed 'our commitment to lasting peace, based on the unity and independence of Ireland.' A speech that was often insipid but more often bitter ended: 'Given that my party, Sinn Féin, is still engaged in democratic debate on this document and all that swirls about it, it is not possible for me to record other than an abstention on the passage of this bill at this juncture.'

But Ó Caoláin wasn't alone in his unease. Dessie O'Malley had a few queries too, and he observed of the murderers of Detective Garda Jerry McCabe that 'these people were described at the recent Sinn Féin ard-fheis as "political prisoners". Sinn Féin's idea of politics and mine are irreconcilably different.' He said the Gardaí are our 'thin blue line', and 'if this state will not stand behind them, at least to the extent of the full enforcement of the law against their assailants, it will ultimately place itself in jeopardy.' O'Malley concluded, 'Civilised nations honour and cherish their fallen. That honour should not end with their funerals.'

O'Malley, the SDLP, David Trimble, the McCabes and many more would soon learn that honour wouldn't be the defining theme of our peace process.

Chapter 39 ↶

THE APOTHEOSIS OF THE DRAGON'S TEETH OF TERRORISM

2 September 1998

After hope came murder. On a balmy Saturday afternoon in August, when the smoke cleared on the main street of the quiet provincial town of Omagh the scene was one of carnage. Water was spraying from burst water mains, and what was unveiled was a street strewn with the twisted wreckage of cars and with limbs torn from bodies by the force of the blast.

Among the dead were a woman pregnant with twins, whose mother and daughter also died, and four children on a Spanish exchange programme. A-level pupils, Sunday-school teachers, young country boys, Oxfam charity workers, an excited child who had turned around that morning to wave what would be a final goodbye to his parents—all lay scattered, in early autumn sunshine, across the street.

The illegitimate children of the newly respectable union of Sinn Féin and the IRA had literally blown asunder the budding but still delicate peace process.

In the aftermath a rattled Gerry Adams and Martin McGuinness hurried to Omagh to be photographed looking concerned. But the reality of what had happened was captured by the mother of young James Barker.

To see him lying there with half his head gone and those beautiful green eyes looking at me was devastating. I never realised how green his eyes were. That image will stay with me for the rest of my life.

In the Dáil debate of 2 December, Bertie Ahern set a tone of sombre realism for possibly the saddest debate in the house since the Civil War. Although only two weeks had passed 'since a street carnival was turned into a massacre . . . as with previous outrages, survivors of the Omagh bombing years from now will still suffer from their injuries.' Ahern also admitted that he was 'under no illusions . . . as to the continuing danger fanatics who remain at liberty can pose to the rest of society.' On this occasion he said clearly to the people of Omagh, 'A terrible wrong was done to you. We will continue to grieve for you and support you in any way we can.'

Ahern was sometimes accused of being too close to Sinn Féin for the comfort of true democrats. On this occasion he warned that 'we in this house, not any small self-appointed elite who would blow their fellow-humans to oblivion, are the democratic successors of the first Dáil—the custodians of the Declaration of Independence of 1919 and other founding acts.'

A Taoiseach who traded in ambivalence on any number of fronts was the very model of clarity as he observed that 'what was done at Omagh was a very far cry from what the people of Ireland—North and South—voted for on the 22nd of May 1998.' It was, Ahern claimed, a denial of 'the hallowed right of the people to freely choose their own destiny,' and the Real IRA were about 'to learn a lesson that will teach them to respect the strength of Irish democracy.'

Ahern noted that 'my predecessor in the last Government faced a somewhat similar threat during the breakdown of the IRA ceasefire', and he recalled that the consequence of this was the tragic deaths of children 'because of blind hatred'. Events such as this, Ahern said, reminded us that 'idealism and vision today is also about building a new future; it is about accommodation, equality and partnership' and ignoring 'the siren voices of the depraved few'.

John Bruton was equally stark. 'The massacre at Omagh was the worst mass murder in modern Irish history.' The former Taoiseach didn't pull his punches, noting that 'it was committed by former members of the Provisional IRA now travelling under the banner of the Real IRA.' A less than impressed Bruton also dismissed a comment by Gerry Adams that violence must be a thing of the past with the observation that this was 'just a statement of a wish, not a statement of what the IRA will do in all circumstances.'

Bruton cut to the core of Sinn Féin's dissimulation by noting that, in spite of all the pious sentiments being expressed by Adams, the IRA was still not decommissioning because of what it said was its concern at the slow pace of movement, 'whatever that means'. It meant that despite all the prayerful photo opportunities in Omagh, Gerry and the IRA were still indulging in an each-way bet. According to Bruton, 'whereas other political parties committed themselves unreservedly to the democratic path, the republican movement said as recently as this week that it will retain its military capacity indefinitely.'

A concerned Bruton said 'the British-Irish Agreement deprives all such violence of any semblance of republican mandate.' He warned that disarmament is 'not some new precondition. It is not a Unionist ploy or a Tory ruse. It is part of the British-Irish Agreement approved by the people of the thirty-two counties of Ireland in an act of national self-determination.'

In that context Bruton welcomed 'the fact that Martin McGuinness has described the Omagh bombing as "indefensible". But for so long

as the IRA's own war cannot be said to be over, the republican movement is saying that there are still some unstated circumstances in which violence might actually be defensible. That continuing ambiguity provides a moral cover for the Real IRA and for its activities at Omagh.

Bruton, however, didn't spare the Government either. Already people were tiring of the 'delicacy' informing its refusal to call on the IRA to issue a clear statement, on the grounds that there was no point wasting time on 'word games' and 'linguistic quagmires'. Many on the Government benches, let alone the opposition benches, were in sympathy with Bruton's question:

What on earth does that mean? Saying a war is over is not a word game or a quagmire. Words are the only tools available to democratic politicians to create meaning.

Simple questions can often be the most dangerous, and answers were slow in coming to Bruton's queries.

Why will the IRA not say the war is over? Why is the Government afraid to ask it to say so? Why is the Government afraid of the answer it will get?

We would be waiting some time for a response.

The intensity of the emotion hanging over the chamber was most clearly captured by the contribution of the normally staid Ruairí Quinn, who told a silent house, 'For so long as I live I will never see a clock at 3:10 p.m. on a Saturday without recalling the sheer evil perpetrated on that day.' He noted that 'in recent months many people who had been too frightened to look over their shoulders have taken the brave step of glimpsing into the future.' Referring to John Hume's critique of the undiluted fascism of a republican movement Hume knew all too intimately, and forgave too graciously, the normally prosaic Quinn, echoing Maya Angelou's denunciation of the shadows cast by the crouching beasts of terror, warned of this particularly toxic variant that 'the republican movement can no longer remain deaf to the voice of the people'.

After Quinn's speech the tone in the Dáil was lowered initially by a hysterical contribution from Mary Harney and still further by the dissembling spin of Caoimhghín Ó Caoláin. The single Sinn Féin representative was, not for the first time, in a lonely place when he distanced himself from a new set of bombers who, apparently unlike their IRA predecessors, were not 'accountable to any community or political constituency.' It was a pretty fine distinction, and as we digested this new concept of the rogue as distinct from the ordinary decent terrorist the sense that it was all getting a bit close to home for Ó Caoláin was intensified by his warning that 'now is not the time for party-politicking and point-scoring, for recriminations or the placing of new obstacles to progress.'

This didn't stop Ó Caoláin from treating us to a moral lecture about how 'the onus is on all those democratically mandated by the people to join together in the creation of a new political dispensation.' In particular he criticised 'how out of step with what is required was the contribution this morning of Deputy John Bruton.'

Happily, Brendan McGahon was no in mood for hearing any such lectures. The veteran opponent of republican extremism proudly stated that 'only two months ago I was the only deputy in this house to oppose the release of prisoners.' On this occasion, however, he believed that, finally,

> the tragedy of Omagh, in which so many women and children were killed, was such that violent republicanism will be dead in Ireland for several years to come. The rats who have murdered people for the last thirty years have retreated into their bolt holes.

Though McGahon colourfully noted that Adams and McGuinness, who were being 'hailed as international statesmen', were 'the bastards who have brought Ireland to its knees', in the end it all turned out well for Messrs Adams and McGuinness. Although Adams, much to his personal disappointment, didn't win the Nobel Peace Prize (it had been awarded to Hume and Trimble), he now leads the second-largest opposition party in the republic he used to call the Free State. And McGuinness, in the wake of a somewhat turbulent campaign for the presidency of Ireland, is the Deputy First Minister of Northern Ireland.

In contrast, a combination of police bungling, political lethargy and the refusal of Sinn Féin figures to co-operate with the investigation means that the relatives of the victims of Omagh are still awaiting justice.

DEATH OF THE REPUBLIC

Chapter 40 ~

A MAN IN FULL: BERTIE LEAPS THE SECOND HURDLE

6 June 2002

Bertie Ahern may not have come to the electorate in 2002 bearing gifts of gold, frankincense and myrrh, but it was a damn close-run thing. It was, however, P. J. Mara who typified the rakish ebullience of the 2002 Fianna Fáil election campaign when he walked into the launch with all the stately grace of a Turkish pasha, clapping his hands, saying, 'It's showtime, folks.' Which, of course, it was. But the greater truth may have been captured by the lyrics of the campaign anthem: 'All together now, in no man's land.'

In truth, despite some unease about the perennial woes of schools and hospitals, the feverishly effusive national mood was captured by Declan Kiberd in the *Irish Times,* who had said that that year 'the real question should not be why the Celtic Tiger happened but why its coming took so long.'

Amidst such praise Ahern was certainly a man in flow. Ireland was the apple of the EU's eye—so much so that the humble ward boss from Drumcondra was now a world statesman. There had been failures in the peace process, and the economy, after that pre-election binge, was looking somewhat jaundiced; but credit was still cheap, and the skyline of the capital, and that of dozens of provincial towns, was black with cranes.

The woes of the opposition, in contrast, had been summarised by John Bruton in his bleak outburst in 2000 that 'it is bizarre that we have a Fianna Fáil party still in office that could select Ray Burke to be Foreign Minister, Deputy [Denis] Foley as its senior representative on a Dáil committee to maintain financial probity, Deputy [Liam] Lawlor as its representative on a Dáil committee on political ethics and Deputy [John] Ellis to head a Dáil committee to protect the financial interests of farmers.' My, but how we laughed!

In truth, the quality of an opposition that under Bruton, at the height of the boom, had launched the infamous 'Celtic Snail' campaign, which promised to 'grab the snail by the horns', went a long way towards explaining why Fine Gael was where it was. Things didn't improve when they ousted Bruton, as Fianna Fáil had destroyed the clever but fatally dated Michael Noonan, so much so that it was described as the election in which 'the electorate voted out the opposition'. Noonan might have dreamt of a Just Society-style social contract, but the Irish voter had voted, as they always do, with their pockets.

As a half-living, half-dying Fine Gael looked nervously in the direction of a confident Labour Party that simply by surviving (and that was all it had done) was now breathing down the necks of the disconsolate Fine Gael ranks, the happiest faces of all were found on the PD benches. Bertie had been tiptoeing in his inimitable way towards an absolute majority until, in what appeared to be a quixotic gesture, Michael McDowell had engaged in the most unlawyerlike activity of shinning up a lamp-post. His *Single-party Government? No thanks!* poster was seen as being decisive in ensuring that the PDS would act as watchdogs over Fianna Fáil, for what that was worth.

The Dáil debate on the second triumph of Bertie was a curious affair. Proposing Ahern, McCreevy noted that 'the Government leaving office today held it longer than any other in peacetime'. In a measure of the performance of its predecessors, and the endemic distrust by the voters of our political elites, he claimed that the new Government was unique in that it 'became the first Government in thirty-three years to receive the people's mandate to continue in office and did so on the basis of increased representation in the house.'

Charlie couldn't be accused of exaggerating when he celebrated the 'steady and clear leadership of Deputy Bertie Ahern.' While Ahern had 'held high office for a significant period, he continues to be in touch with the people, and they continue to have faith in him.' He was a leader who had delivered a 'historic breakthrough for peace, helped the largest sustained period of economic growth in our history and ensured economic growth meant real social progress throughout the country.'

And yet a strange air of unease persisted. It was as though there was something false about the coronation, that we were pledging too much faith in one man for our own good. The alternatives, though, were thin, for the best that Richard Bruton could do, in calling for the election to the Taoiseach's office of 'the new leader of Fine Gael, Deputy Enda Kenny', was to cite 'Enda's good humour and warm-heartedness.' Ultimately the real truth of the political landscape was captured by Bruton's honest admission that 'as a party', when it came to the Taoiseach's office, Fine Gael were 'not so fanciful as to believe that we have yet earned the right to that post.'

Meanwhile, Brendan Howlin was, to put it mildly, even more optimistic in his claim that the Labour Party's nomination of Ruairí Quinn was 'a mark from the outset of this new Dáil of a difference of ideas and policy and an alternative view of politics that is unashamedly of the left.'

In a somewhat self-pitying speech the Tánaiste, Mary Harney, crowed about how the PDS

> were written off until this election by virtually all the commentators and pundits . . . When I telephoned the new leader of Fine Gael yesterday to congratulate him I welcomed him to what I called the lonely leaders' club. I genuinely wish Deputy Enda Kenny every success. He probably has been one of the most popular figures in this house for many years. I am not so certain he can maintain that popularity and be a successful leader.

Harney would certainly discover the truth of that particular process. For now, though, she was content to boast that

> what happened in this election was . . . a very decisive result. It is the first Government since 1969 to have been re-elected. It is the first coalition Government ever to have been re-elected, and the Taoiseach is the first Taoiseach since 1966 to have been re-elected.

Ahern, in contrast, humbly noted that 'public life is something of which we, our families and the organisations who support us can be proud. We can take pride in the fact that we have been given the trust of our neighbours and communities to represent them here in Dáil Éireann.' With the Flood Tribunal not yet even a twinkle in his eye, he promised to continue to earn his place with 'hard work and with integrity', and he advised the new TDS 'to remain true to themselves and close to the people who elected them.'

Ahern was gentle with his fallen foe, Noonan, who had 'marked my cards when I was Minister for Finance a decade ago and again in my period as Taoiseach.' Ahern had 'learnt to respect his abilities as a minister and his forensic capacity as an opposition spokesperson', and the general election campaign Noonan fought had 'deepened my respect for the man and the politician.' The Taoiseach, whose own party strategists had whooped with delight when Noonan was chosen to lead their Civil War rivals, was undoubtedly gilding the lily a little, but given the broken state of Fine Gael there was no harm in engaging in a charitable analysis of how Noonan 'never gave up, and not even for a moment did he give the slightest comfort to his opponents.'

In a rare revelatory moment Ahern, the Fianna Fáil icon, whose real nature would later be cleverly defined by Enda Kenny's claim that Bertie was 'a sociable loner', admitted that 'political leadership is difficult: not only is it a great honour but it is also a great and sometimes lonely responsibility.' While Bertie may have been in a somewhat philosophical mode, he also made it his business to note that Fine Gael's bright new challenger, Kenny, had actually been a TD 'for a longer period of time than me, and he has worked hard in many offices and responsibilities.' Bertie always had a knife hidden somewhere up his sleeve.

As Taoiseach, Ahern promised he would continue to

> to reach out and to listen, to be available and to take account of the people's concerns . . . The office of Taoiseach brings with it not just political responsibilities but personal challenges . . . to remain calm in the face of political turmoil and to remain humble in the midst of public honour.

By now we were skirting dangerously close to the Beatitudes as Ahern mused about the importance of having 'the humility to recognise a mistake has been made and the wisdom to learn from it make real political leadership.' He somewhat optimistically added, 'That is what I myself aspire to, and that is what I ask of my colleagues in Government.' All this in what would evolve into the most arrogant Government in the history of the state.

Ahern noted he was coming into power at 'a time of unprecedented opportunity to build a fair society of equal opportunity and sustained prosperity on an island at peace with itself.' However, there was a certain incipient anxiety evident in his determination to dismiss the concept of any ideological divide. He had

> never met a deputy who has not had working for the people as the foremost of his intentions. Sometimes we talk about right, left and centre; but, on the ground, members of the house might work with different philosophies, but they all work for the people, because it is the people who support them and elect them. The Irish people have a great sense of justice, and while people want to see their own area or sector helped, everyone wants to see justice and equality.

Though he couldn't have known it, the Taoiseach was being prophetic in his warning that 'too often we have enjoyed the beginning of economic progress' only to 'see it disappear' and turn into 'fool's gold'. Ahern's intention on this occasion was to 'manage the economy prudently, not only to meet the needs of today but to safeguard our welfare for many years to come.'

In fairness, given the increasingly sickly state of the peace process, one could hardly blame Ahern for making it a priority. A Taoiseach whose achievements in foreign affairs will be regarded kindly by history noted that his principal concern was that

> too often in our history we have seen the promise of peace only to see it wither away again . . . Building a lasting and just peace on this island is my great political goal—the priority that I have and will continue to put above all else.

Ultimately the real template for the Government was set not by Bertie but by the triumphalism of Harney.

> I remind Deputy Quinn that five years ago, when a minister of the Rainbow Government was leaving his department, that minister told the secretary-general of the department that he would be back in six months. That was five years ago, and Deputy Quinn has still not come to terms with the outcome of this election.

It was a bray that signalled that the arrogant age of hubris was about to begin.

Chapter 41 ∼

MCCREEVY'S LAST HURRAH TURNS INTO A HANDFUL OF DUST

3 December 2003

It may seem strange now, but few people quibbled when Charlie McCreevy was named the greatest Minister for Finance in the history of the state in a survey of businesspeople conducted by the magazine *Finance* in 2004. Given the pretty deplorable performance of his predecessors, the competition wasn't stiff. However, though he had reaped a vast political dividend from the situation in which from 1987 to 2001 the average annual growth rate of the economy had averaged 7 per cent of GNP per annum, the minister's halo had begun to slip, and his slip had begun to show.

McCreevy had dismissed the warning in 2001 by Maurice O'Connell, governor of the Central Bank, that the age of the Celtic Tiger was over. But though he didn't fully know it yet, McCreevy was being sized up for the chop. He might have won the 2002 election for Fianna Fáil, but Bertie was casting cold eyes in his direction. Worse still, so too was the world economy. The luck of the Punchestown-loving king of the punters was running out, and the anonymous briefings were about to begin.

It had been an extended fall, beginning in the wake of the 2002 election, when McCreevy's reputation had been seriously damaged by the accidental release of a Government memo that contradicted his claim before the election that 'no cutbacks whatsoever are being planned, secretly or otherwise.' The subsequent cutbacks, which were couched in the Orwellian language of 'moderations in the increases', were minimal enough. But suddenly a minister whose reputation had been one of plain speaking and honest dealing had been made to look shifty and furtive.

By 2003 McCreevy's biggest problem, outside of Bertie, was that he had grown becalmed. Too many ministerial enemies had been made, and now that the milk and honey was on a go-slow, everyone, both inside and outside the Government, had become sick of his face, and sicker still of his know-all, condescending voice, which seemed to have absolutely nothing new to say. He was, dangerously in a Government run by Bertie Ahern, becoming politically disposable.

In an unusually chilly house McCreevy correctly noted at the beginning of his script that 'the budget comes at a turning-point in our economic prospects' and would 'set the strategic direction which this country will follow for the next few years.' The silence continued to be stony as McCreevy claimed that Ireland had 'come through the recent international economic downturn better than most. This is in no small part due to our sound budgetary policies.'

An embattled minister warned that 'it is easy to forget the progress we have achieved: the defeat of unemployment as an economic scourge', and he was certainly right. There was, however, a dangerous element of self-pity in his claim that 'even if we sometimes forget the progress we have made in recent years, other fair-minded and reputable international organisations do not have any difficulty reminding us.' McCreevy might have been enthusiastic about how the IMF report had commended the Irish authorities for their 'exemplary track record of sound economic policies', but despite his listing of 'enviable achievements' (unemployment reduced from 16 to 4 per cent, huge gains in competitiveness, and public debt reduced from more than 100 per cent of GDP to 33 per cent) none of the spoilt and unnaturally quiet Fianna Fáil benches were biting the spin.

Then, suddenly, clever political ears pricked up at the mention of a 'balanced growth strategy for all areas of the state, which can be progressed through decentralisation.' They pricked up even further when McCreevy piously noted:

> It is important that the growth we expect should be regionally balanced. In this regard I am approving details of the decentralisation of Government departments and agencies, as promised in the budget of 2000. For the first time ever decentralisation will involve the transfer of complete departments, including their ministers and senior management, to provincial locations.

The horror of the senior mandarins was matched only by the joy of the Fianna Fáil TDs. Silence was replaced with a happy hullabaloo as McCreevy announced that 'a total of eight departments and the Office of Public Works will move their headquarters from Dublin to provincial locations'. There was one despairing, insightful cry of 'Back-of-an-envelope job' from the opposition ranks, but few in the Government benches were inclined to listen as McCreevy was in full flow about how 'ministers with headquarters outside

Dublin will be provided with a centralised suite of offices, close to the houses of the Oireachtas, for a small secretariat to allow them to conduct business while in Dublin and when the Dáil is in session.'

As politicians calculated the electoral benefits of the relocation of '10,300 civil and public service jobs to fifty-three centres across twenty-five counties', McCreevy made sure he played the ever-popular rural Ireland versus metropolitan elite card, in the form of a promise of 'radical change of culture in terms of policy formation . . . No longer will policy be made entirely in Dublin on the basis of a Dublin mindset.'

But despite the minister gabbling affably about 'the very significant benefits for the staff', including 'reduced commuting times', 'lower house prices outside Dublin' and 'good transport links' (none of which actually existed), and despite all his chatter about 'viable clusters of work units', not even the great decentralisation stroke could hide fully the declining state of the national finances.

In opposition McCreevy had preached caution in public spending. Now, even at a time of restraint, he announced gross increases in gross spending of 7 per cent, defending benchmarking by saying that 'if we wish to deliver quality public services we have to pay the salaries necessary for their delivery.'

The minister's view that 'we now have a pay-determination system which rewards public servants by reference to the market value of their work' didn't trot along at all well with his anxiety about avoiding 'unsustainable borrowing'.

And not even the hubbub about decentralisation could assuage the fear that the party was definitely ebbing, as that year's tax package came to a humble €287 million. Suddenly the insipid talk of tax credits and of taking the lower paid out of the net had left Charlie sounding like the old Rainbow.

He could claim that the 'public has accepted the need for fiscal restraint', but as the opinion polls plunged for Fianna Fáil even the sanguine minister must have wondered when the far larger spoon of Bertie would begin to stir the budgetary mix as a prelude to winning the next election.

The response of Richard Bruton was remarkably prescient, as Noonan's grandfatherly metaphors were replaced with a forensic exercise in accountancy. Bruton warned that the cost of benchmarking would be €1,000 per household. Other central themes of the succeeding years were raised as he noted that we were also seeing the evolution of 'rip-off Ireland'. While some crumbs had been given to local authorities in an effort to calm the nerves of backbenchers, Bruton asked, 'Whose quality of life will be markedly improved by the budget?' His answer, not too surprisingly, was 'No-one's'.

For Bruton, 'the budget is not about people: it is about keeping the system going, farming it along and feeding it just to mark time.' It was a statement that cut to the core of one of the defining motifs of the second Ahern

Government. Bruton soon identified another, noting of the promise to end hospital waiting-lists that 'this is the sort of approach that has cheapened the currency of political debate.' Even producing decentralisation 'like a rabbit out of the hat' was, he felt, influenced by the lurking presence of a council election the following June.

Bruton, though, was being too pessimistic with the claim that 'we are experiencing the legacy of the "get out and party" years: never did a Government spend so much to achieve so little.' That was yet to come, but the signs of that slowly approaching abyss were there in Bruton's warning that

> there is a significant figure in the budget. After the minister made his budget speech in 2000 he was able to look forward to the following three years in the expectation of a surplus of €6 billion. That was a sound financial position in which to be. That was before the general election spending spree began. What do we see now as we look three years ahead? We see a deficit of €9.5 billion. That turnaround of €15.5 billion reveals much.

It all suggested to Bruton that, far from being 'Keynesian' or 'Friedmanite', McCreevy's principles were 'those of the hog cycle: fuel the boom, suck poorly informed people into taking a chance and, when it gets difficult, renege on the promises, pull all the credit lines and let the innocent be crushed.'

Joan Burton, the Labour Party's spokesperson on finance, was equally unimpressed with a budget that reminded her of the view of the American billionaire Warren Buffett that 'government can't deliver a free lunch to the country as a whole.' Burton noted that the ones 'paying for lunch this year' are 'the extra 62,000 workers who have moved onto the 42 per cent rate courtesy of the Minister for Finance.' Of the tax breaks for rich developers she said, 'Many bottles of pink champagne will be opened today.'

The Taoiseach was a happy pragmatist, however. With an eye to the coming local elections, Ahern claimed that 'with our massive decentralisation programme the budget will ensure that growth is properly distributed around the country.' The socialist gene was also bubbling to the surface as Ahern claimed that this was, 'without argument, a socially progressive budget', one that 'exposes once again the hollow ideological myth that this is a right-wing Government which cares only for the better off.' The greatest irony was reserved for last. He warned that 'the recovery is taking place against the background of historically low interest rates', and that in a situation where 'borrowing is the real stealth tax' . . . 'as a small country it is not in our interest to have any doubts hanging over the soundness of our economic management.'

In retrospect, however, in spite of the publicly stated satisfaction of the ward boss, it is clear that a noose was beginning to be tightened around Charlie's neck. The Taoiseach might have called the budget of 2003 'a budget of hope' and claimed that increasing public spending would have a 'counter-cyclical effect, as noted by the IMF and the OECD,' but simple Bertie's observations about his 'centre-left Government' were signals that couldn't be missed by someone as astute as McCreevy.

The age of non-intervention with the splendid isolation of Finance was over, and the goose of the Minister for Finance was beginning to be slowly cooked. Within a year McCreevy would be gone and Bertie would emerge from his socialist closet and embrace the radically different duo of Father Seán Healy and the academic guru Robert Putnam.

McCreevy, in contrast, was about to be exiled to the Elba of the EU, so Mr Cowen, and all that that meant, could be unleashed on an unsuspecting nation.

At the time, for many, it actually seemed like a good idea.

Chapter 42 ～

APPEASEMENT CHALLENGED: ENDA COMES OF AGE

8 February 2005

It was 2005, and Enda Kenny, three years into his 'leadership' of Fine Gael, was struggling. Little had changed since Vincent Browne had at the time of Enda's first challenge for the leadership somewhat cruelly observed:

> Out of the blue comes a very nice fella offering himself as leader of Fine Gael, Enda Kenny. His name would not have been the first, or second or even 23rd that would have occurred to me as a future leader of Fine Gael ... But now that Enda Kenny himself has thought of the idea maybe it is not so bad. Enda is a nice fella, maybe even a bit nicer than Bertie. He may not know much about BSE ... or who is the PM of India or what is the capital of Djibouti. But people who meet him like him almost immediately.

By the beginning of 2005 the hope that the palpably 'lite' Fine Gael leader would 'out-Bertie' Ahern wasn't the only political concept that was on the ropes. Seven years on from the Belfast Agreement all the idealism that had been engendered by it had been squandered. Instead of bringing peace, appeasement had emboldened Sinn Féin and the IRA to such an extent that the IRA was believed to have participated in the raid on the Northern Bank in Belfast in December 2004. The largest bank robbery in Irish history had been followed by the withdrawal of a previous IRA commitment to begin the decommissioning of arms because of the additional requirement that the acts of decommissioning be photographed. Amidst claims that the IRA had engaged in surveillance of members of the Dáil, even the ever-duplicitous Bertie admitted that 'events have taken a bad turn ... all kinds of things had been ignored.' It was a moment when the Republic needed a Cosgrave-style figure who would end this circus and make a stand for democratic values and the institutions of the state. But was there a Cosgrave to be found?

Kenny had certainly decided that enough was enough and broke with the multi-party consensus by tabling a Dáil motion calling for the bridle to be finally put on the Sinn Féin-IRA axis and for a definitive end to the politics of appeasement.

Fine Gael's Simon Coveney might not up to that point have featured to any great degree in the evolution of Fine Gael's Northern policy. But one of his political strengths (and occasional weaknesses) is his permanent state of high moral seriousness. It was a public stance that was needed when, as Coveney angrily noted, 'faceless people with no legitimate mandate . . . lectured the two governments and the Irish people in a self-righteous manner and threatened to withdraw all co-operation regarding the peace process.'

Other heavy-hitters got stuck in. Billy Timmins of Fine Gael lambasted the spectacle of 'people convicted of the most horrific crimes being freed from prison to the cheers of their associates while the true victims of their appalling deeds watched helplessly on their television screens'.

Pat Rabbitte warned that

> the main obstacle to progress appears increasingly to arise from the fact that Sinn Féin has used the peace process for its own political ends . . . Moral authority . . . now enables us to demand that Sinn Féin contest the political space according to the same rules that apply to the rest of us . . . The proposition that the democratic parties should provide a footbridge to power for a twin-track Sinn Féin is untenable.

The gentler souls of the media also got a little bit of stick. Rabbitte told those who were so enthralled by the 'work on the ground of Sinn Féin public representatives' and their 'new army of "community workers"' to 'take a little time out to locate where, how and by whom the same "community workers" are paid on Thursday evenings.'

In a prescient point Rabbitte said that since the terrorist attacks on New York in 2001 'we live in a new environment'. The age of jesuitical statements was over. We had reached 'make-your-mind-up time', and there was 'no percentage in blaming the DUP, British "securocrats", or the Irish or British governments. Whoever robbed the bank in Belfast, it was not Ian Paisley or Tony Blair or even Deputy McDowell.'

According to Rabbitte, the initial peace process ethos of all-party co-operation had been frayed to such an extent that if 'the Government in its dealings with Sinn Féin has allowed the impression to be created that the occasional bit of criminality would not be contested' it would be a 'shameful indictment'.

The fieriest speech of all, though, came from Kenny, who felt it had taken a motion from Fine Gael the previous Friday to put fire in the belly of the Government. In a rare public example of his usually well-hidden capacity for using his political elbows, Kenny claimed that his 'objective was to achieve a consensus among the democratic parties in this house on what was required to see the will of the Irish people delivered.' But, he added sharply, it was an objective that would be secured, if only partially, on his terms as much as those of any other party.

He agreed that 'the significance of the popular mandate given to the agreement should not be forgotten or underestimated', but in May 1998 the public had believed that decommissioning would be secured in two years. The failure to achieve this, allied to the rest of the concessions that the then Sinn Féin-IRA party responded to with a less than appropriate level of political gratitude, had created a gap in the political market. The public may have wanted peace, but not with dishonour.

In language that was unusually sharp Kenny warned that 'of all the acts of appeasement perpetrated by this Government surely the most reprehensible . . . was the Taoiseach's secret deal with the IRA to release the common criminals who murdered Jerry McCabe'. This had been a 'capitulation of the sovereign Government in the face of IRA intimidation' and the 'worst in a long list of concessions which have corrupted the peace process.'

This corruption was epitomised by the sight of the IRA continuing in its normal activity, but 'tonight the Fine Gael party is shouting "Stop," and I hope the other parties in the house will join us in doing so.' There was no doubt that Kenny was scratching the old Blueshirt itch as he warned that

> the republican movement had, since the foundation of the state, challenged the validity of the institutions of government . . . it challenged the Oireachtas . . . it challenged the authority of the Gardaí, the Irish army, the courts and the Government itself. It challenged the principle of consent.

However, it could also be argued that Kenny was right, at a time when the IRA seemed to believe it could carry out a major bank robbery to secure the pension plan of its members, to disinter the core Fine Gael principle that the institutions of the state be protected at all costs. And few could deny that it was high time that a movement for which 'the 1918 election legitimised . . . its killing of more than two thousand people, its maiming of more than twenty thousand', and which had become 'accustomed to its mandate being disproportionately heard because it comes to us through a megaphone at the end of a gun,' should be warned that 'no democratic party has a mandate for killing, robbery, racketeering, maiming or stalking.'

The new, tough-talking Enda clearly believed his mandate 'to stand up for the truth, to defend and strengthen the institutions of this state and to allow democratic politics to build a country of peace and pride' meant that he couldn't 'endorse an arrangement in which Sinn Féin is sent to the sin bin for a few months and then return to business as usual.'

An acerbic Kenny put a smile on the faces of his backbenchers by dismissing the 'bleating' of Michael McDowell over the last two months. Kenny noted that 'despite his protestations to the contrary the minister had a central part in the October 2003 deal, which, but for the intervention of David Trimble, would have seen the killers of Detective Garda Jerry McCabe set free'. He concluded, 'My party does not want to see Sinn Féin excluded from the democratic process, but unless it completes this journey it will have deluded itself.'

Ahern might have had to be dragged onto the pitch by Kenny, but now that he was there Ahern decided to let Sinn Féin have a taste of the cold steel too. Citing George Mitchell's warning that 'it would be more difficult to implement the agreement than it was to negotiate it', the Taoiseach called the Northern Bank robbery 'a profoundly unwelcome and regrettable act of criminality', which in its essence 'brought into very sharp relief the issues that must be addressed and resolved if that trust was to be restored, namely, ending IRA paramilitarism, including all forms of criminal activity.' In very carefully chosen language Ahern said, 'After more than two years of exhaustive negotiations across the full spectrum of issues it is now impossible to deny that continuing IRA paramilitary and criminal activity are now fundamentally destabilising the peace process.'

The Government was still anxious to avoid seeking to 'humiliate any community or score political points off any party', but, Ahern coldly observed, electoral representation did not in itself 'override the adherence to fundamental democratic norms'. And, for once, instead of genuflecting before the then mysterious deity known as the IRA Army Council statement, Ahern warned that 'threats, no matter how implicit or subtle, have no place in a process of conflict resolution'.

A somewhat happier McDowell warned Sinn Féin that the Republic 'derives its authority from the strong voice of the people, not from some ghostly whisper from history.' The Provisional movement needed to learn that 'marginalisation and exclusion . . . are self-inflicted handicaps.' It was, after all, difficult to 'claim opposition to the use of violence by others if armed robbery, armed punishment beating—which is a euphemism for torture and mutilation—extortion, exiling under threat, attempted murder and murder fall to be viewed by one as things that are not crimes.' In a phrase that would become more well known in somewhat different circumstances McDowell told Sinn Féin and the IRA that 'one cannot hope to participate in the political process while one has those mental reservations.'

McDowell claimed he wasn't saying these things to exclude but to appeal to 'those who hold these views to exit that time warp . . . and to come into the democratic world occupied by the rest of us on equal terms.'

But a furious Ó Caoláin was in no mood to agree with the minister's suggestion that 'equality is a challenging item' and 'a matter of give as well as take'. The loquacious Sinn Féin TD claimed that McDowell's 'heart is still back in the days of section 31, internment without trial and the demonisation of the entire nationalist community in the North.'

But by the close of the debate, though McDowell had treated us to the fancier rhetoric, the greater victory was in the end secured by Kenny. The Fine Gael leader had finally found his authentic voice, and, more critically still, it was a voice that suggested that this dreamy playboy was a politician of some substance—one who, despite what Brian Cowen might think, was fit and able to stand by the Republic.

Chapter 43

THREE-IN-A-ROW SECURED AS DEATH BY TRIBUNAL WAITS

14 June 2007

S ome months after that coveted three-in-a-row had been secured, a reflective Bertie Ahern told the *Nealon's Guide* that 'the Irish electorate has established beyond doubt that it is not prepared to take long-term decisions based on short-term electoral campaigns.' It was the finest display of Fianna Fáil's capacity for hiding in full view that we had seen at a time when we weren't exactly short of such examples.

In fact Fianna Fáil and Bertie weren't just running out of hiding places in the Mahon Tribunal. The Taoiseach was still the little prince of Europe, and the *Economist* could cheerfully note that Ireland had the best quality of life in the world, just ahead of Switzerland and Norway. Such a view was perhaps unsurprising: national economic output since 1995 had increased by 350 per cent, personal disposable income had doubled and exports had increased fivefold. But despite the dizzying economic ode to joy Ahern's accession was infused by a strange elegiac spirit. After a decade the tribunal had come looking for a head, and the one it had cast its eye on was Bertie's. As the most cunning one of all was struggling to escape the snares being set by the tribunal's SC, Des O'Neill, Fianna Fáil, in the run-up to the election, threw everything bar the kitchen sink at the electorate.

Voters were told of a national development plan of €84 billion, and Bertie, thanks to meetings with Ian Paisley at the site of the Battle of the Boyne and to a series of dubious testimonials from Tony Blair and Bill Clinton, wrapped himself in the iconography of being the statesman who had brought peace to Ireland after seven hundred years.

Nothing exemplified Fianna Fáil's mix of desire and desperation more than the chaotic series of events in which, before that year's ard-fheis, the veteran minister Séamus Brennan warned that 'auction politics . . . would bankrupt the country.' Four days later there would be fifty-three promises in Ahern's ard-fheis speech. The strangeness continued with a hunted Ahern seeming to experience what looked remarkably like a nervous collapse during the election.

Though Brian Cowen would claim that Fianna Fáil had won because it had roasted the opposition's economic policies 'on the barbie', the electorate's motives were more circumspect. The initial lead of the alternative Rainbow had been informed by the terror that the boom was flitting away, but in the final week voters returned to Fianna Fáil out of fear that the Fine Gael nurse would inflict something worse.

It was, to put it mildly, an ambivalent mandate, and in an ill-fated beginning John O'Donoghue of Fianna Fáil was appointed Ceann Comhairle. The less than thrilled new occupant would become the first person to resign from that office after a furore about expenses that included such delights as a trip in a Venetian gondola. It would only be one in a series of firsts for the most misfortunate Dáil in the history of the state.

In time, the choice of Cowen to nominate Ahern would acquire an odd synergy, for these more than anyone else were the pair of political Captain Boyles who had driven, and would continue to drive, the Irish economy onto the rocks.

On this occasion Cowen was in ebullient form—at least by his standards. In what was now becoming a stock claim he said that over the previous ten years Ireland had been 'transformed in many ways, the greatest part of which has been the overcoming of the historic challenge of conflict, unemployment and emigration.' And despite the darkening skies few were yet prepared to quibble with the view that we had 'moved from being a nation defined by the problems it faced to one defined by the opportunities it has created.'

Cowen confidently claimed that the status of Ahern's Governments, 'the two longest-serving peacetime administrations in our history,' stands as 'a testament to his ability to lead.' He validated Ahern's reputation as a Taoiseach who was 'close to the people' and who had 'a cool head and a consistent focus'. Sadly, Cowen's claim that 'in the recent election he did not seek a reward for past achievements but a mandate to implement an ambitious and positive programme to keep Ireland moving forward' would turn out to have been optimistic: far from moving on from the past, this Government would be haunted by it.

Trevor Sargent, the politically eccentric Green Party leader, was also looking to the future.

> We are not only voting for Deputy Bertie Ahern to be Taoiseach but for the
> opportunity to play our full part in a Government that will set the country

on a course to being a leader in terms of quality of life, energy, efficiency, renewable energy technology, good food production, equitable health care and good planning.

It was an impressive list of objectives—all of which would be drowned by the great crash.

Fine Gael's eternal Dauphin, Richard Bruton, nominating Enda Kenny, claimed that most voters had not wanted to see 'the same battered vessel or tired crew put back to sea', even if it had been 'patched up and put out with new bunting.' It was a speech steeped in the regret of a generation of politicians whose careers had been choked in their cradles by Ahern's magisterial populism. Bruton claimed 'we should be looking back on a seven-year period in which we created a world-class health service, made it easier for families to bear their burdens and when there were safer streets than at the beginning of the millennium'. And though he didn't say it, the hidden fear among the opposition now was that if they ever actually did return to government there would no longer be the sort of growth that would allow them to achieve these things.

However, Bruton was gilding the lily with his claim that 'in Deputy Kenny we have a man who has made it possible for the Dáil to vote for a complete change of Government.' While Bruton claimed that Kenny, 'rather than being another pastel shade of Fianna Fáil, is committed to serious reform,' the view of the public was that a man of pastel had ended the Fine Gael 'surge'. And three years later Bruton would become a great deal more dubious about Enda's 'hidden' qualities.

A philosophical Pat Rabbitte said of Kenny that he had 'hoped until recently that he would be elected Taoiseach because he and I set out to offer the people a choice of Government in the recent election.' The Mullingar alliance had 'sought to spell out on the big issues confronting our people' and to face the fact that 'it is not healthy in a democracy that a single party dominates'. The tone of pessimistic despair that informed Rabbitte's resigned prophecy that Fianna Fáil was 'likely to dominate politics in the foreseeable future' indicated that, after yet another election defeat, yet another beaten Labour Party leader was preparing to hang up their spurs.

In contrast a gloating Mary Harney noted that the securing of the coveted three-in-a-row was a tribute to Ahern's 'unique personal and political qualities'. Once again, generosity in victory wasn't to feature in her speech, and the leader of a derelict party wheezing its way to a political death delivered a petty lecture to the opposition about how 'today is not a day for robust opposition or heated debate.' She then somewhat inappropriately quoted Edmund Burke's view that 'magnanimity in politics is not seldom the truest wisdom.'

On a subdued day it was perhaps appropriate that the greatest drama was provided by the colourful, though by now somewhat tedious, Co. Kerry independent Jackie Healy-Rae. The sworn political rival of the new, deeply reluctant Ceann Comhairle, John O'Donoghue, was anxious to congratulate the new man 'in a very special way.' Healy-Rae did so

> because I go back to when I directed elections for him in the early years. God knows, I played a leading role in sending him to this house in the first instance. I wish him many long and happy years in the seat in which he is now sitting.

The old Kilgarvan fox was also kind enough to promise that 'if there is a bad pothole around Waterville, on Dursey Island in west County Cork or anywhere in Cahersiveen I will do my very best ... to sort them out, and I will keep him well informed'.

After the Ceann Comhairle anxiously assured the deputy that 'I will never be far away' the most curious episode of all was Ahern's acceptance speech. Normally his respect for the Dáil's trappings and trimmings was equivocal. On this occasion the great ward boss, influenced by the realisation that he was somewhere he knew he wouldn't be again, assumed a valedictory air of high dignity.

Ahern expressed his 'deep gratitude and appreciation to the Dáil for the great honour it has conferred on me' and his deep consciousness of 'the important responsibility this house places on me.' He sombrely observed that 'the exercise of democracy, as prescribed by the Constitution, is fundamental to the stability of our country and the legitimacy of our Government,' and though our free, transparent and peaceful exercise of the democratic franchise is, happily, the norm, it should never be taken for granted.' Ahern continued:

> It is worth remembering today, as we meet for the first time, that Ireland enjoys a longer period of continuity under a single written constitution than any other European country. From a perspective of peace and prosperity the abiding memory today of the 1920s, 1930s and 1940s may be of economic hardship and emigration, but we should recall too that in a world at war and a European continent oppressed by fascism and communism Ireland's proudest achievement then was the establishment of stable democracy.

The sense of a Taoiseach casting around for a legacy was intensified when, after a brief reference to the 'unprecedented peace and prosperity' we were experiencing, Ahern noted that 'through every single day of the last decade the quest for peace has been the single dominating purpose of my public life.' In a line that might almost have been borrowed from Daniel O'Connell, Ahern said that 'the cause of peace will be the cause that is always closest to my heart.' Of course, like any pragmatic Fianna Fáil man, the economy had always come a close second.

However, Fianna Fáil's new philosopher warned that, while we enjoy

> the full employment, good wages and promising opportunities of which the generations that secured our independence and built our democracy could only dream . . . wealth creation is not an end in itself. Rather it is the engine that drives improvements.

As Ahern added that 'in a world with higher interest rates, higher energy costs and increasing competition from emerging economies, success cannot be assumed and prosperity cannot be taken for granted,' observers were already noting that politicians tend to embrace morality only when in opposition or as they reach the end of their careers.

Kenny, whom we thought to be at the end of his career as party leader but who was actually only at the beginning, was phlegmatic about it all. Paraphrasing Einstein, he said, 'Try not to be a man of success; try also to be a man of value.' Kenny added that he hoped, 'by the end of the Taoiseach's term of office, that this is what the people will judge him by.' He also wondered how well a Green Party that had called Bertie a 'dead man walking' would get along with a Fianna Fáil that had said, 'Ireland needs Green economics like a lettuce needs slugs.' Kenny mischievously noted that Fianna Fáil, 'as the Ceann Comhairle will be aware, said, "The Greens are a rabid crowd of tree-hugging, muesli-eating wackos".'

Pat Rabbitte then divined another source of uncertainty. 'The growing assertiveness of the Minister for Finance, and the fact that he is being treated by the Taoiseach as if he were the head of a neighbouring state, confirms my view that the Taoiseach may be taking his leave of us sooner than we thought.'

In truth, we would all be moving far away from these parlour games far sooner than we, and particularly Brian Cowen, would like.

Chapter 44

'THIS IS A WONDERFUL COUNTRY, AND WE ARE A FORTUNATE PEOPLE': SEEING THROUGH A GLASS DARKLY AS BRIAN COWEN BECOMES TAOISEACH

7 May 2008

It is easy to forget now just how much Brian Cowen was the special child of Fianna Fáil. Mind you, it is fairly easy these days to forget about Fianna Fáil altogether. But in his day he was that creature to such an extent that he was described, just before the crown of thorns landed, as being the 'anointed' one. And Cowen hadn't just been anointed by Bertie: he had also been anointed by the party that, in the guise of Conor Lenihan, had shouted 'Ten more years' after Cowen's 2007 budget. The Offaly Dauphin had been anointed more reluctantly by his cabinet rivals, and he had also been anointed by the media.

It is easy to forget, too, that when Cowen took office everyone was desperate for Ahern to be gone, for he had 'dried the marrow' from the bone of power to such an extent that he was already a political husk. The farewell had so much resembled the departure of a beloved monarch that all that was missing was a Viking funeral with a flaming ship sailing down the Liffey. But in spite of all his reinventions Ahern was a man who had been politically destroyed by the tears of his secretary Sandra Cullagh at the Mahon Tribunal and by the increasingly risible explanations he had given for the frequent appearances of large sums of money in his domestic accounts. When you're being called 'Mr Sterling Deposits' and when your 'I won it on the horses' explanations are being compared to the money-laundering exploits of career criminals such as John Gilligan, you've simply run out of political road.

On the day of the anointment, therefore, no-one offered any objection when the disgraced Ahern said the new sorcerer's 'skilled and widely admired engagement in Europe' made him qualified to 'undertake the obligations of the office of Taoiseach with flair and capacity.' When it came to the man who secretly didn't want the job, Ahern wasn't alone in his view that Cowen's successful contribution to partnership government meant he was a 'uniquely well-qualified' candidate to succeed him.

John Gormley, leader of the Green Party, claimed that 'during the protracted and sometimes tense negotiations that led to the formation of the Government I got to know Brian Cowen the politician and the private man.' The debate began to veer towards hagiographical territory as the normally dry Gormley enthused about how 'the Brian Cowen I know is tough but fair-minded and gregarious but thoughtful. He is relaxed but always focused on the task in hand' and knows that 'to complete the task successfully there must be a strong and united Government.' After a brief moment of recognition of the difficult times ahead, a hopeful Gormley claimed that 'the Minister for Finance, Deputy Brian Cowen, is ideally placed to tackle these challenges and turn them into real opportunities for this country. He has the ability to harness the energy and innovation of the Irish people to embrace this transformational agenda.' As Gormley finished by nominating Cowen with a 'sense of pride and hope' it was clear that the Stockholm syndrome really had taken hold.

Richard Bruton and Lucinda Creighton were in a similarly elevated place. Bruton claimed that, in nominating Enda Kenny, Fine Gael was 'opting for a path of radical change', and Creighton said 'it is with great pride that I second the nomination of Deputy Kenny.' This duo would be singing a somewhat different duet before much longer, and Creighton once she got past praising Kenny's 'calm and considered leadership', ran out of steam fairly sharpish.

In spite of Joan Burton's concerns that 'time and time again' the new Taoiseach had 'waved away warning messages that flashed as brightly as neon signs,' and her warning of his propensity to surrender to 'vested interests', the house ignored the 'ominous' precedent set by a 'casual reaction' to 'the decline in the public finances' and elected Cowen by as substantial a margin as that secured by his still-venerated predecessor.

It was a majority that would disappear as swiftly as snow in a July meadow. The *bonhomie* began to disappear almost immediately after Mary Harney expressed her 'great pleasure' in Cowen's success. It was perhaps unsurprising, seeing as she was getting to keep her job.

Meanwhile, the colour provided by Jackie Healy-Rae was now as traditional as the Queen's speech. The independent said he was 'here to support Brian Cowen this evening, as I did in 1997, when I planted the famous man Bertie as a seed.' Jackie wished Ahern luck, noted that 'one thing is certain: no-one will have to ask his name when he goes on journeys' and then issued a plea to Cowen to 'come down to south Kerry to help me with the potholes . . . The weather is getting very hot, and I'm under pressure.'

Enda Kenny began by noting that '*Esto fidelis* is the motto of Offaly, the faithful county.' Then, in an intimation of the direction Fine Gael would be taking, he warned that Cowen

> has always placed great store on political loyalty . . . The challenge facing Deputy Cowen . . . is to balance that loyalty against the requirements of the national interest and all our people, whom he now represents.

It would be excessive to suggest that Kenny was setting psychological traps when he noted that Cowen's position was a 'privilege' tempered by 'enormous responsibility'—a responsibility that would mean 'the Taoiseach elect will have to make decisions in the loneliness of his own office and without the collective energy of those around him.' But for some it seemed as though the leader of the opposition, who was always more effective with psychology than with finances, was ever so subtly stoking fears that Cowen was doing his best to disguise, possibly even from himself.

Kenny touched on another gathering storm when he observed that we were now five weeks from the referendum on the Lisbon Treaty, which would be the first electoral challenge for the Taoiseach elect. In a sharp reference to a previous put-down of himself by Cowen, Kenny said he was 'sure that by now, if he has not done so already, the Taoiseach elect will recognise I am both qualified and able to make a judgement on a matter like that.' Kenny then ended on a typically positive note.

> It was Ronald Reagan who said politics is not a bad profession: if one succeeds there are great rewards, and if one ends up in disgrace one can always write a book. I do not believe this will happen to the Taoiseach elect.

Sadly, the new broom set the tone of his leadership from the start by bellowing out the beginning of his acceptance speech *as Gaeilge*. Those of the public and the media who didn't comprehend a word he was saying experienced a growing sense of apprehension, confusion and irritation—feelings with which they would become increasingly familiar. Cowen's appeal to the *zeitgeist* of the 1950s did more than merely set the tone of nihilistic nostalgia that would become such a curious feature of his odd reign.

His speech was tragically rich with ironies and expressed his view that 'this is a wonderful country, and we are a fortunate people.' He noted with some innocence that 'the scale of the challenge I face is expressed in the quality and achievements of all those who have gone before me . . . not least my immediate predecessor, Deputy Bertie Ahern, whose outstanding contribution to the life of this country has rightly attracted praise and acknowledgement from far and wide'. As Cowen claimed that 'his is an inspirational example . . . I salute him and wish him happiness and fulfilment in the contributions that he will doubtless make over many years ahead,' few of us could ever have expected that Ahern's subsequent career would include such episodes as the advertising of a now-defunct Sunday tabloid from inside a cupboard.

After Bertie, Cowen moved on to future as distinct from historical problems. He warned that 'it is in the context of our . . . membership of the European Union that our place in the international arena and our relationship with other nations . . . find their proper perspective and most potent context.' But as he promised that 'as a member of the European Council I will strive to ensure that our European vocation is a live, engaged, creative thing, not a passive recipient of the fruits of the labours of others,' something strange was already happening to our Taoiseach. Even as Ahern the great communicator slid into history, Cowen had already begun to use that strange bureaucrat-speak that would separate him irredeemably from his people.

Though he didn't fully know it, Cowen was also describing an Ireland that was already a ghost when he triumphantly claimed that 'the movement of our people is now by choice' and that migrants now come to our shores to 'share in the economic miracle of the Celtic Tiger'. We would soon be nostalgic for a time when Cowen could indulge in self-important, de Valera-style musings about how the economy should act as a 'servant of society' and how one of our greatest challenges was 'to temper a rising tendency towards individualism within Irish society.'

For all the bombast, ultimately a real nervousness was evident in his observation that 'on assuming the position of leader-elect of Fianna Fáil I stated that I was excited, if not a little daunted.' There was certainly something of the little boy lost in his concluding sentiments that 'I have assumed the position of Taoiseach with an even greater sense of responsibility' and in his honest plea that he looked forward in the Dáil to securing 'a blanket of goodwill for many months to come.'

In the aftermath of his choice of the Government of the damned it also began to emerge that our new Taoiseach was, to put it kindly, a bit of a talker, as he indulged in yet another lengthy speech. This one mingled the 'reality of an economy in transition to lower levels of growth' with aspirations for moving from 'an unsustainable level of activity in the housing market to a more balanced provision'. Even then, however, there was an element of whistling past the graveyard in the talk about how, other than in the case of housing, 'the economy is . . . very resilient'. As Cowen promised to be 'clear about where we are going as a society' and 'equally clear about how we will achieve our goals,' little did we know that we had already embarked on a journey in the opposite direction.

In the Dáil and outside, the patience of those Fianna Fáil supporters who were preparing for a 'last night' of raucous celebrations was beginning to fray. But as Cowen talked, and talked, about how we would succeed by 'avoiding the mistakes of the past', he was already beginning to resemble a man who was talking a great deal out of a sense of scarcely suppressed terror over what might happen when the talking stopped.

Chapter 45 ~

HANDING OVER THE DEEDS OF THE COUNTRY TO BAIL OUT THE BANKS

30 September 2008

At the height of the Celtic Tiger the financier Derek Quinlan—whose property empire began with an investment in an ice-cream outlet in the Square in Tallaght—on hearing that the Tricolour had been hoisted on the hotel of the famous Savoy Group after its purchase by his syndicate, said, 'I cried. My poor father, who was in the Irish army, would have loved to see this.'

The Savoy purchase was a classic example of how property first enchanted and then destroyed us. During this final stage of the boom it was almost as though we were compensating for our oppressed past, as Ireland colonised the world's property market to such an extent that in 2005 we overtook the United States as the largest investor in foreign property. Then, with the speed of a winter solstice, darkness fell.

The new Government, whose attention had been dominated by the Mahon Tribunal, was at least warned. The lads had barely settled into their easy chairs before that fiscal John the Baptist, Morgan Kelly, claimed that house prices would fall by up to 60 per cent. Ahern may have rubbished such 'cribbing and moaning', later having to apologise for off-colour remarks querying why such 'quibblers' don't 'commit suicide', but by June 2008, weeks after Cowen took charge, trouble had arrived: it was officially declared that Ireland was in recession for the first time in twenty-five years.

As Brian Lenihan bewailed his fate in taking charge of the economy just as 'the boom was coming to a shuddering end', Cowen responded to the emerging crisis by disappearing from public view for an extended period. But with American banking houses tumbling, even Cowen couldn't hide for ever. So it was that on Monday 29 September, Cowen, Lenihan and a rabble of soon to be disgraced banking chiefs and fiscal regulators found themselves engaged in what Matt Cooper subsequently claimed was the closest a Taoiseach has been 'to making a decision on the lines of "Do we go to war?" In their case, the decision was made that instead of going to war the country would surrender unconditionally . . . to the banks.'

Afterwards it was said that the banks had come like thieves in the night, but thieves don't have the keys for the side door of Government Buildings. The decision was all the more shocking, as up to that Monday the citizens had been told they had a functioning banking system. Lenihan had even complained to RTE about concerns raised by the tabloid talk-show 'Liveline' about the safety of bank deposits. Ironically, as it turned out, the callers to Mr Joe Duffy knew more about the state of the Irish banks than the Financial Regulator.

Throughout the subsequent series of debates it became increasingly clear that the Government didn't understand the full import or the even more dangerous consequences of what had happened. Essentially, though it would take time for the scale of the destruction to become apparent, the Valhalla of the Celtic Tiger golden calves was here.

At a hushed leaders' questions that day Enda Kenny promised that Fine Gael would 'respond in the interests of the country, in the interests of protecting our economy and to protect the interests of our taxpayers.' He warned, though, that the Government was effectually 'asking the taxpayers of Ireland to underwrite a €400 billion guarantee . . . the equivalent of up to €250,000 per taxpayer.' An astonished opposition leader noted that 'the Taoiseach has stated on behalf of the Government that normal regulatory requirements will apply, but this is completely insufficient and completely unacceptable.' The taxpayer, he said, 'cannot be expected to underwrite a guarantee of €400 billion without strings attached.'

Cowen's response consisted of the usual mix of belligerence and innocence. He claimed that this action had been taken 'to ensure we maintain the stability of the Irish financial system'. A man who was always quick to condemn others criticised misleading indicators as to the exposures being placed on the taxpayer, claiming that 'we are providing a guarantee as a means of dealing with the basic problem for the banks . . . the question of accessing liquidity in the form of cash in order to conduct their business.'

After Cowen claimed that 'the banking system has assets in Ireland that exceed its liabilities' by approximately €100 billion, what was needed was a latter-day version of that famous boy who asked the emperor about his absence of clothing—one who would ask why, if everything was so rosy in the garden, the banks couldn't access any cash.

In fairness, Eamon Gilmore, leader of the Labour Party, engaged in a fairly good imitation of that precocious child, warning that 'the Taoiseach is proposing to hand over the deeds of the country to bail out the banks'.

He then wondered:

> What are we getting in return? ... What will the decision do to the nation's credit-worthiness? ... What does it do to the perception of the national debt? Will it be seen as the €46 billion? ... Will the €400 billion guarantee be added to it?

Suddenly the Taoiseach began to get terribly twitchy. He claimed that 'what is in it for the taxpayer . . . is to have a stable Irish financial system that is operational.' Then, in a phrase that would haunt him, he issued the lordly proclamation, 'The issue here is that solvent banks . . . are faced with an unprecedented situation whereby there is a credit crunch'.

Cowen's bad political habit in times of uncertainty, mixing indecisiveness with bullish promises, prevailed as he growled about how 'anyone who has a cursory understanding of what has been happening in the European and United States banking systems' would understand that 'if a deficit emerged the sector would pay, not the Irish taxpayer.'

Supportive backbenchers began to gather around the Taoiseach as Seán Power of Fianna Fáil shouted, 'What is the risk if we do nothing?'

An unfazed Gilmore answered, 'Let me tell Deputy Power the Government has been doing nothing for quite a while now.'

The full extent of Cowen's uniquely dreadful school of governance was crystalised in a sentence as he snapped, 'A situation emerged, and it was made clear to me that this was what was required.' There was, of course, no mention of how the situation might have emerged, nor was there an analysis of the consequences of the actions taken to remedy it.

That evening, as a shocked Minister for Finance, Brian Lenihan, was introducing the Credit Institutions (Financial Support) Bill (2008), he told the Dáil, 'This house does not lightly agree to debate emergency legislation of the type that is before us this evening; but when finance, the lifeblood of our economy, is a matter of concern the house will appreciate that we must move swiftly and decisively.' He somewhat optimistically stressed that 'the provisions we are asking the house to approve are in no way a bail-out'.

Lenihan said this guarantee was 'not free ... The terms and conditions on which the guarantee is provided will ensure the taxpayer gets value for money.' And, he claimed, it was 'a strong and decisive response from the Government ... By any measure there is . . . a very significant buffer before there is any question of the guarantee being called upon.' The apotheosis of the patented Lenihan family politics of 'No problem' had just been reached.

Richard Bruton, however, recalled that

> in the 2006 stability report the Regulator drew our attention to the

excessive growth in credit, the excessive reliance on the wholesale market to support that credit growth, the excessive reliance on the property sector as a proportion of the loan book, the falling provision for bad debt and the limitations of stress-testing that were going on in financial institutions.

In short, there had been even back then 'a warning that our financial structure was going down a road that was dangerous'. Bruton didn't dwell on the Government's failure to see what was coming down the tracks. Instead he warned that 'a sound financial system is like the oil running through an engine: if that oil is drained away by a loss of confidence then suddenly that engine seizes'. The priority now was 'to move and to deal with what would be a potential run on the banks.'

Significantly Bruton agreed with the Government response, except for the claim that 'the rules are not being changed dramatically.' Sadly, though, the warning about the danger of an 'institution which is exposed to risk gambling on the chance of "getting out of jail" and believing it will be home free with another roll of the dice' was too late, for, essentially, that had already happened. As Bruton also made the prescient point that €80 billion wasn't such a huge buffer, Joan Burton claimed that the bill offered an 'extraordinary blank cheque to the Minister for Finance in conjunction with the Central Bank and the Financial Regulator.' In common with Bruton, she claimed that if we were not careful 'the exchequer, or some specially created public agency, may become an owner of vast amounts of dodgy debts and the property associated with them.' Burton said 'a simple, "dump it all on the taxpayer" proposal', in which we would 'get the invoice in the post' was, 'in the long term . . . not good enough,' and she was deeply suspicious of the claims by Finance that the €400 billion was merely 'a little note to the bottom of the national debt'.

Micheál Martin, in contrast, wasn't at all concerned by the possibility that some NAMA-type Frankenstein's monster would emerge from the murk. He applauded 'the decision taken by the Taoiseach and the Minister for Finance' and criticised the 'over-simplistic' perception that this was 'a bail-out for the elite at the expense of the person on the street.' The future Fianna Fáil leader concluded with the promise that 'everybody with a stake in our economy—including elderly people, those who are employed, the self-employed, businesspeople and shopkeepers—will benefit from the legislation.' It was a promise he would probably now prefer to forget.

John Gormley, meanwhile, claimed that

for the past month many Irish citizens have been living in daily fear for their jobs, their family's welfare and their homes. We have seen the breathtaking speed with which some of the world's fabled Wall Street investment banks literally vanished. Some of these were a century old and had even survived the 1929 Wall Street Crash. Many of us asked what hope we in Ireland had if finance giants like Merrill Lynch, Goldman Sachs and Morgan Stanley could not withstand the financial hurricane . . . The lack of bank liquidity was threatening to bring longer-term depression to bear on an Irish economy already technically in recession . . . Rather than follow the lead of Britain or the USA, we in Government are convinced that we have a better remedy. We are delivering an Irish solution to a global problem.

It was, of course, hubris on an unprecedented scale.

In contrast, Leo Varadkar of Fine Gael was shushed away like a bold child when he disagreed with the concept that

the main problem with the banking sector is liquidity. I think there is a capital problem as well. The banks have squandered their capital on mistaken loans to the property sector, and I really wonder whether, in all cases, their assets exceed their liabilities.

As the Government broke the deadlines of 6:30, 7:30 and 9 p.m. for the debate on the second stage of the bill, the chaos summoned up reminders of old ghosts such as the day-long prelude to the fall of Albert. Varadkar informed the house that at one stage

it was suggested by the Taoiseach that we should discuss a draft bill that had not even been published . . . We have been told that markets and banking operate on confidence, but I do not have a lot of confidence in a Government that does its business that way. We finally got the bill—and it is still warm, believe it or not—at 9:45 p.m.

After Varadkar warned that this was like being asked 'to read the Lisbon Treaty in fifteen minutes', Mary Coughlan insouciantly claimed that 'Irish institutions have no significant exposure to the kind of assets that have sparked the credit crunch'.

Lenihan continued to make much play about the fact that when he 'telephoned Deputy Kenny at 7 a.m. this morning and explained to him the circumstances in which the state found itself in regard to financial stability he responded without hesitation that he would support any measure the Government brought forward.'

Significantly, though, as we moved into Wednesday, Gilmore was much more cautious. The metaphor might have been homespun, but his observation hit a nerve.

Many people at some stage in their lives have been approached by a family member, friend or business colleague who has asked them to be guarantor for a bank loan. Most people would be cautious and reluctant to do that.

Gilmore's warning that, 'frankly, the Labour Party is not prepared to do with the taxpayers' money what it would not be prepared to do with personal money,' and his threat that if neither the Tánaiste nor the Minister for Finance had satisfactory answers he and his party would not support the bill, differentiated the Labour Party significantly from the political herd, who were so busy donning the green jersey that few were checking to see if it fitted.

He was ably supported by Burton, who claimed that 'this scheme is being toasted by banks and financiers not just throughout Ireland but in Europe.' Those who thought Burton was exaggerating when she lashed 'a carnival of capitalism' that was matched only by 'the eras of Gatsby, the Weimar Republic and France in the 1930s' would soon change their minds. If anything, her analysis was understated.

Michael Noonan, who was just about to make one of the most astonishing comebacks in Irish politics, was still a mere backbencher. However, he made an observation that carried some weight.

> The minister asks us to take a great deal on trust . . . I cannot measure the effectiveness of the bill without knowing this: Was the crisis a liquidity or a solvency crisis?

After Noonan showed his concern over the fact that the governor of the Central Bank and the Regulator came weeks ago and said there was no problem, yet 'we then wake up one morning and there is chaos,' Beverley Flynn confidently observed that 'at a time of global turmoil in all financial markets, the one government that has taken very decisive action that has had a favourable impact on the markets is our own.' In fact, as we now know, it was the last 'roll of the dice' that Bruton had fretted about some hours earlier. Flynn subsequently left politics to run a fish-and-chip shop in Spain, where presumably less weighty matters were discussed over the battered cod.

Rather like Neville Chamberlain, Lenihan, happily, had a piece of paper in his hand.

> I have here the National Treasury Management Agency estimate. This states that the guaranteed liabilities of the relevant banking institutions are estimated to be €440 billion, and the assets are estimated at €520 billion.

When it came to the issue of impaired assets Lenihan, in words that would come back to haunt him and the Government, clearly said, 'I do not accept any degree of impairment.' He reiterated the point that 'the central issue confronting the Government last Monday evening was the liquidity of the Irish banks, not the question of solvency.'

In further assertions that he and the Government would regret, Lenihan promised that 'as a result of this legislation we are going very deep into the banking system, and we must ensure that the taxpayer is protected in regard to that intervention.' He claimed this would include powers in the area of credit and remuneration, and he dismissed the criticisms of the Central Bank and the Financial Regulator on the grounds that our arrangement is the 'envy of many European countries.'

Joan Burton raised an even more enviable set of arrangements. Calling on the Government to ensure that no member of the rescued banks would earn more than the minister, she noted that in the banks

> the masters of the universe have become accustomed to earning extraordinarily large salaries. We know that the managing director of Irish Life and Permanent earns an annual salary of €1.4 million. In AIB the figure is €2.1 million, Anglo Irish Bank €3.3 million, Bank of Ireland €3.1 million and Irish Nationwide €2.3 million . . . If a bank was a delinquent teenager engaged in anti-social behaviour it would be given an ASBO. What about undermining the finances of a country?

Richard Bruton helpfully noted that savings of as much as a billion could be made by stopping dividends. Truly we were living in a different country.

Burton meanwhile expressed concerns over the fact that the deal was being negotiated by a civil service elite responsible for debacles such as the Residential Institutions Redress Scheme.

A bullish Michael Mulcahy of Fianna Fáil, however, dismissed their calls for three experts to report every six months to the Committee of Public Accounts. In a statement he too would probably prefer to forget, Mulcahy said:

> We have people of the highest ability in the Central Bank and in the Financial Regulator's office, and I will be damned if we are going to hire more people. It is an insult to these people to say they are not capable of providing expertise.

On Thursday morning, in a manner typical of the Cowen era, the story moved on to another disaster. In the Dáil, Gilmore noted that 'yesterday, while we were all in here working, a report was published that showed we have the highest rise of unemployment in the history of the state.'

The response to this human tragedy was even more typical, as that debased piece of political currency Mary Harney jeered about how the Labour Party 'did not don the green jersey'. It was a witless comment from a politician whose credit rating would soon resemble that of the banks.

Chapter 46 ～

IRELAND HAS 'TURNED THE CORNER'

9 December 2009

It was a time when, increasingly, the future of the nation was seen to be in the hands of one man. A series of appalling political blunders meant that confidence in Brian Cowen had utterly evaporated. As the economy imploded it looked more and more like we were experiencing our own unique version of GUBU economics. In a reprise of the horror show of the 1980s the emergency budget, mass emigration and unemployment had all returned like the dormant spores of some long-forgotten blight. Cowen's claims on his inauguration about where we were as a country had collapsed like a house of cards. Worse still, a Taoiseach who appeared to be as connected to the plight of his people as an absentee Famine landlord was being revealed to be a man of straw.

The most chilling development of all was the establishment of the National Asset Management Agency. This unique economic nightmare, described by Enda Kenny as a 'secret society' combining the worst economic excesses of communism and civil service interference in the economy, was a tacit admission that the banks, contrary to all claims by the Government at the time of the guarantee, were bust.

It was becoming clear that Ireland was entering a dangerous end game, but in a final desperate attempt to place a barrier in the way of the avalanche of bad news, Brian Lenihan attempted to revitalise the spirit of the nation. In a budget offering the salt and ashes of €4 billion in cuts and a prophecy of 75,000 more people on the dole, however, the only weapon he had was words. His infamous 'We have turned the corner' declaration did echo throughout the world, but no-one believed it, and in truth even the minister was dubious in his secret heart.

For now, though, there was no sign of doubt in what was as ebullient a speech as the Charge of the Light Brigade. Lenihan began by recalling that 'when I presented the supplementary budget to this house last April I said we could work our way through this period of severe economic distress.' The next promise—'Today I can report that, notwithstanding the difficulties of the past eight months, we are now on the road to economic recovery'—was hopeful even by the high standards of optimism embedded in the Lenihan genes, and it was greeted by what is kindly recorded as 'interruptions'. But he was undaunted.

> It is of enormous benefit that the main political parties in this house share a common understanding of the extent of our difficulties, and even if we disagree on how to solve our problems our agreement on the amount of savings required sends a powerful signal to the rest of the world that we are able and willing to put our own house in order.

It was at this point, however, that the script started to veer towards fantasy. Lenihan claimed that although our 'self-confidence as a nation has been shaken, the Government's strategy over the past eighteen months is working, and we can now see the first signs of a recovery here at home and in the main international markets.' There had been, in his view, 'bold, decisive and innovative steps' that had been 'commended by international bodies such as the European Central Bank, the European Commission, the IMF and the OECD.'

Little did Lenihan—or, for that matter, anyone else—know that we would be having a very different relationship with the ECB less than a year later. Although hope continued to be the theme, with Lenihan stating that the measures taken had also 'won the approval of the international markets', the markets, with the active connivance of the ECB, would soon force Ireland to accept a bail-out and the loss of the state's sovereignty.

But this cruel dénouement was a long way from Lenihan's mind. Instead, now that we were 'in a position to stabilise the deficit', he was planning to 'rebuild our nation's self-confidence here at home and our reputation abroad.' A series of infamous phrases that would haunt his political career rolled off the silver-tongued barrister's lips. Lenihan claimed that 'the worst is over . . . The international economy has exited recession.' More ironically still, he expressed the belief that 'recent indicators suggest that economic activity in this country is turning the corner.' In a phrase carrying eerie echoes of those stupid First World War generals in 1916, Lenihan cited his department's expectation of a 'return to positive growth within the next six to nine months' and promised that we were facing into the 'last big push of this crisis'.

He cited the positive result of the second referendum on the Lisbon Treaty and said that 'the single currency has provided huge protection and support to Ireland in the current crisis' by preventing 'speculative attacks on our country' and by providing funding to the banking system. As Lenihan pledged that we would never again 'return to a position where all of our income taxes go to pay interest on the national debt,' an ominous hue entered the speech in the warning that 'international debt markets have become more crowded and more fragile.'

The mood wasn't improved by the delicate introduction of such concepts as water meters and property tax, which would be used to stabilise the deficit 'in a fair way', but the genesis of the fiscal debacle Lenihan was struggling to combat was contained in the part of the speech in which he tried to save Fianna Fáil's progressive image.

He proudly stated that 'since 1997 we have made great strides in expanding the level of public service provision. We did so out of the best of motives and in response to public demand.' But while the minister claimed that 'the Government is proud of its unrivalled record in increasing the level of social welfare payments,' whereby 'over the last twelve years we have increased pension rates by approximately 120 per cent, unemployment benefits by almost 130 per cent and child benefit payments by over 330 per cent,' others thought he was actually unveiling an unprecedented record of fiscal recklessness.

This view wasn't at all undermined by his claim that 'the cost of living has increased by about 40 per cent over the same period.' As he described how Fianna Fáil and, more astonishingly still, the PDS had 'extended coverage, removed barriers and increased entitlements such that the level and extent of social welfare payments has been transformed beyond recognition,' it was clear that the much-trumpeted 15 per cent pay cut for ministers and secretaries-general of departments wouldn't make much of a dent in this lot.

Such was the feeling of despair within the chamber that Lenihan even tried to invoke the ghost of JFK. The country, he admitted, had 'taken a step back', but Lenihan, referring to the death that year of Ted Kennedy, recalled how 'the inauguration of John F. Kennedy as president of the United States in 1961 gave a powerful sense of hope, possibility and self-belief to Irish people all over the world.' As Lenihan observed that a recent survey commissioned by the *Irish Times* found that 84 per cent of those surveyed 'thought Ireland needs to start believing in itself again,' it would have seemed almost impolite to suggest that there was a slight difference between the inspirational qualities of a JFK and a BIFFO.

The shrewdly optimistic Lenihan believed that the realisation that the 'plan is working' and that 'the innate advantages that brought us the boom have survived the downturn' could precipitate such a national renewal. Despite all his efforts, there was more than a slight air of desperation in his repetition of the fact that 'we have in place a plan to take us forward on the path of sustainable economic growth.'

As Lenihan promised that 'unemployment will not be as high as previously forecast,' James Reilly of Fine Gael caught the doubtful mood in the Dáil best in his query, 'Is this another call to patriotic action?' And when Lenihan concluded with the final infamous claim of 'our plan is working. We have turned the corner. I commend the budget to the house,' the reality of where the Government really stood was evident in the taunts after this final promise. As the Fianna Fáil TDs sat resolutely on their hands, Fine Gael and the Labour Party shouted, 'Stand up, stand up,' and Michael Ring chortled, 'Where is the standing ovation this year? Where is the Fianna Fáil choir?'

Richard Bruton was, as ever, both eloquent and prescient, noting that,

> instead of the minister taking the radical steps to recondition an engine that this Government has brought to a standstill, ordinary people are being told to get out and push. That is not fair and is not sufficiently visionary to address the scale of the problems we now face.

Once again the minister had gone back to the 'old reliable of slashing investment not only this year and last year but next year and the following year.' Bruton warned that 'we have never seen an economy come out of depression by slashing investment—the sort of investment that should be creating infrastructure fit for a modern age'. Rather like Mr Haughey, who also had little time for having accountants as Ministers for Finance, Bruton slammed an 'accountant's budget' that was nothing more than 'a recipe for staying in this hole for the next year, looking to the same people for the same sacrifices.'

Bruton claimed that 'we have to break out of this vicious cycle in the public finances,' and 'slide-rule accountancy will not crack it.' As an example of this he noted of the €4 billion in cuts that the 75,000 more people Lenihan forecast would be on the dole 'will cost €1.5 billion in lost revenue . . . Interest on the debt will rise by €2 billion next year, that is, €3.5 billion of the €4 billion that he has pushed people so hard to deliver has just been wiped away.'

Joan Burton, opposition spokesperson on finance, meanwhile observed that, having last month 'had the establishment of NAMA—which was in many ways the bail-out of the guilty, who, aided and abetted by the Fianna Fáil party, drove the economy to ruin—today we have the slaughter of the innocents.' She suggested that, given the time that was in it, 'Fianna Fáil's hit single for Christmas will be "I Saw NAMA Killing Santa Claus",' and she warned parents that 'child benefit is being cut to pay for the bail-out of the banks and developers. That is where the hole is in the budget.'

Kieran O'Donnell of Fine Gael—who was to set the unwanted record of being the shortest-lived opposition spokesperson on finance, being appointed and then resigning and backing the wrong horse (Bruton) in two days during the Kenny heave—warned that the Government couldn't 'bluff its way out'.

Cowen was going to have a damn good try, though, and he warned that the Labour Party 'advocates a new top rate of tax which would mean an effective marginal rate of 59 per cent, which is a reversion to the failed policies of a more socialist past'. Ironically, with the Universal Social Charge his Government would come as close as made no difference to imposing a similar rate in its final budget. Cowen then proudly noted that 'over the next two years we will be spending over €100 billion in this country,' adding that the continuing confidence of the outside world in this country was epitomised by those who 'invest in our capacity as a country by buying our government bonds. They would not be buying these if they did not have confidence in our capacity to recover and did not believe we possess the will to do so.'

Enda Kenny attempted to be positive with the claim that 'the budget may or may not contain all the answers to our economic problems, but it has the appearance of an honest and credible attempt to meet the country's need, that is, to kick-start the restoration of stability, opportunity and competitiveness.' He expressed the hope that we would be 'able to look back on the supplementary budget of April 2009 as the first step in our recovery from economic disaster.' However, he warned the minister that, for all his talk of having turned the corner, 'when the Government faces the wrath of the electorate in the next one hundred weeks it will get its answer in no uncertain terms.'

In fact—and it wasn't necessarily good news for Enda—the electorate would have their say a lot sooner.

Chapter 47 ~

DARKNESS FALLS

23 November 2010

For a brief, flickering moment it even looked as though it might work. As late as March 2010 government bonds were still selling for 4.426 per cent. The exchanges between Government and opposition had become increasingly ferocious in the wake of Eamon Gilmore's claim that Brian Cowen had been guilty of 'economic treason'. Yet normality prevailed to such an extent that Brian Lenihan was emboldened to make his infamous 'riots in the streets' comment, stating that 'our partners in Europe' were 'amazed at our capacity to take pain'.

The auguries began to change in May as Greece went into melt-down. The emergence of Morgan Kelly, brandishing the warning that 'it is no longer a question of whether Ireland will go bust but when,' may even have terrified the Government even more. The skies darkened still further when, in August, the Government finally admitted that the bailing out of Anglo alone would cost €22¼ billion.

As Irish bond prices began to slide, Cowen assured us with his usual prescience that this was all part of the 'ebb and flow' of the market. The truth was that Ireland was attracting some most unwelcome attention, as the medicine wasn't working. In the end it was a very European *coup d'état*, with some input from the US Secretary of the Treasury, Tim Geithner. All the groundwork had been done behind closed doors, where the ECB had slowly turned the ratchet on a bewildered, frightened Irish state that had just been forced to leave the bond markets.

It was also a very Cowenesque crisis. The Government had attempted to peddle the illusion that leaving the bond markets was merely a temporary little inconvenience for a state that was fully funded until the middle of the following year. And in typical Cowen style the truth was kept from the people until it was unavoidable.

Two defining images stand out from that time. One was of a pair of ministerial stumblebums, Dermot Ahern and Noel Dempsey, shaking their heads grimly at the prospect of any bail-out. The other was the moment the 'good civil servant' Patrick Honohan went on 'Morning Ireland' and told the people the truth Cowen either didn't have the stomach for or didn't trust them enough to say.

In the aftermath of the IMF's arrival, Michael Noonan, Fine Gael spokesperson on finance, wasn't exaggerating when he said it was the worst of times for any government since the Civil War. A Fine Gael leader who had resigned from that post half way though the 2002 election count on the RTE news knew everything there was to know about political hard times, but even his travails were a summer picnic compared with what this Government was experiencing.

None of the new half-language of 'adjustments' and 'partnership' could cast a veil over Ireland's status as the pauper of Europe, nor could it disguise the fact that such was the level of the justified collapse of faith in Fianna Fáil that an electorate desperately seeking 'stability' actively welcomed the entry of the IMF.

The Dáil, though strangely calm, was actually in the sort of shock seen in those stags that, even when shot, continue to run for a brief period before the final collapse. The flag might not have been flying at half mast, but it really should have been, for Mr Cowen had lost the state its independence.

His colossal political squandermania also lost him his coalition partners, though the Green Party had offered the wretched Government a stay of execution until after the budget. Mind you, significant elements of Fianna Fáil were hard-pressed to know whether this was a blessing or a curse.

In the Dáil Enda Kenny warned that 'in the past week we have seen the authority of and trust in this Government evaporate.' Having been told there was 'no need for any outside intervention or help with regard to a bail-out, people have watched in horror as the IMF, the ECB and the European Commission arrived in Dublin.' Now the only thing the Taoiseach could do was to offer 'two dates which can restore certainty and a sense of confidence', the first being 'the date of the budget'.

After Kenny suggested that the following week would be a good start, for the budget at least, a defiant Cowen said, 'As I made clear yesterday, there is no question that the characterisation of clinging to office is my motivation . . . My sole motivation is to ensure that a four-year plan is published, as agreed with the people with whom we are dealing.'

The house and, more significantly still, his own party, however, were tiring of specious country-solicitor legalisms about how

> last weekend I refuted specific reports that were put to me and which were untrue at the time. The first of these was the report that we had applied to join a facility. I felt it was very important to confirm that this was not the case.

As a response it really was the epitome of the now-debased politics of 'if you don't ask the right question, don't expect a truthful answer.'

The detachment from reality was, again, grotesque, with Cowen claiming that 'it was unusual that a Government which had been pre-funded until July would have to consider applying for this facility' and stating that the current debacle had been caused by the 'abnormality in the market situation and the perception or view of the G7 and of our EU partners and others.' Once again, disaster was the fault of everyone from the EU to the bond markets, but none of it had anything to do with our BIFFO.

The reinvention of history continued. Cowen claimed that while our 'room for manoeuvre was constrained or limited, what we were trying to do was to ensure we were not bounced into a situation.' In the world according to BIFFO, at least, we had 'looked at the situation calmly, worked with colleagues, listened to concerns and made sure the parameters of the decision we were about to take were consistent with what was best for the country in the circumstances.'

For Kenny what was at stake was 'certainty, stability and the confidence of our people,' and he criticised the claims by some ministers that there might not be an election until April or May. It wasn't perhaps consoling that the only solution the opposition had to the great Irish debacle was to put themselves in government, but Kenny was right to ask, 'Does the Taoiseach have any concept of the reaction this creates in respect of uncertainty?'

The nub of Gilmore's questions was, essentially, 'When will you be going?' He slammed the situation in which the 'governor of the Central Bank told members on Thursday on radio what the Taoiseach should have told them earlier in the week.' The sense that we were talking about a political corpse intensified as Gilmore bluntly asked:

What is the Taoiseach's timeline . . . In particular, when does he envisage the finance bill being presented, voted on and enacted? . . . Since one party in Government already has semi-detached itself from the Government, and because I have heard statements from some independent members who have loyally supported the Government over the past three years that suggest such loyal and continued support may be, at least, in doubt, does the Taoiseach consider that the Government has a sufficient majority to put through the financial resolutions of the budget on budget night itself?

Cowen, with some desperation, attempted to hang on to the normality of the past by talking about the 'November tax returns being an important part of the construction of any budget.' He then noted:

The discussions that have been undertaken with the European Union and the institutions concerned both since the Government formally applied on

Sunday and the focused discussions since Thursday, when they arrived here, are based on, and [are] in the context of, a publication of a four-year plan this week and the ratification of a budget on 7 December.

It was cruelly clear that Ireland didn't really have a choice about whether it would pass a budget or not.

Instead the country was now visibly slipping out of our hands as Cowen said the budget was 'being introduced on the 7th of December for the valid reasons I have given' and pleaded that he wasn't 'trying to be difficult'.

Joan Burton, however, sharply noted of the bail-out that

the proposal that this would merit a mere ninety-minute debate in the Dáil is unbecoming to the Constitution and the people of Ireland. The Taoiseach himself needs to come to the house and explain in detail to the people what his cabinet signed off on, by way of a virtual meeting and video-conference of finance ministers.

Enraged, she added:

Under the proposed arrangements the Labour Party would have one fifteen-minute speaking slot, and only the Minister for Finance would speak for the Government.

After the Ceann Comhairle attempted in vain to chastise Burton for her 'disorderly and inappropriate' behaviour (it being apparently appropriate to debate a national bail-out in ninety minutes), Caoimhghín Ó Caoláin of Sinn Féin poured more oil on the fire, bellowing that the Taoiseach had 'not got the support of either his own party or his coalition partners' and that he 'should have gone to the Park yesterday evening if not a long time before'. In a rare shaft of wit he added that the Green Party was 'the only example I can think of from history where rats have given notice of their intention to abandon the sinking ship some weeks or months in advance.'

After Cowen claimed that 'there will be other opportunities to address this as matters develop' in the debate itself, an astonishingly sanguine Lenihan welcomed 'the opportunity to provide the house with information' about what he chastely called 'developments'. He then assured everyone that 'all deposits in Irish banks are secure' and claimed that 'the initiative for requesting this assistance, both from the European Union and the IMF, rests with the member-state.' In a statement at considerable variance with his subsequent claims that Ireland had been bullied into the deal, Lenihan said 'there is no arrangement whereby a member-state can be invited by the European Commission or the ECB to request such assistance.' Instead, as he had 'told the house last Thursday, we agreed with our euro-area colleagues at the Euro Group meeting on the 16th of November to hold a short and focused consultation between the Irish authorities and the Commission, the ECB and the IMF.'

The purpose of this had apparently been to 'determine the best way to provide any necessary support to address market risks, especially relating to the banking sector, in the context of the four-year budgetary plan and the upcoming budget.' This, Lenihan claimed, 'proved to be very constructive and positive engagement and dialogue. The Government then met on Sunday afternoon to consider the outcome of the engagement' and, just like that, 'agreed to request financial support from the European Union, the euro-area member-states and the IMF in the context of a joint EU-IMF programme.'

Time would show that Lenihan's outwardly blasé approach concealed turbulent emotions. For now, though, this surrender of a state's sovereignty was described as support to be provided 'under a strong policy programme' that would 'address the budgetary challenges of the Irish economy in a decisive manner.' He tried to talk the tombstone up by noting that the EU had pointed to 'the strong fundamentals of the Irish economy.' The genie, however, was let out of the bottle when Lenihan admitted that 'the provision of financial assistance to Ireland is necessary not only to support our banking and budgetary situation but also to safeguard financial stability in the European Union and the euro area.'

This was a deal that had been done in the interest of Europe, not of the Republic. And unlike the conclusion of so many of Lenihan's other speeches, the drab final observations that 'our strong underlying economic performance, combined with the fiscal correction and reform measures contained in the plan to be published tomorrow, will provide the foundation for recovery', together with his claim that 'we will emerge from this programme as a vigorous economy and nation once more,' suggested that Lenihan knew his political death warrant was about to be signed.

Michael Noonan cut to the core of the issue by noting that it was 'an appalling situation where, after running our own affairs for so many years, the Minister for Finance had to go and plead with our colleagues in Europe to come to the assistance of the country.' There was no doubt in Noonan's mind that we could have resolved our own difficulties, but the banks were 'the straw, the bale of straw or the lorryload of straw which broke the camel's back.' They had driven Lenihan

> into the arms of his European colleagues and across the Atlantic to ask the IMF in Washington to come to our assistance. That was a humiliating request for the minister, the cabinet and the country. While his colleagues have not shown any sense of shame, I hope he is suitably embarrassed.

Noonan slammed the extraordinary management of the period preceding the request, during which ministers had ended up in a situation where, 'to put it bluntly, they were either lying through their teeth or they had not been briefed.' He didn't know 'what kind of cabinet has been operating if ministers of long standing were not in the loop,' but given 'that it was certainly embarrassing to watch, it must have been excruciating for the people concerned.' The Green Party came in for a bit of stick as well as Noonan recalled how he had been 'in Governments which broke up', but when 'the Labour Party deputies decided to go they went. This crowd decided to go but stayed.'

After Noonan took the political carving knife to a party that has 'no confidence in the Government' but that wants to 'hang around for another two months,' one could hardly have thought it would get any worse for Cowen and his addled team.

In fact, miraculously, it did, as members of a party that had sold the country into slavery roused themselves enough to complain at the breach of parliamentary etiquette in which Noonan had used the 'lying' word. Noonan magisterially said, 'I withdraw it. They made a series of untruthful statements through their teeth.'

Lenihan conceded that the charge 'was not said with venom', but Joan Burton sank her teeth deeply into his unprotected flank, asking, 'Will the minister tell us at this point what is the amount of the loan, the assistance and the facilities he and the Government propose to seek?' She warned of the Government's continuing love affair with austerity that 'there is no economy in the world of which I am aware where such deflation has succeeded' and added, 'The Great Leap Forward—or whatever it was called—practised at various times by the Soviet Union and China . . . They were accompanied by terrible sufferings in the societies in question.' Burton asked, 'How will the minister deflate this economy back to recovery? It has never been done in economic history.' Instead, according to Burton, we needed to 'grow and recover'. That way we could 'pay the astonishing debts from the banks that have sunk us'.

Pat Rabbitte meanwhile responded to an appeal for responsibility on the opposition benches by observing that 'as we speak in the calm of the chamber there is considerable chaos outside. The television news is full of colleagues of the minister threatening bare-fisted quarrels at the Fianna Fáil parliamentary party meeting, and according to the national broadcaster ministers are at loggerheads and pointing fingers.'

Although the Ceann Comhairle Séamus Kirk wailed about how we were 'under time constraints', the unreality was to continue. Cowen claimed that the four-year plan would act as 'a signpost and a pathway to recovery' that would end the 'frenzy of doubt'.

The reality, however, was captured by the Taoiseach-in-waiting, Kenny, that Thursday. Speaking on the Government's latest National Recovery Plan, he coldly observed that he

> did not know if the Taoiseach saw the television cameras panning across the cabinet during the closing remarks of his speech, but I have never seen such a po-faced, sombre, demotivated and beaten crowd as I saw on that screen . . . Shining from their eyes was not conviction but guilt.

In a poignant codicil to the debate, Lenihan unveiled his inner turmoil. In an interview in the *Irish Times* he recalled

> going to Brussels on the final Monday to sign the agreement and being on my own at the airport and looking at the snow gradually thawing and thinking to myself, 'This is terrible. No Irish minister has ever had to do this before' . . . I had fought for two-and-a-half years to avoid this conclusion. I believed that I had fought the good fight and taken every measure possible to delay such an eventuality, and now hell was at the gates.

Mary Harney, in contrast, felt that 'there is no point in the blame game.' One would have expected nothing more from a politician whose capacity for political escapology rivalled that of Mr Ahern.

Chapter 48 ∾

'WHERE DO WE LEAVE OUR CVS FOR ALL THESE JOBS?'

19 January 2011

The date is Wednesday 19 January, and to all intents and purposes Brian Cowen, the Taoiseach who will go down in history as BIFFO, for once appears to be in charge of his game. Though an internal motion of no confidence in the Fianna Fáil leader has been beaten off, the opposition is inevitably unimpressed. Eamon Gilmore notes that the Taoiseach

> does not enjoy the confidence of a majority of the members of the house
> . . . Some nine out of every ten people in the country have no confidence
> in the Government and want it out of office. The Green Party has clearly
> lost confidence in the future of the Government, because it has announced
> its intended withdrawal from it. Some ministers have clearly lost
> confidence in the ability of the Government to be re-elected, because they
> do not propose to stand for re-election . . . Several of the Taoiseach's
> parliamentary colleagues voted no confidence in him yesterday. Others
> would have done the same, but they thought the timing was wrong.

It was a long list, but for once Cowen was in buoyant humour. He lambasted Gilmore, saying he did not

> know how the deputy intends to instil confidence when he continues to be
> one of the foremost spokespersons for the negativity industry in the
> country . . . He uses phrases such as 'stuck in the mire', 'economic corpse'
> and 'banjaxed'.

After our friend 'interruptions' made a brief appearance on the record, a happy Cowen said he would not accept Deputy Gilmore's confidence motion . . . [because] even Fine Gael thought it was stupid. It was a stunt last Saturday in an effort to see if the deputy could get his face in the paper for Sunday.

For once there were smiles on the Fianna Fáil benches as Cowen chortled about how he knew

> the day would come when Deputy Kenny would realise that a no-confidence motion in this Government was ill-timed and ill-judged . . . I will tell deputies one thing: they are worth it. It is worth coming in here for half an hour.

In the aftermath of the 2011 election the understated Seán O'Rourke captured the essence of what followed as he compared the final death throes of the Cowen administration to a 'rollercoaster ride through hell'. The last debacle began at half five that evening. Cowen initially called in the resignation of Mary Harney, which had been discussed since November. From that point all that was missing was a President smiling like 'moonlight on a tombstone', as the resignations of Dermot Ahern, Noel Dempsey, Tony Killeen and Batt O'Keeffe were sent to the President before midnight.

There was something typical about the spectacle where, now that it was about to collapse, the Taoiseach had decided to freshen up his Government. Sadly, as six ministers went, and as there were two more still to go, it didn't quite work, as, in scenes never before seen, TDs turned down appointments to the Government.

The final moments in Government Buildings on Thursday morning were pathetic. John Gormley asked, 'Has the President accepted the resignations?' and in a desperate attempt to keep some sort of show on the road asked Cowen to 'call the Áras' to try and reverse them.

Brian Lenihan, who would have had bad memories of a different set of phone calls to the Áras, made the somewhat unlikely declaration to Gormley: 'You can bully Fianna Fáil, but you won't bully the President of Ireland.'

But it was, as ever, too late, and soon Cowen had two more resignations from the Green Party to add to a very long list.

The most illuminating encounter of all came in a final meeting of Gormley and Cowen in the Taoiseach's ante-room. Cowen noted of his shreds and patches of a Government, 'That's all that's left, thanks to you.' Even to the end this most addled of all our Taoisigh was utterly unaware of the extent of his collusion in his own fate.

On that chaotic morning things weren't going much better elsewhere. A Dáil by turns agitated and angry was trying to decipher the muddled entrails of the maddest Government reshuffle in the history of the state. That poor, hapless fool of a Tánaiste, Mary Coughlan, hopefully suggested that the house might like to deal with 'number 19, Communications Regulation (Postal Services) Bill (2010)', while the Ceann Comhairle even more prayerfully said, 'There are no proposals to be put to the house.' But on a day on which half the ministries were vacant the opposition had very different ideas.

As Tom Hayes of Fine Gael sardonically asked, 'Where do we leave our cvs for all these jobs?' Enda Kenny noted that 'due to the antiquated standing orders that operate in here, I am precluded from making a proposal to change the order of business.' He then asked, 'Where is the Taoiseach this morning? Why is he not in the chamber of the heart of our democracy to tell us what is going on?' After one TD cruelly noted that 'he is looking for a minister', Kenny added that 'in the long history of this state this situation has never obtained previously, where almost half of the cabinet have resigned.' Kenny was gilding the lily with the claim that 'this was plotted and planned to some extent for the past couple of weeks.' However, he was on somewhat surer ground with the claim that 'the junior partners in the Government have been treated with contempt.'

By now things were beginning to resemble a French farce. Kenny pointed out that 'we do not know . . . whether technically there is a minister in charge of the Department of Justice and Law Reform, the Department of Transport or the Department of Health and Children, where there is a constitutional requirement to have a minister in charge of these departments.'

This, he warned, 'would not have happened even in the days of great dictators.'

As Coughlan stared despairingly at the ceiling it was clear that Kenny was asking the wrong person if he wanted to find out what was going on. The Taoiseach-in-waiting succinctly analysed the state of play and told a bewildered Tánaiste:

> These are the last days of the worst Government in the history of the state . . . It is a cowardly, disgraceful act of the Taoiseach, Deputy Brian Cowen, in refusing to come in here today to tell the people of his country what is happening with a Government that has imploded, is dysfunctional, has disintegrated and let our people down.

Gilmore wondered if Coughlan could

> tell us who has resigned or who is about to resign. Can the full list of resignees be told to us? . . . If the Garda Commissioner or the Chief of Staff of the army has a serious issue of security or of crime to deal with this morning, to whom do they report?

The hapless Ceann Comhairle attempted to move the business on from the apparently minor issue of our missing Government. But he was dismissed by a fuming Gilmore, who snapped:

> I am sorry if I am keeping you from your coffee and biccies . . . [but] the idea that the Tánaiste can come in here and announce that the order of business is the Communications Regulation (Postal Services) Bill, in circumstances where the Government is disintegrating, is eccentric.

After Brendan Howlin chipped in with the fairly obvious suggestion that 'members need to know who is the Minister for Justice and Law Reform—this is a basic question,' an utterly addled Ceann Comhairle took the most sensible option and suspended the Dáil for fifteen minutes.

The chaos continued when the TDs returned. Kenny told the Dáil that he had sent 'the Taoiseach a letter to the effect that it would be appropriate that he attend the house and informed the people and the country what responsibilities various ministers reputed to have resigned now hold.'

Further drama, as if it were needed, wasn't long in coming. Kenny said he understood that, 'as we speak, the Green Party leadership is now in direct contact with the Taoiseach, and I understand the Taoiseach is in Government Buildings.'

A by now despairing Ceann Comhairle suspended the sitting at 11:40 a.m. until 1:30 p.m., at which time Cowen insouciantly wandered in with the air of a man wondering what all the fuss was about. He casually observed that the President, 'acting on my advice, has accepted the resignations of Mary Harney, Noel Dempsey, Dermot Ahern, Batt O'Keeffe and Tony Killeen as members of the Government.' The number of disappeared ministers rose to six, Cowen adding that he had advised the house yesterday about the resignation of Micheál Martin. The good news was that Health was being reassigned to Mary Coughlan, Transport to Pat Carey and Justice to Brendan Smith.

Cowen then noted of the lost ministers that he wanted to put 'on the record of the house my gratitude to each of them for their distinguished contributions to the work of the Government and the country.' And, amazingly, he then did.

The white flag then finally and definitely went up as Cowen said, 'It is my intention in due course to seek a dissolution of Dáil Éireann, with a view to a general election taking place on Friday the 11th of March next.' He added that Fianna Fáil would 'go to the country with a strong front-bench line-up that will put the case of this party to secure the future of our country and to stay with the policies which will bring us success.' Though Cowen promised he would 'not back down from such a challenge now or in the future,' he wouldn't even get that far.

Gratitude, alas, even for the election, was conspicuous by its absence, and it was even harder to discern a week later when, on 25 January, the Taoiseach sombrely announced 'for the information of the Dáil that on Sunday the 23rd of January 2011 the President, on my advice, accepted the resignations of Deputy John Gormley and Deputy Eamon Ryan as members of the Government.' Cowen then assigned the Department of the Environment to Éamon Ó Cuív and the Department of Communications to Pat Carey.

After Cowen, who had resigned the leadership of Fianna Fáil, noted that he had also accepted the resignations of Ciarán Cuffe and Mary White, the Fine Gael backbencher Pádraic McCormack, as was his wont, got under the Taoiseach's skin, snapping, 'They will be a big loss.'

Kenny, who was acquiring more authority by the minute, summed up the desolate state of the rump of this dying Government.

> I have never before attended a Dáil with such a depleted number of ministers on the Government benches. I have never before faced a group of ministers with such enormous constitutional responsibilities on their shoulders.

There was a final desperate attempt at defiance. Cowen tried to claim that, 'despite the fact that we are reduced in number, the workload of the Government is being taken on board by its members.' As the rest of the Dáil wondered what planet this man was now residing on, he claimed that Fianna Fáil wasn't trying to 'cling to office' and that this was actually a Government 'seeking to discharge its responsibilities to the country'.

It all came to a bitter end when the poor, tortured Cowen slammed the 'vacuous, stupid' questioning of his mandate after Pearse Doherty snapped that 'the Taoiseach's mandate disappeared on Sunday.' The astonishing nature of the fall of the 'anointed one' was epitomised by Cowen's plea that he expected that 'basic respect and courtesy will be accorded to me, even if it comes from the most unlikely quarters.' There weren't many takers.

In the end, nothing captured the essence of those despairing days so well as the moment in the aftermath of Cowen's resignation that previous Sunday as leader of Fianna Fáil when Mary Coughlan, the designated Marie Antoinette of the Government, was left waiting on the street for her state car. Her recorded snap of 'Where the fuck is my car?' meant it could at least be said that they were loyal to the trappings of power right up to the deluge.

Chapter 49 ⌒

MR COWEN SIPS FROM THE BITTER CUP FOR A FINAL TIME

1 February 2011

History may yet record it as the last day a Fianna Fáil leader sat in the Taoiseach's seat. But just before he flitted from public life Brian Cowen spoke for one last time in the public theatre of the nation. As his party shivered waiting for the inevitable deluge, Cowen began his valedictory address by noting that 'fifty years ago, almost to the day, on the 30th of January 1961, President John F. Kennedy delivered his first state of the union message, noting that the members of the Congress "were among [his] oldest friends, and this house is [his] oldest home".'

Only someone with such an utter lack of self-awareness as Cowen could, given his status as the last, bloated scion of a dead party, seek to gather such a symbol of hope about himself. Kennedy had created Camelot. Cowen, in contrast, had turned the nation into a fiscal charnel house.

Yet there was a modicum of truth in the analogy as Cowen noted that 'these words resonate with me here today. I have made many friends in this house and this parliament, and its traditions will always have my deepest respect.' The enclosed safety of Leinster House was, in truth, the closest thing Cowen had to a home. And at a deeper level Cowen's identification with Kennedy was undoubtedly informed by JFK's status, in common with the Pope and the Sacred Heart of Jesus, as an icon for the gauche, contentedly impoverished, unquestioning Ireland of the late 1950s, which was Cowen's personal nirvana.

In the sullen chamber a Taoiseach who was more governed by sentiment than was recognised added that those friends, who were frankly conspicuous by their absence, 'go beyond politics and any debates or disagreements that we may have had about the issues of the day.' It was for that reason that 'I decided to come to the house so that the thirtieth Dáil could conclude in plenary assembly.'

As the last grains of sand ran through the darkened glass of Cowen's political career, few even in that Dáil could argue with his claim that 'my overriding objective was to do my best by the Irish people.' We were even offered a rare glimpse into his secret soul as Cowen quoted

> the wise words of a man I came to know through his friendship with my late uncle . . . I refer to the poet and philosopher John O'Donohue, whose book 'Benedictus' contains a poem called 'For a Leader'. I recommend it to all in the house and particularly to those who will be in positions of leadership in the thirty-first Dáil.

What followed was loaded with accidental ironies. Cowen urged his successor to

> have the grace and wisdom to act kindly, learning to distinguish between what is personal and what is not.
> May you be hospitable to criticism.
> May you never put yourself at the centre of things.
> May you act not from arrogance but out of service.
> May you work on yourself, building up and refining the ways of your mind.
> May those who work for you know you see and respect them.
> May you learn to cultivate the art of presence in order to engage with those who meet you.
> May you have a mind that loves frontiers, so that you can evoke the bright fields that lie beyond the view of the regular eye.
> May you have good friends to mirror your blind spots.
> May leadership be for you a true adventure of growth.

The tragedy for poor Cowen was of course that he possessed none of those qualities. And even in these final minutes his defining trait of estrangement from reality continued to be the dominant theme. The politically bankrupt Taoiseach of a fiscally bankrupt country lugubriously observed that

> today is not a day for me to list achievements or engage in contentious debate . . . Politics is about serving the interests of the people first and last . . . and I stayed true to it right to the very end.

The Taoiseach also retained his capacity for reciting indigestible reams of statistics that bore no relation to the world the rest of the country resided in. So it was that the speaking political ghost claimed that 'Ireland's economy retains very significant strengths'. We were 'the fifth-best country in the world, as measured by the United Nations human development index', we had 'the highest proportion of graduates in the European Union among the 25 to 34 years age group', and our exports were 'performing better than ever.'

On and on went the list about American investment in Ireland being 'greater than what it has invested in Brazil, Russia, India and China combined,' about Ireland's stock of direct inward investment, about improved competitiveness and about our 'clusters of the world's leading international companies, including household names such as IBM, Google, eBay, Intel and Facebook.'

After Cowen claimed that 'Ireland is consistently in the world's top ten places in which to open, start and grow a business,' you would in truth wonder why after that grandiose list everyone wanted him to go. Cowen, as he reluctantly sat down, certainly did.

It would have been normal at that stage for kindly wishes to be expressed for the departing Taoiseach. But on the last day, on which the Fianna Fáil benches would be thronged, the game had moved on much too far for sentiment. There was a brief moment of light in a touching personal observation by Enda Kenny.

> I wish the Taoiseach, his wife, Mary, and daughters, Sinéad and Maedhbh, well as he retires from this house. Last year I sat beside little Maedhbh at the national celebration in Kilmainham. When the Taoiseach came in with a guard of honour I asked her, 'Who is that man?' and she said, 'That's my Daddy.' The Taoiseach has one strong supporter there, and rightly so.

From then on, however, the mood was set by Kenny's claim that the Taoiseach was

> retiring after leading what many people consider to have been the worst Government in living memory . . . His colleagues in Fianna Fáil are required to be accountable for their collective governance of this country . . . None of them will be able to dodge responsibility for driving Ireland into the arms of the IMF.

The aspirant Taoiseach, in contrast, hoped to 'replace old government cynicism with new government compassion, and old government indifference with new government insights.' Fine Gael would, he said, 'replace the old dysfunction and disorder at the heart of government with a Government that holds the hearts and the needs of the people within its own heart.'

An unrepentant Eamon Gilmore, who had shocked Cowen to the core with his claim that he had been guilty of economic treason, coldly observed that they had 'clashed in robust debate'. For Gilmore, Cowen had always 'stood by his position, and I have stood by mine, and now the time has come to put our case to the verdict of the people.' He noted that the voters now had a unique opportunity to elect a non-Civil War party, and he sharply told Fianna Fáil that

> government is not a hospitality tent, roped off for VIPS . . . Government is not a big house shielded from the people by high walls. Government is not the business of the insiders: it is the business of us all.

It all ended on an astonishing note. The Ceann Comhairle, Séamus Kirk, said of the outgoing TDs that he would 'like to pay tribute to you now and to thank you for your work, some spanning many, many years. You can be proud of your achievements.'

It was praise that, like so many other events of this unique period, attracted from the outside world nothing more than a stunned contemptuous silence.

EPILOGUE

Chapter 50 ～

HANGING OUT OUR BRIGHTEST COLOURS FOR ENDA

9 March 2011

Comparisons between Dáil Éireann and the surreal world of *Alice in Wonderland* are made too frequently in Irish politics. But on 9 March 2011 not even Lewis Carroll on speed could have dreamt up the tableau that unveiled itself. In 2002 Charlie McCreevy had cruelly summed up the election result with the pithy observation that the electorate had voted out the opposition. They were, less than a decade later, to do a great deal more to Fianna Fáil, and to the Green Party. The harrowing both parties experienced was epitomised by the fate of Brian Cowen's final Government of the damned. Six of them, if we include Cowen, had wisely decided not to run in the election. Along with Cowen's departure, where for the first time an outgoing Taoiseach hadn't faced the judgement of the citizens, Mary Harney had slunk away to a multi-pensioned existence and a fat libel settlement, and Batt O'Keeffe, Dermot Ahern, Tony Killeen and Noel Dempsey also left politics.

Of those who had faced the electorate, the Tánaiste (Mary Coughlan), a possible future leader (Mary Hanafin), the Green Party leader (John Gormley) and his successor (Eamon Ryan) had all lost their seats. The Government chief whip, John Curran, and the Minister of State for Children, Barry Andrews, were also rejected by the electorate, as was Pat Carey.

The only outgoing ministers to return were the seriously ill Brian Lenihan, the peripheral Brendan Smith and the frankly eccentric Éamon Ó Cuív. Micheál Martin had also survived, though by the time the election had been called he had left the Government.

Within the Dáil bullpen a curious collection of independent political curios such as Mattie McGrath, Mick Wallace (a long-haired, near-bankrupt builder), Luke 'Ming' Flanagan (a former cannabis-smoking community activist) and Michael Healy-Rae (son of Jackie) occupied as much space as the decimated ranks of Fianna Fáil, while Sinn Féin, incorporating at least two suspected former members of the Army Council of the IRA, completed the menacing circle that surrounded the cowed Fianna Fáil.

In contrast, that party was faced by a Government that had the biggest majority in the history of the state. Fine Gael had won more Dáil seats than Fianna Fáil for the first time since September 1927, and the Labour Party had won more seats than Fianna Fáil for the first time ever. In 1977 Jack Lynch had spoken warily of the dangers of 'carrying a full jug' when Fianna Fáil had returned with 84 seats. After this election Fine Gael and the Labour Party had a combined total of 113 seats. It was 12 more than the ill-fated Reynolds-Spring Government could muster in 1993. Fine Gael, indeed, had contended for an absolute majority (or, at a minimum, the prospect of single-party government), before the prize was snatched, amidst a final desperate flurry of promises by the Labour Party, from their sweaty palms.

After all that, the unnervingly youthful Simon Harris, just twenty-four, told the Dáil that 'at a time when my generation is faced with the grim prospect of forced emigration, and when unemployment blights our society yet again, we need a Taoiseach determined to restore stability, credibility and hope to this country.' Harris then showed some innocence about the nature of the task in which he was engaged with the claim that 'I am sure that my predecessors who stood here and nominated a person to be Taoiseach have hoped that at the core of a nominee was an honesty and a decency,' for George Colley might have been harbouring slightly different thoughts when he nominated Haughey, and Heaven only knows what Oliver J was thinking when he nominated Garret the Good. Still, Harris's innocence was a change from the smothering darkness of Cowen as he noted that 'the period of mourning is over for Ireland: today we hang out our brightest colours, and together, under Deputy Kenny's leadership, we move forward yet again as a nation.'

Ciara Conway of the Labour Party, who seconded the nomination, lauded the 'historic moment . . . when the two largest parties in the state have joined together in the national interest to form a strong and stable Government . . . [which] will have the strongest mandate in the history of our state.' The air was certainly thick with aspiration as Conway pledged that the Government's purpose now, 'as it was in the democratic programme of the first Dáil, will be to ensure that Ireland's economic strengths are used to benefit all of her people.' Conway promised that,

> in the words of that programme, written by Tom Johnson some ninety-two years ago, our purpose must also be 'to secure that no child shall suffer hunger or cold from lack of food, clothing or shelter' and to provide the 'care of the nation's aged and infirm, who shall not be regarded as a

burden but rather entitled to the nation's gratitude and consideration.'

Fianna Fáil had already made their own bit of unwanted history earlier when, for the first time before an election, they didn't run enough candidates to win a majority. The party would provide a second in the Dáil as a subdued Micheál Martin said a 'habit has developed of nominating people for the position of Taoiseach for the sake of doing so rather than in the belief that the person has a right to assume the office.' Today, however, it was his intention 'to break with that precedent. It is clear that Deputy Kenny has been given a mandate by the people'. In truth, as Fianna Fáil had lost sixty seats, Martin, unless he wanted to turn the nomination into a farce, had no other option.

Joe Higgins introduced a more bracing tone to a debate that was veering dangerously towards the sentimental with his observation that 'the very first sentence of the Programme for Government states that a democratic revolution took place in Ireland on the 25th of February.' The ascetic socialist declared that 'the Oxford dictionary defines "revolution" as the overthrow of a government or social order in favour of a new system,' adding that if this was correct

> the programme presented by Deputy Kenny is a grotesque betrayal of that revolution, because it proposes, almost to the letter, to continue the reactionary programme of the old order of the late and unlamented regime of Fianna Fáil and the Green Party, a regime that was rightly reviled, rejected and sent to oblivion.

Smirks began to fade as Higgins added:

> This is not the first time an Irish political establishment responded to an Irish and Europe-wide crisis by sacrificing its people. Nearly a hundred years ago the forebears of today's speculating European financiers and their political clients plunged into war in a vicious competition for markets, raw materials and profits. The Irish Parliamentary Party of the day will forever be remembered in infamy for its campaign to dragoon a generation of youth to feed the insatiable appetite of the imperial warmakers.

Lest we be left in any doubt, Higgins made it clear that today,

> by sacrificing our people, our services and our youth to feed the equally insatiable appetite of the wolves in the European and world financial markets . . . first Fianna Fáil and the Greens, then Fine Gael and Labour play an equally shameful role as the Irish Parliamentary Party.

The mood was further depressed for the new TDs when Gerry Adams observed that 'it is appropriate that we gather here at the beginning of Lent, given what is coming for the citizens of the state.' In fairness, a dubious Adams did qualify his dog-in-the-manger mood with the pledge that 'if, by fluke, positive proposals are brought forward we will support them.'

One of the consequences of the implosion of Fianna Fáil and the rawness of Sinn Féin was that, when it came to the Dáil looking-glass, a colourful cacophony of independents dominated proceedings to an unwonted degree. Shane Ross at least brought some logic to the affair, pointing out that there were 'so many reviews and fudges that we do not know exactly what is being promised at all, except that the Labour Party and Fine Gael will be the Government over the next few years and will stick together come hell or high water.'

The uncrowned king of the independent mixum-gatherums was typically colourful. Ming Flanagan wished Enda 'the best of luck on behalf of my two children, because if he has good luck and he does well they will not have to take the boat or the aeroplane to London like nineteen out of twenty members of my family and my wife's family.' In a somewhat touching speech he observed:

> I am terrified of the prospect that they will have to take the same road. I am conscious of the fact that parents in Germany, Denmark, Holland, Belgium and other countries do not have to tell their sons or daughters when they turn eighteen that the best thing they can do is leave their country.

After a record vote of 117 to 27 for Kenny it was the winner's turn. The new Taoiseach initially spoke simply about how his Government's tasks were 'rescuing our economy, resuscitating our reputation and restoring our society.' The 'renewal of what political leadership in Ireland should be about' would be a central theme of a Government commencing work in 'the most economically difficult days since Ireland's independence . . . I do not say this to be negative or excusing but to be real and true, to tell the truth of the Ireland of today.'

Kenny got into dangerous territory only when he promised to 'enter into a covenant with the Irish people' that 'in these times of crisis, full of many unknowns, honesty is not alone our best policy but our only policy.' John Bruton had tried that line before, and it had come back to bite him, but Enda was hardly the first emboldened new Taoiseach to promise to 'tell the people the truth regardless of how unwelcome or difficult that might be.' And, in fairness, few could gainsay Kenny's belief that 'the old ways of politics damaged us not alone financially but emotionally, psychologically and spiritually.'

He made sure to describe in detail the damage that had been done, for even Fianna Fáil—well, especially Fianna Fáil—flinched when Kenny said, 'The IMF arrived at our door, and because it did our Republic is betrayed.' Others too had been betrayed.

> Parents are rendered speechless at the sight of their children boarding planes to countries where spring is autumn, and our today is their tomorrow. Employers are traumatised by laying off staff and shutting down businesses. Workers pray for invisibility as they queue for the dole. Families worry that the neighbours might see the Vincent de Paul calling to their door, dreading the postman dropping bills like stealth bombs into the hall.

Ultimately, amidst all the rhetoric about how 'the people and the Government are one again,' perhaps the canniest remark was borrowed from Seamus Heaney: 'You have to try to make sense of what comes. Remember everything and keep your head.'

Still, after the short, bleak Dark Age of Cowen one could almost dare to hope momentarily as Kenny called on us to 'lift our heads, turn our faces to the sun and, as has already been said, hang out our brightest colours.'

BIBLIOGRAPHY

Newspapers and periodicals
Irish Examiner
Irish Independent
Irish Times
Magill
Sunday Independent

Books

Aldous, Richard (ed.), *Great Irish Speeches*, London: Quercus Publishing, 2009.

Arnold, Bruce, *Haughey: His Life and Unlucky Deeds*, London: Harper Collins, 1993.

Arnold, Bruce, and O'Toole, Jason, *The End of the Party: How Fianna Fáil Finally Lost Its Grip on Power*, Dublin: Gill & Macmillan, 2011.

Brennan, Pat, and Kerrigan, Gene, *This Great Little Nation: The A–Z of Irish Scandals and Controversies*, Dublin: Gill & Macmillan, 1999.

Collins, Stephen, *Spring and the Labour Story*, Dublin: O'Brien Press, 1993.

Collins, Stephen, *The Cosgrave Legacy*, Dublin: Blackwater Press, 1996.

Collins, Stephen, *The Power Game: Fianna Fáil since Lemass*, Dublin: O'Brien Press, 2000.

Collins, Stephen (ed.), *Nealon's Guide to the 30th Dáil and 23rd Seanad*, Dublin: Gill & Macmillan, 2007.

Collins, Stephen (ed.), *Nealon's Guide to the 31st Dáil and 24th Seanad*, Dublin: Gill & Macmillan, 2012.

Cooney, John, *Battleship Bertie: Politics in Ahern's Ireland*, Dublin: Blantyremoy Publications, 2008.

Cooper, Matt, *How Ireland Really Went Bust*, Dublin: Penguin Ireland, 2011.

Cooper, Matt, *Who Really Runs Ireland?: The Story of the Elite Who Led Ireland from Bust to Boom . . . and Back Again*, Dublin: Penguin Ireland, 2009.

Cullen, Paul, *With a Little Help from My Friends: Planning Corruption in Ireland*, Dublin: Gill & Macmillan, 2002.

Duignan, Seán, *One Spin on the Merry-Go-Round*, Dublin: Blackwater Press, 1995.

Dunlop, Frank, *Yes, Taoiseach: Irish Politics from Behind Closed Doors*, Dublin: Penguin Ireland, 2004.

Ferriter, Diarmaid, *The Transformation of Ireland, 1900–2000*, London: Profile Books, 2004.

Finlay, Fergus, *Snakes and Ladders*, Dublin: New Island Books, 1998.

Foster, R. F., *Luck and the Irish: A Brief History of Change, c. 1970–2000*, London: Penguin, 2008.

Foster, R. F., *Modern Ireland, 1600–1972*, London: Penguin, 1988.

Garvin, Tom, *Preventing the Future: Why Was Ireland So Poor for So Long?* Dublin: Gill & Macmillan, 2004.

Hannon, Katie, *The Naked Politician*, Dublin: Gill & Macmillan, 2004.

Hannon, Philip, and Jackie, Gallagher (eds.), *Taking the Long View: 70 Years of Fianna Fáil*, Dublin: Blackwater Press, 1996.

Horgan, John, *Noël Browne: Passionate Outsider*, Dublin: Gill & Macmillan, 2000.

Horgan, John, *Seán Lemass: The Enigmatic Patriot*, Dublin: Gill & Macmillan, 1997.

Hussey, Gemma, *At the Cutting Edge: Cabinet Diaries, 1982–1987*, Dublin: Gill & Macmillan, 1990.

Joyce, Joe, and Murtagh, Peter, *The Boss: Charles J. Haughey in Government*, Dublin: Poolbeg Press, 1985.

Kavanagh, Ray, *Spring, Summer and Fall: The Rise and Fall of the Labour Party, 1986–1999*, Dublin: Blackwater Press, 2001.

Keena, Colm, *Bertie: Power and Money*, Dublin: Gill & Macmillan, 2011.

Keena, Colm, *Haughey's Millions: Charlie's Money Trail*, Dublin: Gill & Macmillan, 2001.

Kelly, J. M. (ed. John Flanagan), *Belling the Cats: Selected Speeches and Articles of John Kelly*, Dublin: Moytura Press, in association with Fine Gael, 1992.

Kennedy, Geraldine (ed.), *Nealon's Guide to the 29th Dáil and Seanad*, Dublin: Gill & Macmillan, 2002.

Kenny, Shane, *Go Dance on Somebody Else's Grave*, Dublin: Kildanore Press, 1990.

Keogh, Dermot, *Jack Lynch: A Biography*, Dublin: Gill & Macmillan, 2008.

Leahy, Pat, *Showtime: The Inside Story of Fianna Fáil in Power*, Dublin: Penguin Ireland, 2009.

Lee, Joseph, and Ó Tuathaigh, Gearóid, *The Age of de Valera*, Dublin: Ward River Press, 1982.

Lysaght, Charles (ed.), *The 'Times' Great Irish Lives*, London: Times Books, 2008.

McCarthy, Deirdre (ed.), RTÉ: *The Week in Politics: Election 2011 and the 31st Dáil*, Dublin: RTÉ Publishing, 2012.

McDonald, Frank, and Sheridan, Kathy, *The Builders: How a Small Group of Property Developers Fuelled the Building Boom and Transformed Ireland*, Dublin and New York: Penguin Ireland, 2008.

McLoughlin, Michael (ed.), *Great Irish Speeches of the Twentieth Century*, Dublin: Poolbeg Press, 1996.

Manning, Maurice, *James Dillon: A Biography*, Dublin: Wolfhound Press, 2000.

Minihan, Mary, *Dáil Spats*, Dunshaughlin (Co. Meath): Maverick House, 2005.

Minihan, Mary, *The Green Party in Government*, Dunshaughlin (Co. Meath): Maverick House, 2011.

Ó hEithir, Breandán, *The Begrudger's Guide to Irish Politics*, Dublin: Poolbeg, 1986.

O'Leary, Olivia, *Party Animals*, Dublin: O'Brien Press, 2006.

O'Leary, Olivia, *Politicians and Other Animals*, Dublin: O'Brien Press, 2004.

O'Reilly, Emily, *Candidate: The Truth behind the Presidential Campaign*, Dublin: Attic Press, 1991.

O'Toole, Fintan, *Meanwhile Back at the Ranch: The Politics of Irish Beef*, London: Vintage, 1995.

O'Toole, Jason, *Brian Cowen: The Path to Power*, Dublin: Transworld Ireland, 2008.

Powell, Jonathan, *Great Hatred, Little Room: Making Peace in Northern Ireland*, London: Bodley Head, 2008.

Rafter, Kevin, *Fine Gael: Party at the Crossroads*, Dublin: New Island Books, 2009.

Reid, Gerard (ed.), *Great Irish Voices: Over 400 Years of Irish Oratory*, Dublin: Irish Academic Press, 1999.

Ross, Shane, *The Bankers: How the Banks Brought Ireland to Its Knees*, Dublin: Penguin Ireland, 2009.

Smith, Raymond, *Garret, the Enigma: Dr Garret FitzGerald*, Dublin: Aherlow Publishers, 1985.

Smyth, Sam, *Thanks a Million, Big Fella*, Dublin: Blackwater Press, 1977.

Waters, John, *Jiving at the Crossroads*, Belfast: Blackstaff Press, 1991.

Whelan, Noel, *Fianna Fáil: A Biography of the Party*, Dublin: Gill & Macmillan, 2011.

INDEX

Act of Union, 209

Adams, Gerry, 213, 214, 216, 278

Ahern, Bertie, 150–51, 177, 181, 189–90, 219, 227–8
  and the Belfast Agreement, 209–10
  and Burke, 193, 198–200
  and the Mahon Tribunal, 239–40
  and Omagh bombing, 213–14
  and the peace process, 222–3, 237–8
  on the Rainbow Coalition, 183–4, 192
  and Sinn Féin, 232
  as Taoiseach, 190–92, 220, 221–3, 234-8

Ahern, Dermot, 193, 200, 200–201, 257, 265, 275

AIB (Allied Irish Banks), 250

Aiken, Frank, 19, 39, 82

Andrews, Barry, 275

Andrews, David, 74, 84, 184, 190, 200, 211

Andrews, Niall, 117, 134

Angelou, Maya, 215

Anglo Irish Bank, 257

Anglo-Irish Agreement, 139

Arms Trial, 2, 100, 106, 128

Arnold, Bruce, 124, 136

Artane, St Joseph's Industrial School, 33–4, 64

Artane Boys' Band, 33

Bailey, Michael, 193, 194, 198

Bailey, Tom, 198

Balfour, Arthur James Balfour, Earl of, 68

Bank of Ireland, 250

Barker, James, victim of Omagh bombing, 213

Barry, Peter, 176

Beckett, Samuel, 82

Beef Tribunal Report (1994), 180

Behan, Brendan, 81, 170

Belfast Agreement, 3, 107, 209, 210, 229

Bell, Michael, 142, 160

Belton, Louis J., 206

Berry, Peter, 94, 96

Bhreathnach, Niamh, 189

Blair, Tony, 209, 234

Blaney, Neil, 45, 68, 113, 128–9, 136-7
  and the Arms Crisis, 93–4, 96, 97, 98

Blowick, Joe, 8, 49

Blueshirts, 8, 29, 105

Blythe, Ernest, 152

Boland, Gerald, 65

Boland, Kevin, 94, 95–6

Bord na Móna, 50

The Boss (Joyce and Murtagh), 138, 171

Bovale Developments Ltd, 194

Brennan, Séamus, 111, 136, 186, 234

British Commonwealth, 15, 16

Broadcasting Authority Act (1960), Section 31, 14

Brooke, Rupert, 111

Browne, Noël, 36, 48, 131
  and Archbishop McQuaid, 22, 24, 25, 26
  autobiography *Against the Tide*, 30
  criticism of Haughey, 123, 128
  and de Valera, 42–3, 48
  and Dillon's critique of, 31–2
  and free education, 42–3
  and Health (Family Planning) Bill, 118
  and Mother and Child Scheme, 20, 21–7
  views on Lemass, 49–50

Browne, Vincent, 229

Broy, Ned, 29

Bruton, John, 140, 141, 180, 190, 191, 194
  and the Belfast Agreement, 210, 211
  and Budget (1982), 132–3, 136
  and Burke, 161, 200, 219
  on Fianna Fáil, 161, 176, 219
  and Haughey, 156, 173

Bruton, John, *continued*
  and nomination as Taoiseach, 181
  and Omagh bombing, 214–15
  in opposition, 176, 220
  and Rainbow Coalition, 181–4, 185
  and Sinn Féin, 1, 214
Bruton, Richard, 180
  analysis of Lenihan's 2009 Budget, 255
  analysis of McCreevy's 2003 Budget, 226–7
  and banking crisis, 246–7, 250
  nomination of Kenny, 220, 236, 240
Budget 1967 (Haughey), 76–80
Budget 1982 (John Bruton), 132–3, 136
Budget 1987 (MacSharry), 152–5
Budget 1997 (Quinn), 185–8
Budget 1997 (McCreevy), 203–7
Budget 2003 (McCreevy), 225–8
Buffett, Warren, 227
Burke, Edmund, 236
Burke, Liam, 105
Burke, Paddy 'the Bishop', 19, 197
Burke, Raphael (Ray), 135, 136, 169, 175, 183, 185
  and Ahern 190, 198–200
  and allegations, 193, 194–7, 201
  and John Bruton, 161, 200, 219
  and Communications portfolio, 161
  resignation from politics, 198–9
Burton, Joan
  analysis of McCreevy's 2003 Budget, 227
  on banking bail-out, 260, 262
  and financial crisis, 247, 249, 250
  and NAMA, 255
  views on Cowen, 240
Bush, George, 207
Byrne, Alfie, 16

Carey, Donal, 205
Carey, Pat, 267, 268, 275
Carroll, Lewis, *Alice in Wonderland*, 275
Carson, Edward, 31
Catholic Church, 20, 144, 149, 179
  see also McQuaid, Archbishop John Charles

Celtic Tiger, 189, 203–7, 219, 224, 242, 244
Censorship of Films Act (1923), 81
Censorship of Publications Act (1929), 81, 83
Censorship of Publications Act (1967), 82–5, 116
Censorship of Publications Board, 81–2, 83
Central Bank, 78, 188, 224, 249, 250, 259
Childers, Erskine, 37
Christian Brothers, 33, 34, 35, 36
CIE (Córas Iompair Éireann), 77, 123
Civil War, 2, 7, 14, 17, 33, 38
Clann na Poblachta, 8, 9, 17, 21, 29
Clann na Talmhan, 8
Clarke, Austin, 81
  'Burial of an Irish President', 20
Clarke, Thomas, 38
Clinton, Bill, 234
Clinton, Mark, 94
Cluskey, Frank, 75, 87, 122–3
Coffey, Betty, 195
Cogan, James, 29
Colley, George, 66, 67, 68, 103, 123, 128
Collins, Gerry, 175
Collins, Michael, 17, 26, 95
Collins, Stephen, 94, 105
Connolly, James, 31, 38, 66, 211
Connolly, Patrick, 138
Connolly, Roddy, 18
Constitution of Ireland
  Article 6, 143–4
  Articles 2 and 3, 209, 211
Conway, Ciara, 276–7
Cooper, Matt, 245
Corish, Brendan, 50, 59, 66, 68, 106, 108
Corry, Martin, 69
Cosgrave, Liam, 79, 102, 105
  and the arms crisis, 93–6, 99
  and coalition with Labour, 110–11
  as Taoiseach, 52, 106, 108–9, 114
  views on Fianna Fáil, 67–8, 108
Costello, John A., 1, 8, 9, 28, 29
  and Archbishop McQuaid, 23–4, 26–7
  and Browne's Mother and Child Scheme, 22, 23–7

and coalition government, 40–41, 42
critique of Fianna Fáil, 48–9, 51
election as Taoiseach, 9–11, 12–13, 38
and Fianna Fáil in opposition, 46–7
and Irish Medical Association, 22, 24, 25
and Lemass, 44
and Republic of Ireland Bill (1948), 14–17
views on inter-party government, 31–2
Coughlan, Mary, 248, 266, 267, 268, 275
Coveney, Simon, 230
Cowan, Peadar, 17, 19, 27, 30, 31, 33–5
Cowen, Brian, 168–9, 178, 184, 228, 239
and Ahern, 235, 242
dissolution of Dáil, 267–8
final address to Dáil, 269–71
and the financial crisis, 244–6, 252, 257, 258–61
and Gilmore, 264–5, 271–2
and leadership of Fianna Fáil, 240, 241–3, 268
and ministerial resignations, 265, 267, 268
retirement from politics, 275
and Supplementary 2009 Budget, 256
Credit Institutions (Financial Support) Bill (2008), 246
Creighton, Lucinda, 240
Criminal Law Amendment Act (1935), 81
Cuffe, Ciarán, 268
Cullagh, Sandra, 239
Cuomo, Mario, 144
Curran, John, 275

Daly, Brendan, 161
Davern, Noel, 178, 204
de Gaulle, Charles, 100
de Rossa, Proinsias, 160, 181, 190, 200
de Valera, Éamon, 15, 28, 31, 39–40, 210
and economic policies, 7–8, 37
and free education, 42–3
and IMF delegation, 55–6
and Ireland's status, 15, 16
and the Irish Press, 8, 48
Uachtarán na hÉireann, 48, 51

views on coalition, 31, 39, 40
de Valera, Vivion, 123
Democratic Left, 182
Dempsey, Noel, 201, 257, 265, 267, 275
Derrig, Tom, 71
Desmond, Barry, 113, 142–5, 149
Desmond, Dan, 44–5, 49
Dickens, Charles, 64
Dillon, James, 8, 9, 11, 47
critique of Browne, 31–2
and de Valera, 15
and Fianna Fáil, 31, 50, 57, 74, 79
and independent TDS, 32
and Lemass, 50, 51, 68
and mentally ill prisoner, 61–4
views on Haughey, 68–9
views on Lynch, 69
Disraeli, Benjamin, 73
Dockrell, Maurice E., 16–17
Doherty, Pearse, 268
Doherty, Seán, 139, 153, 171, 180
Donegan, Paddy, 103, 110
Dooge, Jim, 94
Doyle, Joe, 142
Dublin County Council, 195
Duffy, James, 165
Duffy, Joe, 245
Duignan, Seán, 175, 182–3
Dukes, Alan, 158, 159–60, 166, 180, 201
and Belfast Agreement, 211–12
and the divorce referendum, 147, 150
views on Cowen, 178
Dunlop, Frank, 111
Dunne, Ben, 174, 194
Dunne, Seán, 16, 66, 68, 84, 85
Dunphy, Eamon, 170

Economist, 234
Eden, Anthony (Earl of Avon), 50
Einstein, Albert, 238
Ellis, John, 219
Enda, Reverend Mother, 88
ESRI (Economic and Social Research Institute), 127
European Central Bank, 253, 257, 258, 261

European Commission, 253, 258
European Council, 242
European Union, 2, 219, 242
Everett, James, 29, 40, 84
External Relations Act (1936), 16

Ferriter, Diarmaid (historian), 55
Fianna Fáil, 8, 28–9, 42–3, 119, 219
    and the arms crisis, 93–9
    and censorship, 81–5
    and coalition with Labour, 179–80
    and coalition with PDS, 157–61, 190
    and election (2007), 234–8
    and election (2010), 275–6, 277
    and free second-level education, 71–5
    and the Green Party, 235, 238, 258, 264,
        265, 267
    and McCreevy's 2003 Budget, 225–6
    in opposition, 12, 46–7, 129–30
    and proportional representation, 48–9
    and Rainbow Coalition 1997 Budget,
        185–8
    and taxation, 56–8
Finance, 224
Financial Regulator, 245, 246, 247, 249,
    250
Fine Gael, 8, 220
    and censorship, 83–4
    and debate on divorce, 146–50
    and election contributions, 196
    and historic majority, 276
    and Labour, 105–6, 110–11
    Northern policy, 230
    and Republic of Ireland Bill (1948),
        14–17
    see also Rainbow Coalition
Finlay, Fergus, 180
FitzGerald, Garret, 105, 109, 146, 169
    and the arms crisis, 97–8
    and John Bruton's 1982 Budget, 132–3,
        135, 136
    critique of Haughey, 3, 120–22
    and the divorce debate, 146–7
    and EEC membership, 104
    and Haughey, 137, 166
    and Kemmy, 128, 131, 135

    and peace process, 208
    praise for Lynch, 120
    as Taoiseach, 127, 129–30, 139–40, 141
    views on Fianna Fáil policies, 112–13
Fitzgerald, Gene, 155
Fitzsimons, Eoghan, 179
Flaherty, Mary, 148
Flanagan, Luke 'Ming', 275, 278
Flanagan, Oliver J., 10, 18, 128, 143, 149
    and criticism of Lemass, 50
    and defence of Haughey, 137–8
    and EEC membership, 103–4
    suitability of school text book, 86–9
Flanagan, Seán, 27
Flood Tribunal, 197, 201–2
Flynn, Beverley, 249
Flynn, Eileen, 141–2
Flynn, Pádraig, 111, 120, 149–50, 158, 169
Foley, Denis, 219
Foster, Roy (historian), 209
Fox, Mildred, 190
Franco, General Francisco, 30
Free State, 7, 8, 37

G7, 259
Gallagher, Matt, 78
Gallagher, Patrick, 78
Garda Síochána, 29, 62, 110, 139, 168
    and IRA, 212, 231, 232
    and O'Malley, 212
    and raid on clinic, 142
Garland, Roger, 176
Garvin, Tom (historian), 21, 48, 71
Geithner, Tim, 257
Geoghegan-Quinn, Máire, 76
Gilligan, John, 240
Gilmore, Eamon
    and Fianna Fáil resignations, 266–7
    and the financial crisis, 245–6, 248–9,
        250, 259
    and the Green Party, 264
    views on Cowen, 257, 271
Gladstone, William Ewart, 7
Glenn, Alice, 148
Gogarty, James, 193, 194
Goldman Sachs, 248

Goodman, Larry, 166
Gormley, John, 200–201, 240, 247–8, 265, 268, 275
Government of Ireland Act (1920), 209
Grattan's Parliament, 46
Green Party, 238, 258, 260, 262, 275
  and Ahern, 235–6, 238
  and Cowen, 240
  and Fianna Fáil, 235, 258, 264, 265, 267
Gregory, Tony, 136, 137, 161
Griffin, Brendan, 143
Griffith, Arthur, 38, 95

'Hall's Pictorial Weekly' (RTE), 110–11
Hanafin, Mary, 275
Harney, Mary, 150, 190, 216, 223, 250–51, 263
  and Ahern, 191, 192, 236
  and Burke, 193, 194, 199, 200
  and Cowen, 240
  and the PDS, 181, 188, 221
  on the Rainbow Coalition, 181–2, 188
  resignation, 265, 267
  retirement from politics, 275
Harris, Simon, 276
Harte, Paddy, 181
Harvard Summer School, 120
Haughey, Charles, 2, 50, 111, 119–20, 151
  and Archbishop McQuaid, 114
  and the arms crisis, 93–4, 96, 97, 98, 99
  and Browne's views on, 128
  and John Bruton's 1982 Budget, 134
  and Budget (1967) 76–80
  and coalition with PDS, 157–9
  and Cosgrave's views on, 67
  defence of Lenihan, 166
  and Dillon's views on, 68–9
  and divorce debate, 149
  and the economy, 127–9
  and election (1987), 152
  and Fitzgerald's critique, 120–22
  and the Gregory Deal, 136, 137, 139
  and Health (Family Planning) Bill, 114–18
  and Lenihan's resignation, 169–70
  nomination as Taoiseach, 120–24

perception of, 65, 123
personal finances, 76–7, 120, 127, 132
resignation as Taoiseach, 171–4
and second Government, 136–9
and Spring's critique, 3, 165, 167–8
on taxation, 77–8
Haughey, Maureen (née Lemass), 174
Hayes, Brian, 205–6
Hayes, Joanne, 141
Hayes, Tom, 266
Health (Amendment) Bill, 141–5
Health (Family Planning) Bill, 114–18
Healy, Fr Seán, 228
Healy-Rae, Jackie, 191, 237, 240–41
Healy-Rae, Michael, 276
Heaney, Seamus, 279
Higgins, Joe, 210, 277
Higgins, Michael D., 168–9
Hillery, Patrick (Paddy), 65, 68, 71, 72, 94
Honohan, Patrick, 258
Horgan, John, 55–6, 117, 123
Howlin, Brendan, 160, 181, 221, 267
Hughes, James, 9
Hume, John, 210, 212, 215, 216
Hussey, Gemma, 145, 149, 150
Hyde, Douglas, 20, 21

IBEC report, 37–8
IDA, 28, 186
IMF (International Monetary Fund), 166, 225, 253
  and Britain, 129
  delegation (1958), 55–6
  EU-IMF bailout, 3, 258, 260–61, 271, 279
Intoxicating Liquor Act (1924), 81
Intoxicating Liquor Act (1927), 81
IRA, 8, 19, 29, 98, 229
  and Ahern, 232
  and John Bruton, 215
  and decommissioning, 214, 231
  and Fine Gael, 230
  and Kenny, 231
  and McDowell, 232–3
Irish Free State, 7, 8, 37
Irish Life and Permanent, 250

Irish Medical Association, 20, 21, 22
Irish Nationwide, 250
Irish News Agency, 27
Irish Press, 8, 79, 208
Irish Press Group, 48
Irish Times, 41, 123, 150, 219, 254, 263
  and Mother and Child Scheme, 20, 21
Irish Volunteers, 29

Johnson, Lyndon B., 74
Johnson, Tom, 276–7
Joyce, James, *Ulysses*, 82
Joyce, Joe, 138

Keane, Seán, 30
Keating, Justin, 2, 102
Kelly, John M., 1, 113, 143
  and John Bruton's 1982 Budget, 134
  and the divorce debate, 146, 150
  and Haughey's nomination as
    Taoiseach, 123
  and Health (Family Planning) Bill,
    116–17
  views on Ahern, 150–51
Kelly, Morgan, 244, 257
Kemmy, Jim, 128, 131, 135, 137
Kennedy, Edward (Ted), 254
Kennedy, John F., 254, 269
Kenny, Enda, 184, 221, 229, 263
  on Ahern, 221–2, 238
  and Cowen, 241, 265, 266, 267, 271
  and Fianna Fáil resignations, 266, 267,
    268
  and the financial crisis, 245, 248, 252,
    258, 259
  and Lenihan's 2009 Budget, 256
  and nomination as Taoiseach, 220,
    236, 240
  on Sinn Féin and IRA, 230, 231, 232
  as Taoiseach, 276, 277, 278–9
Kerrigan, Gene, 33
Kerryman, 196
Kiberd, Declan, 219
Killeen, Tony, 265, 267, 275
Killilea, Mark, Jnr, 130
Kirk, Séamus, 262, 272

Knights of St Columbanus, 86

Labour Party, 8, 10, 40, 66, 220, 276
  and Budget (1997), 185–8
  and censorship, 84
  and coalition, 45
  and education, 59
  and EEC membership, 100, 102
  and Fianna Fáil, 179–80
  and Fine Gael, 105–6, 110–11
  see also Rainbow Coalition
Labour Party (British), 16, 110
Larkin, Jim, Jnr, 19
'Late Late Show' (RTE), 168
Lawlor, Liam, 168, 190, 199, 219
Lee, Joe (historian), 14, 37, 111
Lehane, Con, 19
Lemass, Seán, 11–12, 17, 41, 66, 71, 82
  and achievements, 55–6
  and Budget (1963), 57–60
  and de Valera, 29
  and education policy, 71–2
  and EEC membership, 100
  election as Taoiseach, 48–52
  and Northern Ireland, 208
  and policies, 28, 30, 37, 43–5
  retirement as Taoiseach, 65, 67
Lenehan, Joe, 102–3
Lenihan, Brian, Jnr, 257, 265, 275
  and December 2009 Budget, 252–5
  and EU–IMF bail-out, 260–61, 263
  and financial crisis, 244–5, 246, 249–
    50, 248
Lenihan, Brian, Snr, 57, 61, 128, 142, 167,
    168
  and censorship reform, 82–5
  and the divorce debate, 148
  and Haughey, 68, 86, 127, 139, 165, 166
  and mentally ill prisoner, 63–4
  resignation as Tánaiste, 169–70
  and taped interview, 165
Lenihan, Conor, 170
Leyden, Terry, 147
Lindsay, Paddy, 47, 73
Lisbon Treaty, 241, 253
'Live Mike' (RTE), 179

'Liveline' (RTE), 245
Locke Tribunal, 50, 137
Locke's Distillery, 8
Loftus, Sean 'Dublin Bay', 128, 131
Long Kesh, 129
Lourdes, 134
Lovett, Ann, 141
Lowry, Michael, 180, 190, 194
Lynch, Jack, 17–18, 36, 105–6, 119
    and the arms crisis, 93–9
    and the Arms Trial, 106
    and EEC membership, 100–102
    and Northern Ireland, 107, 208
    and O'Malley, 74
    as Taoiseach, 65–70, 79–80, 111–13

MacArthur, Malcolm, 138
MacBride, Seán, 9, 10, 19, 26, 27, 29, 31
    and exchanges with MacEntee, 46
    and national government, 38-9
McCabe, Detective Garda Jerry, 212, 231,
    232
McCartan, Pat, 177
McCormack, Pádraic, 268
McCreevy, Charlie, 3, 176, 220, 224
    and benchmarking, 226
    and Budget (1997), 203–7
    and Budget (2003), 225–8
    and decentralisation, 225–6
    and the divorce debate, 148
    on Rainbow Coalition 1997 Budget,
    187
McDowell, Derek, 207
McDowell, Michael, 155–6, 183, 187–8,
    220, 232–3
MacEntee, Seán, 18, 30, 33, 51, 82, 106
    and policies, 37, 45, 46
Mac Eoin, Seán, 39
McGahon, Brendan, 205, 216
McGee, Mary, 114
Mac Giolla, Tomás, 140
McGrath, Mattie, 275
McGuinness, Martin, 213, 215, 216
McQuaid, Archbishop John Charles, 106
    and censorship, 81, 82, 114
    and Costello, 23–4, 26–7

and Lemass, 82
and Mother and Child Scheme, 22,
    23–4, 25, 26
McQuillan, Jack, 31, 39, 48
MacSharry, Ray, 152–5
Magill, 198
Mahon Tribunal, 197, 234, 239–40
Major, John, 208–9
Mallon, Seamus, 210
Manley, Tadhg, 46
Mara, P.J., 100, 193, 219
Marshall Aid, 28
Martin, Micheál, 189, 247, 267, 275, 277
Merrill Lynch, 248
Mitchell, George, 232
Mitchell, Jim, 176
Molloy, Bobby, 134
Molony, David, 149
Moore, Seán, 84–5
Morgan Stanley, 248
'Morning Ireland' (RTE), 258
Mother and Child Scheme, 20–27
Mountjoy Prison, 62, 63
Moylan, Seán, 33, 35
Mulcahy, Michael, 250
Mulcahy, Richard, 9, 11, 19, 71
    and Costello, 9–10, 29, 38
Murphy Group, 198
Murtagh, Peter, 138

National Anthem, 28
National Asset Management Agency
    (NAMA), 252, 255
National Association of the Ovulation
    Method Ireland (NAOMI), 115
National Labour Party, 8
National Lottery, 155
National Treasury Management Agency
    (NTMA), 249
National Union of Journalists (NUJ), 72
Nationality, 38
Nealon's Guide, 234
New Ireland Forum, 141
9/11 attacks, 230
Nixon, Richard Milhous, 120, 123
Nobel Peace Prize, 216

Nobel Prize in Literature, 84
Noonan, Michael, 155, 161, 206, 220, 221
  and EU-IMF bail-out, 258, 261–2
  and the financial crisis, 249
North-South Ministerial Council, 210
Northern Bank, robbery, 229, 232
Northern Ireland, 110, 128–9, 138, 141, 144
  and arms crisis, 94
  and atrocities, 178, 213–16
  and Belfast Agreement, 3, 107, 209, 210,
    229
  and British White Paper, 107
  and peace process, 179, 208–9, 210
Norton, William, 10, 17, 19, 22, 30–31, 40

O'Brien, Conor Cruise, 97, 103
O'Brien, Edna, *The Country Girls*, 114
O'Brien, Flann (Brian Ó Nualláin), 86,
  173
O'Brien, Sergeant, 17
Ó Caoláin, Caoimhghín, 212, 216, 233,
  260
O'Connell, Daniel, 50, 111
O'Connell, John, 135, 168, 177, 178
O'Connell, Maurice, 224
O'Connor, Frank, 81, 89
  'Guests of the Nation', 87
Ó Cuív, Éamon, 268, 275
Ó Dálaigh, Cearbhall, 110
O'Donnell, Kieran, 255–6
O'Donnell, Liz, 21
O'Donnell, Tom, 74
O'Donoghue, John, 189, 235, 237
O'Donoghue, Martin, 111, 119, 134, 153
O'Donohue, John, 'For a Leader', 270
OECD, 228, 253
Ó Faoláin, Seán, 'The Trout', 88, 89
O'Hanlon, Rory, 142
Ó hEithir, Breandán, 8, 65
  Begrudger's Guide to Irish Politics, 42
O'Higgins, M.J., 51, 83–4, 94
O'Higgins, T.F. (Tom), 21, 24, 73–4, 78–9,
  94, 96
O'Keeffe, Batt, 265, 267, 275
O'Keeffe, Jim, 180, 196, 205
O'Leary, Michael, 97, 111

O'Leary, Olivia, 203
Omagh, bombing (1998), 213–16
O'Malley, Desmond (Dessie), 2, 14
  and the Gardaí, 212
  and Haughey's resignation, 174
  and Health (Amendment) Bill, 142–5
  and PD coalition with FF, 158, 159, 161,
    176
O'Malley, Donogh, 50, 68, 71, 82
  and Flanagan, 86–9
  and free second-level education, 72–5,
    77
Ombudsman, 132
Ó Móráin, Micheál, 93, 94, 110
O'Neill, Des, 234
O'Neill, Terence (Baron O'Neill of the
  Maine), 208
Order of St Gregory the Great, 86
O'Rourke, Mary, 175, 190
O'Rourke, Seán, 265
Owen, Nora, 181

Paisley, Ian, 234
Parnell, Charles Stewart, 7, 50
PAYE, 56, 57, 119
Pearse, Pádraig, 18, 38
Pike Theatre, 81
Poe, Edgar Allan, 166
Powell, Jonathan, 209
Power, Seán, 246
Progressive Democrats (PDS), 142, 145,
  155, 169, 179, 180
  and Fianna Fáil, 157–61, 176, 188, 190,
    220, 254
  and Haughey, 166, 171
  and Rainbow Coalition 1997 Budget,
    186
Proportional Representation (PR), and
  Fianna Fáil, 48–9
Provisional IRA, 94, 214
Public Dance Halls Act (1935), 81
Public Service Advisory Council, 112
Putnam, Robert, 228

'Questions and Answers' (RTE), 165
Quinlan, Derek, 244

Quinn, Ruairí, 123, 155, 160, 180–81, 182
   and Budget (1997), 185–8
   and Burke's resignation, 200
   on McCreevy's first Budget, 204
   and Omagh bombing, 215–16
   and the peace process, 211
   and Reynolds, 179–80

Rabbitte, Pat, 178, 179, 196, 238
   on Fianna Fáil, 236, 262
   on the PDS, 169
   and Sinn Féin, 230
Rainbow Coalition, 180–84, 192, 203, 223
   and 1997 Budget, 185–8
Reagan, Ronald, 241
Real IRA, 214, 215
Reilly, James, 255
Report of the Commission to Inquire
   into Child Abuse, see Ryan
   Commission
Republic of Ireland Bill (1948), 14–17
Residential Institutions Redress Scheme,
   250
Revenue Commissioners, 78
Reynolds, Albert, 149, 157, 158, 166, 181
   and John Bruton, 156
   and cabinet appointments, 176–8
   and Labour, 179–80
   nomination as Taoiseach, 175–6
   and peace process, 208–9, 211
Ring, Michael, 255
Robinson, Mary, 150
Rogers, Kenny, 179
Roman Catholic Church, see Catholic
   Church
Ross, Shane, 278
RTE (Raidió Teilifís Éireann), 110–11, 165,
   168, 179, 245, 258
Ryan Commission, 35–6
Ryan, Eamon, 268, 275
Ryan, James, 51
Ryan, John, 198
Ryan, Richie, 79, 96, 105, 110, 113

St Joseph's Industrial School, Artane, 33–
   4, 64

Salisbury, Robert Gascoyne-Cecil,
   Marquess of, 68
Sargent, Trevor, 235–6
Savoy Group, 244
SDLP (Social Democratic and Labour
   Party), 209, 210, 212
Shakespeare, William
   Julius Caesar, 173
   Othello, 172
Shatter, Alan, 143, 169, 180
Sherwin, Frank, 50, 51
Sinn Féin, 209, 212, 214, 230, 232, 276
   and Ó Caoláin, 216, 233, 260
Sinn Féin the Workers' Party, 181
Skelly, Liam, 148
Smith, Brendan, 267, 275
Smith, Michael, 198
Smith, Raymond, 135
Smyth, Brendan, 179
Society of St Vincent de Paul, 279
Spring, Dick, 148, 160, 170, 179, 180, 181
   and John Bruton, 190
   critique of Haughey, 3, 165, 167–8
   and Haughey's resignation, 173–4
   and Healy-Rae, 191
   and political donations, 196
   and Reynolds' cabinet, 176–7
   views on Lenihan, 167, 168
Stagg, Emmet, 160
Stallone, Sylvester, 190
Storme, Michael, 84
Suez Crisis, 42
Sunday Independent, 170
Sunningdale Agreement, 110
Supreme Court, and the McGee case, 114
Sweetman, Gerard, 42, 46, 56–7, 66, 72,
   79

Taca, 61, 77, 79
Thatcher, Margaret, 141, 208
Thomas (inmate Artane Industrial
   School), 36
Thornley, David, 96–7
Timmins, Billy, 230
Traynor, Des, 78
Traynor, Oscar, 65

Treacy, Seán, 148–9
Treaty, The, 17–18
Trimble, David, 210, 212, 216, 232
Tully, Jimmy, 68, 79–80, 85, 102–3, 106

Ulster Workers' Council, 110

Varadkar, Leo, 248
Veale, Fr Joe, 88

Wall Street, 247–8
Wallace, Mick, 275
War of Independence, 7, 98
    veterans and widows, 132
Whelan, Noel, 66

Whelehan, Harry, 180
Whitaker, Ken, 56, 73, 100
    'Has Ireland a Future?', 55
White, Mary, 268
Wilde, Oscar, 84
Williams, Tennessee, 81
Wilson, Harold, 110
Woods, Michael, 147–8, 169
Wordsworth, William, 183
Workers' Party, 140, 160, 177
World Health Organisation (WHO), 115
World War II, 7
Wyse, Pearse, 142

Yates, Ivan, 128